GREAT LIVES OBSERVED

Gerald Emanuel Stearn, *General Editor*

EACH VOLUME IN THE SERIES VIEWS THE CHARACTER AND ACHIEVEMENT OF A GREAT WORLD FIGURE IN THREE PERSPECTIVES—THROUGH HIS OWN WORDS, THROUGH THE OPINIONS OF HIS CONTEMPORARIES, AND THROUGH RETROSPECTIVE JUDGMENTS—THUS COMBINING THE INTIMACY OF AUTOBIOGRAPHY, THE IMMEDIACY OF EYEWITNESS OBSERVATION, AND THE OBJECTIVITY OF MODERN SCHOLARSHIP.

ISAAC KRAMNICK, *editor of this volume in the Great Lives Observed series, is Professor of Government at Cornell University. Author of* Bolingbroke and His Circle: The Politics of Nostalgia in the Age of Walpole, *Professor Kramnick is now at work on a study of English social thought in the second half of the eighteenth century.*

GREAT LIVES OBSERVED

Edmund Burke

Edited by ISAAC KRAMNICK

*I am not going to make an idle panegyric on Burke (he has
no need of it); but I cannot help looking upon him as the chief
boast and ornament of the English House of Commons.
What has been said of him is, I think, strictly true, that "he
was the most eloquent man of his time: his wisdom
was greater than his eloquence."*

—WILLIAM HAZLITT, 1807

A SPECTRUM BOOK

PRENTICE-HALL, INC., ENGLEWOOD CLIFFS, N.J.

Library of Congress Cataloging in Publication Data

KRAMNICK, ISAAC, comp.
  Edmund Burke.

  (Great lives observed) (A Spectrum Book)
  Bibliography: p.
  1. Burke, Edmund, 1729?–1797.
  DA506.B9K65 1974   942.07'3'0924 [B]   74–12324
  ISBN 0–13–090597–6
  ISBN 0–13–090589–5 (pbk.)

Unless otherwise indicated,
all quotations from Burke's writings
are from the twelve-volume "Boston" edition,
which was published in 1865–67.

10 9 8 7 6 5 4 3 2 1

Printed in the United States of America

PRENTICE-HALL INTERNATIONAL, INC. (*London*)
PRENTICE-HALL OF AUSTRALIA, PTY. LTD. (*Sydney*)
PRENTICE-HALL OF CANADA, LTD. (*Toronto*)
PRENTICE-HALL OF INDIA PRIVATE LIMITED (*New Delhi*)
PRENTICE-HALL OF JAPAN, INC. (*Tokyo*)

Contents

v

Preface

My interest in Burke is not derived from any particular conviction about his relevance for our time or all times, as is claimed by some. Burke is of his own right a towering figure to be reckoned with by the student of eighteenth-century English life and thought. He represents, on the one hand, the continuation of a nostalgic repudiation of modernity found earlier in the century, which I have investigated in some of my previous work. And he is also the archenemy of the radical bourgeois circle of dissenters around Price and Priestley, whose ideological relationship to the Industrial Revolution of the second half of the century I am presently investigating. I have tried in this *Great Lives Observed* volume to rescue the English aspect of Burke from what I take to be the traditional overemphasis on him as simply the commentator on the foibles of the French.

For help in the preparation of this volume I would like to thank Mrs. Deborah Astell of London, England, who was of invaluable assistance as she quickly mastered the British Museum, its intricacies of cataloguing and idiosyncrasies of staff; Mrs. Virginia Brehm for worthy clerical assistance; and finally, the publisher's anonymous reader for points well made.

Introduction

Edmund Burke (1729–1797) played a central role in the political history of England during the first forty years of George III's long reign. In the House of Commons, he defended the cause of the American colonies, championed the rights of persecuted Catholics in England and Ireland, criticized the parliamentary meddling of the Hanoverian monarchy, and decried the rape of the Indian subcontinent by English adventurers. In that same House, he also rejected pleas for the reform of the archaic English constitution, ridiculed efforts to lift the civil restrictions on unitarian and other protestant dissenters, and, most famously, he called down the wrath of God and right-thinking Englishmen on the French Revolutionaries and their Jacobin sympathizers in England. Burke's claim to be a "great life observed" rests, however, on more than this fascinating and controversial career; he stands, after all, as the intellectual source of one of the modern world's most influential political visions—conservatism. His writings and speeches are the bible, and he the prophet of that ideology, in much the same way that *The Second Treatise of Civil Government*, or *The Communist Manifesto* and Locke and Marx are the bibles and prophets of liberalism and Communism respectively. In reviewing and assessing the historical person, role, and impact of Burke one must, thus, confront both the statesman of Georgian England and the philosopher of conservatism.

Had he not become the philosopher of conservatism and been only the Whig statesman, his parliamentary role would have itself been worthy of a "great life observed." His was a great success story: an outsider of no great means rises by dint of his own wits, skills, and energy to the inner circles of power in a closed aristocratic political community. To be sure, he never quite made it to the real pinnacles of power; he became the articulate defender of a class that refused to accept him as one of them. Still his career is linked closely with much of consequence that transpired in the public life of England in the second half of the eighteenth century. The chronology at the end of the introduction carefully traces these biographical details, but the main contours deserve mention here.

His Irish birth and schooling as well as his early essays behind him, Burke entered the English public scene in the middle 1760s as private secretary to the great Whig magnate, the Marquis of Rockingham. For the next ten years, as part of Lord Rockingham's "political con-

nection," he defended the American colonies in their developing clash
with English commercial and imperial policy. By 1780, he had also
emerged as the principal critic of what was considered George III's
corrupt interference with the independence of the House of Commons.
Although Burke saw the power of the Crown as a threat to the ancient
English Constitution and its sacred principles of mixed government
and the separation of power, in the 1780s he also spoke out strongly
against the radical agitation associated with the Yorkshire movement
and the reform effort of the younger Pitt. Democratic enlargement of
the suffrage was, he argued, also a threat to the perfectly balanced
English Constitution; it would admit the people to too great a share
of power. In the late 1780s, Burke turned much of his parliamentary
energy to two causes, the impeachment proceedings against Warren
Hastings, the former governor-general of the East India Company, and
legislative efforts to improve the status of Catholics in both England
and Ireland. These efforts paled in significance, however, as the French
Revolution dominated the last years of his life. More than any other
figure in English public life, Burke mobilized sentiment against the
Jacobin cause at home and abroad. In the course of this, he split the
Whig party, denouncing his former colleagues for their continued
sympathy with the French experiment. As one can see in part two
below, few of his contemporaries had neutral views on this amazing
public career. Burke was passionately worshipped and with equal passion hated. With puffy cheeks, fiery red hair, and excessive emotion,
he held forth in the Senate forum that was the unreformed House of
Commons. Some would be moved by this fount of Republican wisdom and others would rush for the exits. Perhaps this lay behind his
ultimate failure in achieving the heights of political success: his intensity and passionate involvement were not the style appropriate for
the pragmatic world of political management and leadership. But this
is Burke the statesman; there is also Burke the enduring philosopher
of conservatism.

II

And, how he has endured! On St. Patrick's Day, 1973, the American liberal magazine, the *New Republic* ran a lengthy review recon-
sidering the writings and achievements of this Irish conservative born
nearly two and a half centuries earlier. The author, Alexander Bickel,
a Yale Law Professor, saw "much to learn from Burke." In an age of
Right and Left extremists Burke had come into his own in the winter
of 1973. Several weeks earlier, Andrew Hacker, a distinguished political scientist, had written of Burke in a long article in the liberal
New York Times. Burke's deep pessimism about human nature, his
vision of sinful man was, Hacker wrote, a necessary antidote to native

American optimism. American liberalism had rediscovered Burke, and with a vengeance. How sweet Burke's triumph, for but a generation earlier he was the prize discovery of the American Right. At the height of the cold war, it was Burke around whom American conservatives gathered. In 1949, Alfred Knopf published the selected writings and speeches of Burke, edited by Ross Hoffman and Paul Levack. According to the editors, Burke:

> began as a champion of public morality in England; he ended as the protagonist of Christendom against Jacobin imperialism. . . . Englishmen alive today, and facing darker prospects than any their country has confronted since Burke's age, may perhaps draw encouragement from . . . (his) counsels. There is no doubt that the whole Western world, and especially our own Republic, can drink healthfully from the fountain of wisdom that gushed forth from this man and will not run dry as long as his masterpieces remain in the libraries of our civilization. Never have his great maxims been more contemptuously ignored than during the catastrophic last half century.[1]

Five years later, Russell Kirk, the dean of postwar "new-conservatives," also recommended Burke for the spiritual crisis besetting America.

> Burke's ideas did more than establish islands in the sea of radical thought; they provided the defenses of conservatism, on a grand scale, that still stand and are not liable to fall in our time . . . Our age . . . seems to be groping for certain of the ideas which Burke's inspiration formed into a system of social preservation.[2]

During the cold war, the Right had turned to Burke as ideological savior from the sins of atheistic communism. In 1973, liberals came to Burke as intellectual foil to a decade of unfulfilled Great Society reformist programs. In the minds of both camps—the cold war conservatives and the liberals of '73—was the memory of Burke the thundering critic of the French Revolution, who alone said no to western man's zealous (and prideful) pursuit of perfection on this earth. This heroic conception of Burke was, however, a relatively new reading of Burke's achievement. It required the twentieth century with its apocalyptic visions of reconstructed society provided by Fascism and Communism. In the nineteenth century, Burke was seen as a man of lesser accomplishments. Far from his fame resting on his conservative assault on the revolution of the French Jacobin, to the nineteenth century he was remembered as the liberal critic of George III, or as liberal champion of the Americans. Some remembered him as the champion of the persecuted Irish and the disenfranchised Catholics, or as the eloquent

---

1 *Burke's Politics* (New York: 1949), p. xxiv.
2 *The Conservative Mind from Burke to Santayana* (New York, 1953), p. 61.

defender of an Indian subcontinent plundered by English adventurers like Warren Hastings. But few observers in the nineteenth century saw him as the great conservative ideologue. This could come only after Dachau, Stalin, and—yes, for some—only after the collapse of the Great Society. Then and only then could heroic Burke emerge— Burke the author of the *Reflections on the Revolution in France,* wherein all efforts of rational men to remake society according to preconceived and abstract plans are ridiculed.

This is, in fact, the essence of Burke's conservatism—his skepticism. It is this skepticism that explains the appeal of his conservative message both to the cold warrior and the disillusioned liberal, and it is this skepticism I want to analyse for the remainder of this introduction.

Burke is the political skeptic *par excellence.* He stands in revolt against the eighteenth century and, as Burke saw it, the "smuggness of adulterated metaphysics." The "faith in the dogmatism of philosophers" had led Enlightenment thinkers to place faith in reason and abstract ideas, in speculation and *a priori* principles of natural right, freedom, and equality as the basis on which to reform existing government. The English had no such illusions, he argued; they understood the complexity and fragility of human nature and human institutions; they were not "the converts of Rousseau . . . the disciples of Voltaire; Helvetius (had) made no progress amongst (them)." The English, according to Burke, regarded the rampant rationalism of the French philosophers and their quest for an ideal and perfect political order with sluggish skepticism. They understood that since the nature of man was intricate and society complex, "simple governments are fundamentally defective." [3]

Burke's political skepticism was, however, by no means simply a reaction to the trauma of the French Revolution. His opposition to abstract reasoning in philosophy and social matters appeared as early as his undergraduate years in Trinity College, Dublin, during the late 1740s. It also appeared in the religious and philosophical essays he produced between his graduation and the publication, in 1756, of his attack on Bolingbroke's religious rationalism as politically extrapolated. We know, for example, that in these years Burke attacked "great subtleties and refinements of reasoning" which, he felt, produced disorders of the brain. "Custom is to be regarded with great deference" as "a more sure guide than our theories." [4] The conservative thrust of the skepticism found in the *Reflections* is also seen writ large in Burke's response to radical demands in England for democratic re-

3 Burke, *Reflections on the Revolution in France,* pp. 10, 66, 70, 97, 180.
4 Edmund Burke, "Several Scattered Hints Concerning Philosophy and Learning Collected Here from My Papers," in Burke, *A Notebook of Edmund Burke,* edited by H. V. F. Somerset (Cambridge, 1957), pp. 90–91.

form of Parliament in the early 1780s. The agitation, he declared, approached the constitution totally oblivious to the fact that the "House of Commons is a legislative body, corporate by prescription, not made upon any given theory." The English radicals assumed that legislators could remake governments, when all wise men knew that "a prescriptive government never was made upon any foregone theory." How ridiculous, then, to put governments on Procrustean beds and make them fit "the theories which learned and speculative men have made." [5] Such speculators, with their ideal blueprints, were political magicians cutting up the constitution into pieces "in order to boil it, with the puddle of their compounds, into youth and vigor." [6]

But this is by no means the full measure of Burke's skepticism. It can be seen even more completely in his conception of the art of governing, and in his views on the limited rational capacity of mankind. The conservative skeptic like Burke is deeply interested in the character and style of those who govern. He is convinced that pursuit of policies, of preconceived speculative plans, in short, of what we might call today ideology, is inappropriate behavior for political leadership. The major function of a magistrate is seen as prudential manager. Stable government must eschew ideology. What matters most is not the pursuit of policy but the quality of leadership. In Burke's writings, this theme of the importance of prudential management is carefully developed.

Government for Burke was not a science with exact and precise methods and conclusions; government was an art, practiced by artists skilled in prudence. "Constitute governments how you please, infinitely the greater part of it must depend on the exercise of the powers which are left at large to the prudence and uprightness of ministers of state." [7] Governors had to approach political issues according to "the true nature and the peculiar circumstances of the object which we have before us," not in light of "abstract ideas of right" or "general theories of government." [8] The French had devised speculative projects and plans without taking into account the "fixed and the momentary circumstances." [9] In his speeches on America and the taxation issue, Burke repeatedly insisted that "metaphysical distinctions" of abstract right be kept out of the deliberation and that prudence and virtuous discretion rule the day.[10] Prudential political leadership

[5] Edmund Burke, "Speech on the Reform of the Representation of the Commons in Parliament," in *The Works of the Right Honorable Edmund Burke* (Boston, 1865–67), VII, 96–97.

[6] Burke, *Reflections on the Revolution in France*, p. 98.

[7] "Speech on Moving Resolutions for Conciliation with the Colonies," *Works*, II, 170.

[8] "Thoughts on the Cause of the Present Discontents," *Works*, I, 470.

[9] *Reflections*, p. 44.

[10] *Works*, II, 138, 140.

was informed by principle, not ruled by it; and, more importantly, it was guided by circumstances. The prudential magistrate, Burke argues in *A Regicide Peace*, ought to respect the temper and opinions of a particular people, the spirit of their age; and, particularly, to respect and not tamper with the manners of their people, which in many ways formed the basis of their laws.[11] Burke has drunk deep at the fountain of Aristotelian wisdom, for the prudential magistrate is in many ways the modern counterpart to Aristotle's temperate man. There is no doubt, however, that ultimately this model of a compromising, prudential, and temperate set of governors follows from the fundamental premise shared by all skeptics: the disdain for abstract, speculative, and perfectionist thought in politics. Burke skillfully draws the inextricable relationship:

> It is, besides, a very great mistake to imagine that mankind follow up practically any speculative principle, either of government or freedom, as far as it will go in argument, and logical illation. We Englishmen stop very short of the principles upon which we support any given part of our constitution, or even the whole of it together . . . All governments, indeed every human benefit and enjoyment, every virtue and every prudent act, is founded on compromise and barter. We balance inconveniences; we give and take; we remit some rights that we may enjoy others; and we choose rather to be happy citizens than subtle disputants.[12]

Gerald Chapman, a recent writer on Burke, has argued that Burke himself lived the life of prudential magistrate. He contends that a study of the statesman's political career focusing on five case studies (America, Ireland, English radicalism, the French Revolution, and India) reveals that Burke, when all about him sought extreme solutions or pat formulas, succeeded because of what Chapman calls Burke's "practical imagination" (which I take to be the same as "prudential management"). In each instance, Burke, Chapman argues, possessed the ability, lacking in his contemporaries, "to experience a thing in its concrete complexity." His practical imagination "grasps and draws in the actual relation of things." Burke concerned himself "with the relation of concrete values to practice." In each of these political crises, his practical imagination produced "successful and humane compromises within the flux of the actual."[13] However accurately his own career demonstrates the ideal of prudential governing, Burke would still admit that the likes of himself were not those rightly destined to be England's prudential rulers. No matter how

11 *Works*, V, 310.
12 *Works*, II, 173.
13 Gerald Chapman, *Edmund Burke, The Practical Imagination* (Cambridge, Mass., 1967), pp. 81, 131, 241, 280.

much he might proclaim himself "no friend to aristocracy," [14] the overwhelming thrust of his writings proclaimed that only men of breeding possessed this quality of prudence so fundamental to the art of governing. This, after all, was the ultimate sin of the French, their failure to recognize the prescriptive role of aristocracy—its production of qualified governors. Governors ought "to see nothing low and sordid from one's infancy," ought to stand upon "elevated ground," "to have leisure to read, to reflect, to converse." [15] Before the great families, Burke humbly denied his capacity to possess the quality of character and skills of learning required to make a prudential magistrate; thus, he writes to the Duke of Richmond:

> Persons in your station of life ought to have long views. You people of great families in hereditary trusts and fortunes, are not like such as I am, who, whatever we may be by the rapidity of our growth, and even by the fruit we bear, and flatter ourselves that while we creep on the ground, we belly into mellons that are exquisite for size and flavor, yet still are but annual plants, that perish without season, and leave no sort of traces behind us. You, if you are what you ought to be, are in my eye the great oaks that shade a country, and perpetuate your benefits from generation to generation.[16]

The final theme of Burke's skepticism is its assumptions about human nature, specifically its limited potential. Rationalists, the skeptic Burke holds, have too exalted a view of man and of his rational capacities. The restlessness of mind which produced the tumult of ideological politics is seen as symptomatic of a general malady that besets modern man, his prideful belief in his own superiority. Burke's is really the most developed and articulate of all indictments of ideology and of what the skeptic perceives as the prideful quest for perfect schemes and ideal politics. Burke saw the stock of reason in man as small. Despite this, men still fled their basic limitations in flights of ideological fancy. They recognized no barrier to their powers and sought in politics to make reality match their speculative visions. Burke devoutly wished that men would appreciate the weakness of their own minds, their "subordinate rank in the creation." [17] The cosmology embodied in the medieval concept of the chain of being was revived in all its glory by Burke to remind man of his lowly place in God's divine scheme; for Burke "assumes that the awful Author of our being is the Author of our place in the order of existence." In doing this, God has "subjected us to act the part which belongs to the place assigned us." And that place is to know the limits of one's ra-

14 *Works*, I, 458.
15 "Appeal from the New to the Old Whigs," *Works*, IV, 196.
16 Quoted in Chapman, *op. cit.*, p. 65.
17 *Vindication of Natural Society*, p. 5.

tional and speculative faculties.[18] They cannot be used, for example, to cure the world of all its ills:

> Never expecting to find perfection in men, and not looking for Divine attributes in created beings, in my commerce with my contemporaries, I have found much human virtue . . . Am I not to avail myself of whatever good is to be found in the world, because of the mixture of evil that will always be in it?

Burke is convinced that so small is man's own supply of reason that he ought to "avail himself of the general bank and capital of nations and of ages." [19] It is because men forget this that they weave rational schemes of reform far beyond their power to implement. The rationalists are presumptuous men, oblivious to the reality of man's limitations. Men live less by reason than by "untaught feelings," and "old prejudices"; indeed, they love these old prejudices the longer they have lasted. Several times in the *Reflections* Burke returns to the theme of naked and shivering man exposed only in his bare rational power. He needs to cover this bare self with the "coat of prejudice." Other things may also help to cover this puny, naked, and rational self. The prejudice of religion may do this, for example. To those who attack religion and the church, Burke responds: "we should uncover our nakedness by throwing off that Christian religion which has hitherto been our boast and comfort." The prescriptive institutions of aristocracy, honor, and rank also serve this function. To destroy hierarchy would have "all the decent drapery of life rudely torn off . . . all which is necessary to cover the defects of our naked, shivering nature." When the mob, on the sixth of October, 1789, awoke the King and Queen of France, she was forced "to fly almost naked." Take away the genteel clothes of royalty and rank and all men and women are equal in their basic limitations. "On this scheme of things, a king is but a man, a queen is but a woman; a woman is but an animal, and an animal not of the highest order." [20] Here is the rub. When the clothes of prescription and prejudice are torn off, men and women stand naked and equal before their God. Earlier, Rousseau had declared this his very objective: "I demolished the petty lies of mankind; I dared to strip man's nature naked."

By way of concluding this description of Burke as a skeptic it might be useful to note once again the enduring appeal of his message. Conservative skeptics to this day envision government as primarily an act

---

18 "Appeal from the New to the Old Whigs," in *Works*, IV, 165.
19 *Reflections*, 99.
20 *Reflections*, 82, 87, 98–99, 103.

of management and administration. Burke's theory of "prudential management" as the true art of government has been stated most succinctly in the contemporary age by Michael Oakeshott, the English political philosopher. While not dealing with Burke, Oakeshott does call upon political leaders to take the ship of state to no particular port of call, no abstract or ideological ideal. Their task is to manage prudentially the crises that arise out of day-to-day developments—to keep the ship afloat: "in political activity, then, men sail a boundless and bottomless sea; there is neither harbor for shelter, nor floor for anchorage, neither starting place nor appointed destination. The enterprise is to keep afloat on an even keel." [21] Such skills, of course, require men of a high quality and character not found among the democratic citizenry.

Skepticism also involves a specific orientation to change, as we have seen. Change and development are inevitable in any body, and the body politic is no exception. What the skeptic fears, however, is planned change, change which is informed by some ideal, some abstract *a priori* blueprint. Self-consciously tampering and tinkering with the given structure out of a concern for efficiency, justice, or economy is fraught with danger. Better to suffer apparent inequity and imperfection than tempt the possible disorder and unpredictability of planned change. Any attempt to rationalize social or political life raises this spectre of chaos for the conservative skeptic. The social order, he holds, is complex and fragile; who knows what hell will break loose should men set about to structure it according to their abstract notions. This seemed tragically borne out for Burke when he reflected on the French having unleashed a monstrous nightmare on all Europe in their misguided zeal to change the apparently few defects and corruptions of their constitution. The skeptic Burke, then, cautions against zealous efforts to remedy evil lest these very efforts create even greater unintended evil. The position is echoed by a contemporary American conservative skeptic, the political scientist Edward Banfield. In an essay criticizing plans to rationalize and reorganize the American party system, he argues with pure Burkean skepticism:

A political system is an accident. It is an accumulation of habits, customs, prejudices and principles that have survived a long process of trial and error and of ceaseless response to changing circumstance. If the system works well on the whole, it is a lucky accident—the luckiest, indeed, that can befall a society . . . To meddle with the structure and operation of a successful political system is therefore the greatest foolishness that men are capable of. Because the system is intricate

21 *Rationalism in Politics* (London, 1962), p. 127.

beyond comprehension, the chance of improving it in the ways intended is slight, whereas the danger of disturbing its working and of
setting off a succession of unwanted effects that will extend throughout
the whole society is great.[22]

It is the same plea as that of the American liberal skeptic, Professor
Bickel, who, in his St. Patrick's Day piece in the *New Republic*, contends:

> Our problem, as much as Burke's, is that we cannot govern, and should
> not, in submission to the dictates of abstract theories, and that we
> cannot live, much less govern, without some "uniform rule and scheme
> of life," without principles, however provisionally and skeptically held.
> Burke's conservatism, if that is what it was, which at any rate belongs
> to the liberal tradition properly understood and translated to our time,
> is the way.[23]

It was his skepticism that drove the Whig Burke from his alliance
with the liberals like Charles James Fox and that defined his unique
vision of conservatism. So it is this same skepticism that appeals to a
1970s liberal like Bickel and drives him in conservative flight from
the reformer's zeal. The legitimacy and ethical justification of such
skeptical nay-saying is not our concern here. All that needs be insisted
upon is the unquestionable legacy of Burke's formulations—for better
or for worse.

[22] "In Defense of the American Party System," in Robert Goldwin ed., *Political
Parties, U.S.A.* (Chicago, 1964), pp. 37–8.
[23] "Reconsideration: Edmund Burke," in *New Republic*, March 17, 1973.

Chronology of the Life of Edmund Burke

1729   Born in Dublin of Irish parents; his father, a solicitor of good standing and a Protestant; his mother (maiden name Nagle), a Roman Catholic. With his two brothers he is brought up in the father's creed; his only sister in the mother's.

1743—48   At Trinity College, Dublin.

1750   Migrates to London, and lives at first in the Middle Temple as a student of law; abandons his study for literature. Period of obscurity and poverty follows.

1756   Marries Jane Mary Nugent, an Irishwoman, and, until her marriage, a Roman Catholic. (Their eldest son, Richard, is born 1758; a second son died in infancy.) Publishes A *Vindication of Natural Society* and *An Inquiry into the Origin of Our Ideas on the Sublime and Beautiful.*

1758   Undertakes the production of the *Annual Register,* for which he continued to write until about 1788.

1759   Makes acquaintance of William Gerard Hamilton, "Single-Speech Hamilton," a prominent politician, and becomes his private assistant.

1764   Burke leaves Ireland with Hamilton, who had lost his office. Becomes a member, with Johnson, Reynolds, Goldsmith, and others, of the "Literary Club."

1765   Parliament passes the Stamp Act for America. Burke breaks with Hamilton, and becomes private secretary to the Marquis of Rockingham on the formation of his first Ministry. Enters Parliament as member for Wendover (December).

1766   Temporary settlement of the American question by Rockingham's Ministry through (a) a Declaratory Act, affirming authority of Britain over the Colonies in legislation and taxation, and (b) the repeal of the Stamp Act. Rockingham dismissed (June 7). A coalition government is now formed by Pitt under the Duke of Grafton as nominal chief. Burke is offered a place in the new Ministry, but decides to follow his friends.

1768   Chatham leaves the Ministry (October). Burke purchases the estate of Gregories at Beaconsfield for a considerable sum.

1768—69   Struggle of the House of Commons with the constituency of Middlesex over the election of Wilkes.

1769   *Observations on a late Publication of the Present State of the Nation.*

1770	All the American import duties, except that on tea, are removed (March). *Thoughts on the Cause of the Present Discontents* published in April. New Ministry under Lord North.
1772	Opposes petition of certain of the clergy to be relieved from subscription to the articles.
1773	Visits France.
1774	*Speech on American Taxation* (April 19). Fox, having left North's Ministry in 1772, joins the Rockingham Whigs under Burke's influence. Burke returned for Bristol at the general election (November).
1775	His resolutions for conciliation with the colonies proposed and lost (March 22). War in America begins with the Battle of Lexington (April).
1777	*Letter to the Sheriffs of Bristol.*
1780	Brings in bill for economical reform which would reduce patronage power of the Crown, and thus reduce its power to control the House of Commons. Loses his seat at Bristol (September), and is elected for Malton.
1782	North resigns (March); Rockingham Ministry, with Burke Paymaster of the Forces. His economical reforms, in a reduced form, become law. July 1, death of Rockingham. Shelburne Ministry. Resignation of Fox and Burke. Britain acknowledges independence of the United States (December).
1783	Pitt Prime Minister.
1786	Burke moves impeachment of Warren Hastings (June 1).
1788	Trial of Warren Hastings begins (February 13). Burke supports motion for inquiry into the slave trade, and desires its total abolition (May).
1789	Meeting of the Estates General at Versailles (May). Storm of the Bastille (July 14). Abolition of feudal rights in France (August 4). The king and queen forced to ride in triumphal procession from Versailles to Paris (October 6).
1790	Debate in House of Commons on army estimates; Burke differs from Fox on conduct of French Army, and breaks with Sheridan (February 9). *Reflections on the Revolution in France* (published November 1).
1791	Burke renounces his friendship with Fox (May 6). Flight of Louis XVI to Varennes (June). *Appeal from the New to the Old Whigs* (published August). *Thoughts on French Affairs* (written December).
1792	*Letter to Sir Hercules Langrishe* on Roman Catholic disabilities in Ireland (written January). France declares war on Austria and Prussia (April). Overthrow of the French Monarchy (August 10).
1793	Execution of Louis XVI (January 21). France declares war on England (February 1). Committee of Public Safety instituted

(April). Fall of the Girondins (June); execution of Marie Antoinette (October); Reign of Terror (begins November).

1794   Burke retires from Parliament (July). Fall of Robespierre (July 28); death of Burke's son Richard (August). Grant of his first pension of 1,200 pounds.

1795   Grant of two further pensions, amounting together to 2,500 pounds. Peace concluded at Basel between Prussia and France (April 5). Acquittal of Hastings (April 23). Emergence of Napoleon Bonaparte. *Thoughts and Details on Scarcity* (presented to Pitt, November).

1796   *A Letter to a Noble Lord* (February). *Letters on a Regicide Peace,* i and ii.

1797   Burke dies, July 9.

BURKE LOOKS AT THE WORLD

Burke's correspondence, essays, and parliamentary speeches fill numerous volumes. It is difficult to single out parts of this vast repository as indicative of his personality or his attitude to the crises of his era, let alone his world view. These problems of selectivity notwithstanding, in this first part of the book Burke will speak for himself, stating his views on the English Constitution, events in America, England, and France. His is a mastery of English prose seldom equalled by a public figure; in its rich metaphorical cadences there emerges the conservative vision so indelibly linked to his name.

1

Parliamentary Government

Burke sat in the House of Commons from 1765 until 1794. It was a crucial era in the evolution of the British Parliament and, thus, of the general principles of parliamentary government. In these years, Burke articulated many of the fundamental assumptions that would come to characterize modern constitutional regimes.

"THE VIRTUE, SPIRIT, AND ESSENCE OF A HOUSE OF COMMONS"

The British Constitution, according to Burke, provided for popular government. At the center of the political process stood the deliberations of the popular assembly—the Commons. This sacred principle of popular government was threatened, according to Burke, if the independence of Commons was violated by the crown. Against the reality of George III's efforts to influence the popular assembly by controlling the election of some of its members or through the distribution of royal patronage to others, Burke posits the ideal of an independent Commons. This is illustrated in the following selection from his pamphlet Thoughts on the Cause of the Present Discontents *(1770).*

In speaking of this body, I have my eye chiefly on the House of Commons. I hope I shall be indulged in a few observations on the nature and character of that assembly; not with regard to its *legal form and power,* but to its *spirit,* and to the purposes it is meant to answer in the constitution.

The House of Commons was supposed originally to be *no part of the standing government of this country.* It was considered as a *control* issuing *immediately* from the people, and speedily to be resolved into the mass from whence it arose. In this respect it was in the higher part of government what juries are in the lower. The capacity of a magistrate being transitory, and that of a citizen permanent, the latter capacity it was hoped would of course preponderate in all discussions, not only between the people and the standing authority of the crown, but between the people and the fleeting authority of the House of Commons itself. It was hoped that, being of a middle nature between subject and government, they would feel with a more tender and a nearer interest everything that concerned the people than the other remoter and more permanent parts of legislature.

Whatever alterations time and the necessary accommodation of business may have introduced, this character can never be sustained unless the House of Commons shall be made to bear some stamp of the actual disposition of the people at large. It would (among public misfortunes) be an evil more natural and tolerable that the House of Commons should be infected with every epidemical frenzy of the people, as this would indicate some consanguinity, some sympathy of nature with their constituents, than that they should in all cases be wholly untouched by the opinions and feelings of the people out of doors. By this want of sympathy they would cease to be a House of Commons. For it is not the derivation of the power of that House from the people which makes it in a distinct sense their representative. The king is the representative of the people; so are the lords; so are the judges. They all are trustees for the people, as well as the commons; because no power is given for the sole sake of the holder; and although government certainly is an institution of divine authority, yet its forms, and the persons who administer it, all originate from the people.

A popular origin cannot therefore be the characteristical distinction of a popular representative. This belongs equally to all parts of government and in all forms. The virtue, spirit, and essence of a House of Commons consists in its being the express image of the feelings of the nation. It was not instituted to be a control *upon* the people, as of late it has been taught, by a doctrine of the most pernicious tendency. It was designed as a control *for* the people. Other institutions have been formed for the purpose of checking popular excesses; and they are, I apprehend, fully adequate to their object. If not, they ought to be made so. The House of Commons, as it was never intended for the support of peace and subordination, is miserably appointed for that service; having no stronger weapon than its mace, and no better officer than its serjeant-at-arms, which it can command of its own proper authority. A vigilant and jealous eye over executory and judicial magistracy; an anxious care of public money; an openness, approaching towards facility, to public complaint: these seem to be the true characteristics of a House of Commons. But an addressing House of Commons, and a petitioning nation; a House of Commons full of confidence when the nation is plunged in despair; in the utmost harmony with ministers whom the people regard with the utmost abhorrence; who vote thanks when the public opinion calls them for impeachments; who are eager to grant when the general voice demands account; who, in all disputes between the people and administration, presume against the people; who punish their disorders, but refuse even to inquire into the provocations to them; this is an unnatural, a monstrous state of things in this constitution. Such an assembly may be a great, wise, awful senate; but it is not, to any popular purpose, a House of Commons. This change from an immediate state of procuration and delegation to a course of acting as from original power is the way in which all the popular magistracies in the world have been perverted from their purposes. It is indeed their greatest and sometimes their incurable corruption. For there is a material distinction between that corruption by which particular points are carried against reason (this is a thing which cannot be prevented by human wisdom, and is of less consequence) and the corruption of the principle itself. . . .

For my part, I shall be compelled to conclude the principle of Parliament to be totally corrupted, and therefore its ends entirely defeated, when I see two symptoms: first, a rule of indiscriminate support to all ministers, because this destroys the very end of Parliament as a control, and is a general, previous sanction to misgovernment; and secondly, the setting up any claims adverse to the right of free election, for this tends to subvert the legal authority by which the House of Commons sits.

"PARTY IS A BODY OF MEN"

In this same pamphlet, Burke describes the importance in Parliamentary government of political parties. It was a bold step, for parties and factions were almost unanimously despised in the eighteenth century. Not only does Burke see their importance, but he insists on their legitimacy and value. This defense of party must of course be seen in the context of 1770. The Thoughts on the Cause of the Present Discontents *was prompted by the Wilkes*

*affair, the troubles with the American colonies, and resentment
with George III. Burke believes that such discontents can be
resolved and remedied not by the model of personal leadership
provided by the elder Pitt, but by the party or "body of men"
associated with the Marquis of Rockingham, to which he of
course belongs. Despite these partisan origins, Burke's defense of
party is an important landmark in the evolution of modern constitutional doctrine.*

Party is a body of men united for promoting by their joint endeavors the national interest upon some particular principle in which
they are all agreed. For my part, I find it impossible to conceive, that
any one believes in his own politics, or thinks them to be of any weight,
who refuses to adopt the means of having them reduced into practice.
It is the business of the speculative philosopher to mark the proper
ends of government. It is the business of the politician, who is the
philosopher in action, to find out proper means toward those ends,
and to employ them with effect. Therefore every honorable connection
will avow it is their first purpose, to pursue every just method to put
the men who hold their opinions into such a condition as may enable
them to carry their common plans into execution, with all the power
and authority of the state. As this power is attached to certain situations, it is their duty to contend for these situations. Without a pro-
scription of others, they are bound to give to their own party the
preference in all things; and by no means, for private considerations,
to accept any offers of power in which the whole body is not included;
nor to suffer themselves to be led, or to be controlled, or to be over-
balanced, in office or in council, by those who contradict the very fundamental principles on which their party is formed, and even those
upon which every fair connection must stand. Such a generous contention for power, on such manly and honorable maxims, will easily
be distinguished from the mean and interested struggle for place and
emolument. The very style of such persons will serve to discriminate
them from those numberless impostors, who have deluded the ignorant
with professions incompatible with human practice, and have afterwards incensed them by practices below the level of vulgar rectitude.
It is an advantage to all narrow wisdom and narrow morals, that
their maxims have a plausible air: and, on a cursory view, appear
equal to first principles. They are light and portable. They are as
current as copper coin; and about as valuable. They serve equally the
first capacities and the lowest; and they are, at least, as useful to the
worst men as to the best. Of this stamp is the cant of *Not men, but
measures;* a sort of charm by which many people get loose from every

honorable engagement. When I see a man acting this desultory and disconnected part, with as much detriment to his own fortune as prejudice to the cause of any party, I am not persuaded that he is right; but I am ready to believe he is in earnest. I respect virtue in all its situations; even when it is found in the unsuitable company of weakness. I lament to see qualities, rare and valuable, squandered away without any public utility. But when a gentleman with great visible emoluments abandons the party in which he has long acted, and tells you, it is because he proceeds upon his own judgment; that he acts on the merits of the several measures as they arise; and that he is obliged to follow his own conscience, and not that of others; he gives reasons which it is impossible to controvert, and discovers a character which it is impossible to mistake. What shall we think of him who never differed from a certain set of men until the moment they lost their power, and who never agreed with them in a single instance afterwards? Would not such a coincidence of interest and opinion be rather fortunate? . . .

In order to throw an odium on political connection, these politicians suppose it a necessary incident to it, that you are blindly to follow the opinions of your party, when in direct opposition to your own clear ideas; a degree of servitude that no worthy man could bear the thought of submitting to; and such as, I believe, no connections (except some court factions) ever could be so senselessly tyrannical as to impose. Men thinking freely, will, in particular instances, think differently. But still as the greater part of the measures which arise in the course of public business are related to, or dependent on, some great, *leading, general principles in government,* a man must be peculiarly unfortunate in the choice of his political company, if he does not agree with them at least nine times in ten. If he does not concur in these general principles upon which the party is founded, and which necessarily draw on a concurrence in their application, he ought from the beginning to have chosen some other, more conformable to his opinions. When the question is in its nature doubtful, or not very material, the modesty which becomes an individual, and, (in spite of our court moralists) that partiality which becomes a well-chosen friendship, will frequently bring on an acquiescence in the general sentiment. Thus the disagreement will naturally be rare; it will be only enough to indulge freedom, without violating concord, or disturbing arrangement. And this is all that ever was required for a character of the greatest uniformity and steadiness in connection. How men can proceed without any connection at all, is to me utterly incomprehensible.

"THE HAPPINESS AND GLORY OF A REPRESENTATIVE"

In 1774, Burke was invited to stand for election from the city of Bristol. The merchants of this great port city, very much dependent on trade with America, were impressed with Burke's efforts to mediate American affairs and to avoid a crisis harmful to their business dealings with the colonies. After he was elected, Burke spoke to his constituents on his conception of the role and responsibilities of a legislator in a popularly elected assembly. This speech on November 3, 1774 set forth what has remained the classic statement of the independence of the representative in contrast to what Burke saw as the opposing radical claim that the representative was simply the delegate of his constituents.

I am sorry I cannot conclude without saying a word on a topic touched upon by my worthy colleague. I wish that topic had been passed by at a time when I have so little leisure to discuss it. But since he has thought proper to throw it out, I owe you a clear explanation of my poor sentiments on that subject.

He tells you that "the topic of instructions has occasioned much altercation and uneasiness in this city"; and he expresses himself (if I understand him rightly) in favor of the coercive authority of such instructions.

Certainly, Gentlemen, it ought to be the happiness and glory of a representative to live in the strictest union, the closest correspondence, and the most unreserved communication with his constituents. Their wishes ought to have great weight with him; their opinions high respect; their business unremitted attention. It is his duty to sacrifice his repose, his pleasure, his satisfactions, to theirs—and above all, ever, and in all cases, to prefer their interest to his own.

But his unbiased opinion, his mature judgment, his enlightened conscience, he ought not to sacrifice to you, to any man, or to any set of men living. These he does not derive from your pleasure—no, nor from the law and the constitution. They are a trust from Providence, for the abuse of which he is deeply answerable. Your representative owes you, not his industry only, but his judgment; and he betrays, instead of serving you, if he sacrifices it to your opinion.

My worthy colleague says his will ought to be subservient to yours. If that be all, the thing is innocent. If government were a matter of will upon any side, yours, without question, ought to be superior. But government and legislation are matters of reason and judgment, and not of inclination; and what sort of reason is that in which the determination precedes the discussion, in which one set of men deliberate and another decide, and where those who form the conclusion are perhaps three hundred miles distant from those who hear the arguments?

To deliver an opinion is the right of all men; that of constituents is a weighty and respectable opinion, which a representative ought always to rejoice to hear, and which he ought always most seriously to consider. But *authoritative* instructions, *mandates* issued, which a member is bound blindly and implicitly to obey, to vote, and to argue for, though contrary to the clearest conviction of his judgment and conscience; these are things utterly unknown to the laws of this land, and which arise from a fundamental mistake of the whole order and tenor of our constitution.

Parliament is not a *congress* of ambassadors from different and hostile interests, which interests each must maintain, as an agent and advocate, against other agents and advocates; but Parliament is a *deliberative* assembly of *one* nation, with *one* interest, that of the whole—where not local purposes, not local prejudices, ought to guide, but the general good, resulting from the general reason of the whole. You choose a member, indeed; but when you have chosen him he is not a member of Bristol, but he is a member of *Parliament*. If the local constituent should have an interest or should form a hasty opinion evidently opposite to the real good of the rest of the community, the member for that place ought to be as far as any other from any endeavor to give it effect. . . . Your faithful friend, your devoted servant, I shall be to the end of my life: a flatterer you do not wish for. . . .

2
The American Revolution

Burke's was one of the stronger voices, along with Chatham, heard in Parliament pleading for understanding of and compromise with the American colonies. His early patron in Commons, Lord Rockingham, had, in fact, effected the repeal of the Stamp Act in 1766 during his short tenure as the King's first minister. Burke's defense of the colonists stood by no means as a contradiction with his later attacks on the French. The Americans were not innovators, or zealous ideologues, in his opinion; they were simply calling for a return to original rights which they considered revoked by recent British innovations.

"LEAVE THE AMERICANS AS THEY ANCIENTLY STOOD"

As the crisis neared in the 1770s, Burke, in a series of remarkable speeches, warned his colleagues in Commons about their dangerous course. The first selection below is from the Speech on American Taxation *in 1774. The second is excerpted from the* Speech on Moving Resolutions for Conciliation with the Colonies *in 1775. The final selection is a defense of his views on America against charges of disloyalty addressed to some of his constituents in* A Letter to the Sheriffs of the City of Bristol on the Affairs of America *(1777). These selections on America contain some of Burke's most passionate defense of precedent and tradition. Years before the French Revolution, he was critical of abstract speculation and insistent on the need for prudential and practical statesmanship.*

Speech on American Taxation (1774)

Again, and again, revert to your old principles—seek peace and ensure it—leave America, if she has taxable matter in her, to tax herself. I am not here going into the distinctions of rights, nor attempting to mark their boundaries. I do not enter into these metaphysical distinctions; I hate the very sound of them. Leave the Americans as they anciently stood, and these distinctions, born of our unhappy contest, will die along with it. They and we, and their and our ancestors, have been happy under that system. Let the memory of all actions in contradiction to that good old mode, on both sides, be extinguished forever. Be content to bind America by laws of trade; you have always done it. Let this be your reason for binding their trade. Do not burden them by taxes; you were not used to do so from the beginning. Let this be your reason for not taxing. These are the arguments of states and kingdoms. Leave the rest to the schools; for there only they may be discussed with safety. But if, intemperately, unwisely, fatally, you sophisticate and poison the very source of government, by urging subtle deductions, and consequences odious to those you govern, from the unlimited and illimitable nature of supreme sovereignty, you will teach them by these means to call that sovereignty itself in question. When you drive him hard, the boar will surely turn upon the hunters. If that sovereignty and their freedom cannot be reconciled, which will they take? They will cast your sovereignty in your face. Nobody will be argued into slavery. Sir, let the gentlemen on the other side call forth all their ability; let the best of them get up and tell me what one character of liberty the Americans have, and what one brand of slavery they are free from, if they are bound in their property and industry by all the restraints you can imagine on commerce, and at the same time are made pack-horses of every tax you choose to impose, without the least share in granting them. When they bear the burdens of unlimited monopoly, will you bring them to bear the burdens of unlimited revenue too? The Englishman in America will feel that this is slavery; that it is *legal* slavery will be no compensation either to his feelings or his understanding.

. . . Reflect how you are to govern a people who think they ought to be free, and think they are not. Your scheme yields no revenue; it yields nothing but discontent, disorder, disobedience; and such is the state of America that, after wading up to your eyes in blood, you could only end just where you begun—that is, to tax where no revenue is to be found, to—My voice fails me; my inclination, indeed, carries me no further; all is confusion beyond it.

Speech on Moving Resolutions for Conciliation with the Colonies (1775)

One fact is clear and indisputable: the public and avowed origin of this quarrel was on taxation. This quarrel has, indeed, brought on new disputes on new questions, but certainly the least bitter, and the fewest of all, on the trade laws. To judge which of the two be the real, radical cause of quarrel, we have to see whether the commercial dispute did, in order of time, precede the dispute on taxation. There is not a shadow of evidence for it. Next, to enable us to judge whether at this moment a dislike to the trade laws be the real cause of quarrel, it is absolutely necessary to put the taxes out of the question by a repeal. See how the Americans act in this position, and then you will be able to discern correctly what is the true object of the controversy, or whether any controversy at all will remain. Unless you consent to remove this cause of difference, it is impossible, with decency, to assert that the dispute is not upon what it is avowed to be. And I would, Sir, recommend to your serious consideration whether it be prudent to form a rule for punishing people, not on their own acts, but on your conjectures. . . . Alas! alas! when will this speculating against fact and reason end? What will quiet these panic fears which we entertain of the hostile effect of a conciliatory conduct? Is it true that no case can exist in which it is proper for the sovereign to accede to the desires of his discontented subjects? Is there anything peculiar in this case, to make a rule for itself? Is all authority of course lost when it is not pushed to the extreme? Is it a certain maxim that the fewer causes of dissatisfaction are left by government, the more the subject will be inclined to resist and rebel?

All these objections being in fact no more than suspicions, conjectures, divinations, formed in defiance of fact and experience, they did not, Sir, discourage me from entertaining the idea of a conciliatory concession, founded on the principles which I have just stated.

In forming a plan for this purpose, I endeavored to put myself in that frame of mind which was the most natural and the most reasonable, and which was certainly the most probable means of securing me from all error. I set out with a perfect distrust of my own abilities, a total renunciation of every speculation of my own, and with a profound reverence for the wisdom of our ancestors, who have left us the inheritance of so happy a constitution and so flourishing an empire, and, what is a thousand times more valuable, the treasury of the maxims and principles which formed the one and obtained the other. . . .

You will now, Sir, perhaps imagine that I am on the point of proposing to you a scheme for a representation of the colonies in Parliament. Perhaps I might be inclined to entertain some such thought; but a great flood stops me in my course. *Opposuit natura.* I cannot remove the eternal barriers of the creation. The thing, in that mode, I do not know to be possible. As I meddle with no theory, I do not absolutely assert the impracticability of such a representation; but I do not see my way to it; and those who have been more confident have not been more successful. However, the arm of public benevolence is not shortened; and there are often several means to the same end. What nature has disjoined in one way wisdom may unite in another. When we cannot give the benefit as we would wish, let us not refuse it altogether. If we cannot give the principal, let us find a substitute. But how? where? what substitute?

Fortunately, I am not obliged, for the ways and means of this substitute, to tax my own unproductive invention. I am not even obliged to go to the rich treasury of the fertile framers of imaginary commonwealths: not to the Republic of Plato, not to the Utopia of More, not to the Oceana of Harrington. . . . I only wish you to recognize, for the theory, the ancient constitutional policy of this kingdom with regard to representation, as that policy has been declared in acts of Parliament—and as to the practice, to return to that mode which a uniform experience has marked out to you as best, and in which you walked with security, advantage, and honor until the year 1763.

My resolutions, therefore, mean to establish the equity and justice of a taxation of America by *grant*, and not by *imposition;* to mark the *legal competency* of the colony assemblies for the support of their government in peace, and for public aids in time of war; to acknowledge that this legal competency has had *a dutiful and beneficial exercise,* and that experience has shown *the benefit of their grants,* and *the futility of parliamentary taxation, as a method of supply.*

These solid truths compose six fundamental propositions. . . . I think these six massive pillars will be of strength sufficient to support the temple of British concord. I have no more doubt than I entertain of my existence that, if you admitted these, you would command an immediate peace, and, with but tolerable future management, a lasting obedience in America. . . .

The first is a resolution: "That the colonies and plantations of Great Britain in North America, consisting of fourteen separate governments, and containing two millions and upwards of free inhabitants, have not had the liberty and privilege of electing and sending any knights and burgesses, or others, to represent them in the high court of Parliament." This is a plain matter of fact, necessary to be laid down, and (excepting the description) it is laid down in the language of the constitution; it is taken nearly *verbatim* from acts of Parliament.

The second is like unto the first: "That the said colonies and plantations have been made liable to, and bounden by, several subsidies, payments, rates, and taxes, given and granted by Parliament, though the said colonies and plantations have not their knights and burgesses in the said high court of Parliament, of their own election, to represent the condition of their country; by lack whereof they have been oftentimes touched and grieved by subsidies, given, granted, and assented to, in the said court, in a manner prejudicial to the common wealth, quietness, rest, and peace of the subjects inhabiting within the same."

Is this description too hot or too cold, too strong or too weak? Does it arrogate too much to the supreme legislature? Does it lean too much to the claims of the people? If it runs into any of these errors, the fault is not mine. It is the language of your own ancient acts of Parliament. . . . It is the genuine produce of the ancient, rustic, manly, home-bred sense of this country. I did not dare to rub off a particle of the venerable rust that rather adorns and preserves than destroys the metal. It would be a profanation to touch with a tool the stones which construct the sacred altar of peace. I would not violate with modern polish the ingenuous and noble roughness of these truly constitutional materials. Above all things, I was resolved not to be guilty of tampering—the odious vice of restless and unstable minds. I put my foot in the tracks of our forefathers, where I can neither wander nor stumble. . . .

The next proposition is: "That, from the distance of the said colonies, and from other circumstances, no method hath hitherto been devised for procuring a representation in Parliament for the said colonies." This is an assertion of a fact. I go no further on the paper; though, in my private judgment, a useful representation is impossible; I am sure it is not desired by them, nor ought it, perhaps, by us; but I abstain from opinions.

The fourth resolution is: "That each of the said colonies hath within itself a body, chosen, in part or in the whole, by the freemen, freeholders, or other free inhabitants thereof, commonly called the General Assembly, or General Court, with powers legally to raise, levy, and assess, according to the several usages of such colonies, duties and taxes towards defraying all sorts of public services." This competence in the colony assemblies is certain. It is proved by the whole tenor of their acts of supply in all the assemblies, in which the constant style of granting is: "An aid to his Majesty"; and acts granting to the crown have regularly, for near a century, passed the public offices without dispute. . . .

The fifth resolution is also a resolution of fact: "That the said general assemblies, general courts, or other bodies legally qualified as aforesaid, have at sundry times freely granted several large subsidies and public aids for his Majesty's service, according to their abilities, when required thereto by letter from one of his Majesty's principal Secretaries of State; and that their right to grant the same, and their cheerfulness and sufficiency in the said grants, have been at sundry times acknowledged by Parliament."

To say nothing of their great expenses in the Indian wars, and not to take their exertion in foreign ones, so high as the supplies in the year 1695, not to go back to their public contributions in the year 1710. . . .

I think, then, I am, from those journals, justified in the sixth and last resolution, which is: "That it hath been found by experience, that the manner of granting the said supplies and aids by the said general assemblies hath been more agreeable to the inhabitants of the said colonies, and more beneficial and conducive to the public service, than the mode of giving and granting aids and subsidies in Parliament, to be raised and paid in the said colonies."

This makes the whole of the fundamental part of the plan. The conclusion is irresistible. You cannot say that you were driven by any necessity to an exercise of the utmost rights of legislature. You cannot assert that you took on yourselves the task of imposing colony taxes from the want of another legal body that is competent to the purpose of supplying the exigencies of the state without wounding the prejudices of the people. Neither is it true that the body so qualified, and having that competence, had neglected the duty.

The question now, on all this accumulated matter, is whether you will choose to abide by a profitable experience or a mischievous theory? whether you choose to build on imagination or fact? whether you prefer enjoyment or hope? satisfaction in your subjects, or discontent?

If these propositions are accepted, everything which has been made to enforce a contrary system must, I take it for granted, fall along with it. . . .

I do not know that the colonies have, in any general way, or in any cool hour, gone much beyond the demand of immunity in relation to taxes. It is not fair to judge of the temper or dispositions of any man or any set of men, when they are composed and at rest, from their conduct or their expressions in a state of disturbance and irritation. It is, besides, a very great mistake to imagine that mankind follow up practically any speculative principle, either of government or of freedom, as far as it will go in argument and logical illation. We Englishmen stop very short of the principles upon which we support any given part of our constitution, or even the whole of it together. . . . All government, indeed every human benefit and enjoyment, every virtue and every prudent act, is founded on compromise and barter. We balance inconveniences; we give and take; we remit some rights that we may enjoy others; and we choose rather to be happy citizens than subtle disputants. As we must give away some natural liberty to enjoy civil advantages, so we must sacrifice some civil liberties for the advantages to be derived from the communion and fellowship of a great empire. But, in all fair dealings, the thing bought must bear some proportion to the purchase paid. None will barter away the immediate jewel of his soul. . . . None of us who would not risk his life rather than fall under a government purely arbitrary. But although there are some amongst us who think our constitution wants many improvements to make it a complete system of liberty, perhaps none who are of that opinion would think it right to aim at such improvement by disturbing his country and risking everything that is dear to him. In every arduous enterprise we consider what we are to lose as well as what we are to gain; and the more and better stake of liberty every people possess, the less they will hazard in a vain attempt to make it more. These are *the cords of man*. Man acts from adequate motives relative to his interest, and not on metaphysical speculations.

Aristotle, the great master of reasoning, cautions us, and with great weight and propriety, against this species of delusive geometrical accuracy in moral arguments, as the most fallacious of all sophistry.

A Letter to the Sheriffs of the City of Bristol on the Affairs of America (1777)

I am charged with being an American. If warm affection towards those over whom I claim any share of authority be a crime, I am guilty of this charge. But I do assure you (and they who know me publicly and privately will bear witness to me) that if ever one man lived more zealous than another for the supremacy of Parliament and the rights of this imperial crown, it was myself. Many others, indeed, might be more knowing in the extent of the foundation of these rights. I do not pretend to be an antiquary, a lawyer, or qualified for the chair of professor in metaphysics. I never ventured to put your solid interests upon speculative grounds. My having constantly declined to do so has been attributed to my incapacity for such disquisitions; and I am inclined to believe it is partly the cause. I never shall be ashamed to confess that where I am ignorant, I am diffident. I am, indeed, not very solicitous to clear myself of this imputed incapacity; because men even less conversant than I am in this kind of subtleties, and placed in stations to which I ought not to aspire, have, by the mere force of civil discretion, often conducted the affairs of great nations with distinguished felicity and glory.

When I first came into a public trust, I found your Parliament in possession of an unlimited legislative power over the colonies. I could not open the statute-book without seeing the actual exercise of it, more or less, in all cases whatsoever. This possession passed with me for a title. It does so in all human affairs. No man examines into the defects of his title to his paternal estate or to his established government. Indeed, common sense taught me that a legislative authority not actually limited by the express terms of its foundation, or by its own subsequent acts, cannot have its powers parcelled out by argumentative distinctions, so as to enable us to say that here they can and there they cannot bind. . . .

These were the considerations, Gentlemen, which led me early to think that, in the comprehensive dominion which the Divine Providence had put into our hands, instead of troubling our understandings with speculations concerning the unity of empire and the identity or distinction of legislative powers, and inflaming our passions with the heat and pride of controversy, it was our duty, in all soberness, to conform our government to the character and circumstances of the several people who composed this mighty and strangely diversified mass. I never was wild enough to conceive that one method would serve for the whole, that the natives of Hindostan and those of Virginia could be ordered in the same manner, or that the Cutchery court and the grand jury of Salem could be regulated on a similar plan. I was persuaded that government was a practical thing, made for the happiness of mankind, and not to furnish out a spectacle of uniformity to gratify the schemes of visionary politicians. Our business was to rule, not to wrangle; and it would have been a poor compensation that we had triumphed in a dispute whilst we lost an empire.

If there be one fact in the world perfectly clear, it is this: "that the disposition of the people of America is wholly averse to any other than a free government"; and this is indication enough to any honest statesman how he ought to adapt whatever power he finds in his hands to their case. If any ask me what a free government is, I answer that, for any practical purpose, it is what the people think so—and that they, and not I, are the natural, lawful, and competent judges of this matter. If they practically allow me a greater degree of authority over them than is consistent with any correct ideas of perfect freedom, I ought to thank them for so great a trust, and not to endeavor to prove from thence that they have reasoned amiss, and that, having gone so far, by analogy they must hereafter have no enjoyment but by my pleasure.

If we had seen this done by any others, we should have concluded them far gone in madness. It is melancholy, as well as ridiculous, to observe the kind of reasoning with which the public has been amused, in order to divert our minds from the common sense of our American policy. There are people who have split and anatomized the doctrine of free government, as if it were an abstract question concerning metaphysical liberty and necessity, and not a matter of moral prudence and natural feeling. They have disputed whether liberty be a positive or a negative idea; whether it does not consist in being governed by laws, without considering what are the laws, or who are the makers; whether man has any rights by nature; and whether all the property he enjoys be not the alms of his government, and his life itself their favor and indulgence. Others, corrupting religion as these have perverted philosophy, contend that Christians are redeemed into captivity, and the blood of the Saviour of mankind has been shed to make them the slaves of a few proud and insolent sinners. These shocking extremes provoking to extremes of another kind, speculations are let loose as destructive to all authority as the former are to all freedom; and every government is called tyranny and usurpation which is not formed on their fancies. In this manner the stirrers-up of this contention, not satisfied with distracting our dependencies and filling them with blood and slaughter, are corrupting our understanding: they are endeavoring to tear up, along with practical liberty, all the foundations of human society, all equity and justice, religion and order.

Civil freedom, Gentlemen, is not, as many have endeavored to persuade you, a thing that lies hid in the depth of abstruse science. It is a blessing and a benefit, not an abstract speculation; and all the just reasoning that can be upon it is of so coarse a texture as perfectly to suit the ordinary capacities of those who are to enjoy, and of those who are to defend it. Far from any resemblance to those propositions in geometry and metaphysics which admit no medium, but must be true or false in all their latitude, social and civil freedom, like all other things in common life, are variously mixed and modified, enjoyed in very different degrees, and shaped into an infinite diversity of forms, according to the temper and circumstances of every community. The *extreme* of liberty (which is its abstract perfection, but its real fault) obtains nowhere, nor ought to obtain anywhere; because extremes, as we all know, in every point which relates either to our duties or satisfactions in life, are destructive both to virtue and enjoyment. Liberty, too, must be limited in order to be possessed. The degree of restraint it is impossible in any case to settle precisely. But it ought to be the constant aim of every wise public counsel to find out by cautious experiments, and rational, cool endeavors, with how little, not how much, of this restraint the community can subsist: for liberty is a good to be improved, and not an evil to be lessened. It is not only a private blessing of the first order, but the vital spring and energy of the state itself, which has just so much life and vigor as there is liberty in it. But whether liberty be advantageous or not (for I know it is a fashion to decry the very principle), none will dispute that peace is a blessing; and peace must, in the course of human affairs, be frequently bought by some indulgence and toleration at least to liberty; for as the Sabbath (though of divine institution) was made for man, not man for the Sabbath, government, which can claim no higher origin or authority, in its exercise at least, ought to conform to the exigencies of the time, and the temper and character of the people with whom it is concerned, and not always to attempt violently to bend the people to their theories of subjection. The bulk of mankind, on their part, are not excessively curious concerning any theories whilst they are really happy; and one sure symptom of an ill-conducted state is the propensity of the people to resort to them.

But when subjects, by a long course of such ill conduct, are once thoroughly inflamed, and the state itself violently distempered, the people must have some satisfaction to their feelings more solid than a sophistical speculation on law and government. Such was our situation: and such a satisfaction was necessary to prevent recourse to arms; it was necessary towards laying them down; it will be necessary to prevent the taking them up again and again. Of what nature this satisfaction ought to be I wish it had been the disposition of Parliament seriously to consider. It was certainly a deliberation that called for the exertion of all their wisdom.

3
Radicalism and the Threat to the British Constitution

Agitation for the reform of the British Constitution had been growing since the 1760s, when the Wilkes affair gave rise to the Bill of Rights Association. A great deal of the reform effort was directed at the archaic system of representation, which narrowly confined the electorate and left whole geographical areas like the newer northern cities wholly unrepresented. These inequities were rendered all the more glaring in the 1770s as radicals like Price and Priestley used the slogan of the Americans, "no taxation without representation" in their own demands. Much of this effort to reform Parliament came to a head in the early 1780s with the campaign organized by the Yorkshire Association led by respectable gentlemen like Christopher Wyvill. The association sought passage of a reform bill that would increase both county and urban representation. Young William Pitt also emerged in these years as a champion of reform, introducing legislation to reform the House of Commons. Burke opposed all such efforts. Although he agreed with curbing the excesses of George III, he stood adamant against efforts to tamper with the glorious traditions of the British Constitution.

"I WILL NURSE ITS VENERABLE AGE"

In a speech before Commons in 1782, Burke carefully refuted the various radical and reform positions. Nearly a decade before his more famous denunciation of the French radicals, he takes his stand against democratic reform in the Speech on Reform of Representation of the Commons in Parliament. *Any settled arrangement is preferable to any untried experiment.*

We have now discovered, at the close of the eighteenth century, that the Constitution of England, which for a series of ages had been the proud distinction of this country, always the admiration and sometimes the envy of the wise and learned in every other nation,—we have

discovered that this boasted Constitution, in the most boasted part of
it, is a gross imposition upon the understanding of mankind, an insult
to their feelings, and acting by contrivances destructive to the best and
most valuable interests of the people. Our political architects have
taken a survey of the fabric of the British Constitution. It is singular
that they report nothing against the crown, nothing against the lords:
but in the House of Commons everything is unsound; it is ruinous in
every part; it is infested by the dry rot, and ready to tumble about our
ears without their immediate help. You know by the faults they find
what are their ideas of the alteration. As all government stands upon
opinion, they know that the way utterly to destroy it is to remove that
opinion, to take away all reverence, all confidence from it; and then,
at the first blast of public discontent and popular tumult, it tumbles
to the ground.

In considering this question, they who oppose it oppose it on different grounds. One is in the nature of a previous question: that some
alterations may be expedient, but that this is not the time for making
them. The other is, that no essential alterations are at all wanting,
and that neither *now* nor at *any* time is it prudent or safe to be meddling with the fundamental principles and ancient tried usages of our
Constitution,—that our representation is as nearly perfect as the necessary imperfection of human affairs and of human creatures will suffer
it to be,—and that it is a subject of prudent and honest use and thank-
ful enjoyment, and not of captious criticism and rash experiment.

On the other side there are two parties, who proceed on two
grounds, in my opinion, as they state them, utterly irreconcilable. The
one is juridical, the other political. The one is in the nature of a
claim of right, on the supposed rights of man as man: this party desire
the decision of a suit. The other ground, as far as I can divine what
it directly means, is, that the representation is not so politically framed
as to answer the theory of its institution. As to the claim of *right,* the
meanest petitioner, the most gross and ignorant, is as good as the best:
in some respects his claim is more favorable, on account of his ignorance; his weakness, his poverty, and distress only add to his titles; he
sues *in forma pauperis;* he ought to be a favorite of the court. But
when the *other* ground is taken, when the question is political, when
a new constitution is to be made on a sound theory of government,
then the presumptuous pride of didactic ignorance is to be excluded
from the counsel in this high and arduous matter, which often bids
defiance to the experience of the wisest. The first claims a personal
representation; the latter rejects it with scorn and fervor. The language of the first party is plain and intelligible; they who plead an
absolute right cannot be satisfied with anything short of personal representation, because all *natural* rights must be the rights of individuals, as by *nature* there is no such thing as politic or corporate per-

sonality: all these ideas are mere fictions of law, they are creatures of voluntary institution; men as men are individuals, and nothing else. They, therefore, who reject the principle of natural and personal representation are essentially and eternally at variance with those who claim it. As to the first sort of reformers, it is ridiculous to talk to them of the British Constitution upon any or upon all of its bases: for they lay it down, that every man ought to govern, himself, and that, where he cannot go, himself, he must send his representative; that all other government is usurpation, and is so far from having a claim to our obedience, it is not only our right, but our duty, to resist it. Nine tenths of the reformers argue thus,—that is, on the natural right.

It is impossible not to make some reflection on the nature of this claim, or avoid a comparison between the extent of the principle and the present object of the demand. If this claim be founded, it is clear to what it goes. The House of Commons, in that light, undoubtedly, is no representative of the people, as a collection of individuals. Nobody pretends it, nobody can justify such an assertion. When you come to examine into this claim of right, founded on the right of self-government in each individual, you find the thing demanded infinitely short of the principle of the demand. What! *one third* only of the legislature, and of the government no share at all? What sort of treaty of partition is this for those who have an inherent right to the whole? Give them all they ask, and your grant is still a cheat: for how comes only a third to be their younger-children's fortune in this settlement? How came they neither to have the choice of kings, or lords, or judges, or generals, or admirals, or bishops, or priests, or ministers, or justices of peace? Why, what have you to answer in favor of the prior rights of the crown and peerage but this: Our Constitution is a prescriptive constitution; it is a constitution whose sole authority is, that it has existed time out of mind? It is settled in these *two* portions against one, legislatively,—and in the whole of the judicature, the whole of the federal capacity, of the executive, the prudential, and the financial administration, in one alone. Nor was your House of Lords and the prerogatives of the crown settled on any adjudication in favor of natural rights: for they could never be so partitioned. Your king, your lords, your judges, your juries, grand and little, all are prescriptive; and what proves it is the disputes, not yet concluded, and never near becoming so, when any of them first originated. Prescription is the most solid of all titles, not only to property, but, which is to secure that property, to government. They harmonize with each other, and give mutual aid to one another. It is accompanied with another ground of authority in the constitution of the human mind, presumption. It is a presumption in favor of any settled scheme of government against any untried project, that a nation has long existed and flourished under it. It is a better presumption even of the *choice* of a nation,—far better than any sudden and temporary arrangement by actual election. Because a nation is not an idea only of local extent and individual momentary aggregation, but it is an idea of continuity which extends in time as well as in numbers and in space. And this is a choice not of one day or one set of people, not a tumultuary and giddy choice; it is a deliberate election of ages and of generations; it is a constitution made by what is ten thousand times better than choice; it is made by the peculiar circumstances, occasions, tempers, dispositions, and moral, civil, and social habitudes of the people, which disclose themselves only in a long space of time. It is a vestment which accommodates itself to the body. Nor is prescription of government formed upon blind, unmeaning prejudices. For man is a most unwise and a most wise being. The individual is foolish; the multitude, for the moment, is foolish, when they act without deliberation; but the species is wise, and, when time is given to it, as a species, it almost always acts right.

The reason for the crown as it is, for the lords as they are, is my reason for the commons as they are, the electors as they are. Now if the crown, and the lords, and the judicatures are all prescriptive, so is the House of Commons of the very same origin, and of no other. We and our electors have their powers and privileges both made and circumscribed by prescription, as much to the full as the other parts; and as such we have always claimed them, and on no other title. The House of Commons is a legislative body corporate by prescription, not made upon any given theory, but existing prescriptively,—just like the rest. This prescription has made it essentially what it is, an aggregate collection of three parts, knights, citizens, burgesses. The question is, whether this has been always so, since the House of Commons has taken its present shape and circumstances, and has been an essential operative part of the Constitution,—which, I take it, it has been for at least five hundred years.

This I resolve to myself in the affirmative; and then another question arises:—Whether this House stands firm upon its ancient foundations, and is not, by time and accidents, so declined from its perpendicular as to want the hand of the wise and experienced architects of the day to set it upright again, and to prop and buttress it up for duration;—whether it continues true to the principles upon which it has hitherto stood;—whether this be *de facto* the constitution of the House of Commons, as it has been since the time that the House of Commons has without dispute become a necessary and an efficient part of the British Constitution. To ask whether a thing which has always been the same stands to its usual principle seems to me to be perfectly absurd: for how do you know the principles, but from the construction? and if that remains the same, the principles remain the same. It is true that to say your Constitution is what it has been is no sufficient defence for those who say it is a bad constitution. It is an answer to those who say that it is a degenerate constitution. To those who say it is a bad one, I answer, Look to its effects. In all moral machinery, the moral results are its test.

On what grounds do we go to restore our Constitution to what it has been at some given period, or to reform and reconstruct it upon principles more conformable to a sound theory of government? A prescriptive government, such as ours, never was the work of any legislator, never was made upon any foregone theory. It seems to me a preposterous way of reasoning, and a perfect confusion of ideas, to take the theories which learned and speculative men have made from that government, and then, supposing it made on those theories which were made from it, to accuse the government as not corresponding with them. I do not vilify theory and speculation: no, because that would be to vilify reason itself. . . . No,—whenever I speak against theory, I mean always a weak, erroneous, fallacious, unfounded, or imperfect theory; and one of the ways of discovering that it is a false theory is by comparing it with practice. This is the true touchstone of all theories which regard man and the affairs of men,—Does it suit his nature in general?—does it suit his nature as modified by his habits?

The more frequently this affair is discussed, the stronger the case appears to the sense and the feelings of mankind. I have no more doubt than I entertain of my existence, that this very thing, which is stated as an horrible thing, is the means of the preservation of our Constitution whilst it lasts,—of curing it of many of the disorders which, attending every species of institution, would attend the principle of an exact local representation, or a representation on the principle of numbers. If you reject personal representation, you are pushed upon expedience; and then what they wish us to do is, to prefer their speculations on that subject to the happy experience of this country, of a growing liberty and a growing prosperity for five hundred years. Whatever respect I have for their talents, this, for one, I will not do. Then what is the standard of expedience? Expedience is that which is good for the community, and good for every individual in it. Now this expedience is the *desideratum,* to be sought either without the experience of means or with that experience. If without, as in case of the fabrication of a new commonwealth, I will hear the learned arguing what promises to be expedient; but if we are to judge of a commonwealth actually existing, the first thing I inquire is, What has been *found* expedient or inexpedient? And I will not take their *promise* rather than the *performance* of the Constitution. . . .

In every political proposal we must not leave out of the question the political views and object of the proposer; and these we discover, not by what he says, but by the principles he lays down. "I mean," says he, "a moderate and temperate reform: that is, I mean to do as little good as possible." If the Constitution be what you represent it, and there be no danger in the change, you do wrong not to make the reform commensurate to the abuse. Fine reformer, indeed! generous donor! What is the cause of this parsimony of the liberty which you dole out to the people? Why all this limitation in giving blessings and benefits to mankind? You admit that there is an extreme in liberty, which may be infinitely noxious to those who are to receive it, and which in the end will leave them no liberty at all. I think so, too. They know it, and they feel it. The question is, then, What is the standard of that extreme? What that gentleman, and the associations, or some parts of their phalanxes, think proper? Then our liberties are in their pleasure; it depends on their arbitrary will how far I shall be free. I will have none of that freedom. If, therefore, the standard of moderation be sought for, I will seek for it. Where? Not in their fancies, nor in my own: I will seek for it where I know it is to be found,—in the Constitution I actually enjoy. Here it says to an en-croaching prerogative,—"Your sceptre has its length; you cannot add an hair to your head, or a gem to your crown, but what an eternal law has given to it." Here it says to an overweening peerage,—"Your pride finds banks that it cannot overflow": here to a tumultuous and giddy people,—"There is a bound to the raging of the sea." Our Con-stitution is like our island, which uses and restrains its subject sea; in vain the waves roar. In that Constitution, I know, and exultingly I feel, both that I am free, and that I am not free dangerously to my-self or to others. I know that no power on earth, acting as I ought to do, can touch my life, my liberty, or my property. I have that inward and dignified consciousness of my own security and independence, which constitutes, and is the only thing which does constitute, the proud and comfortable sentiment of freedom in the human breast. I know, too, and I bless God for, my safe mediocrity: I know, that, if I possessed all the talents of the gentlemen on the side of the House I sit, and on the other, I cannot, by royal favor, or by popular delusion, or by oligarchical cabal, elevate myself above a certain very limited point, so as to endanger my own fall, or the ruin of my country. I know there is an order that keeps things fast in their place: it is made to us, and we are made to it. Why not ask another wife, other chil-dren, another body, another mind? . . .

There is a difference between a moral or political exposure of a public evil relative to the administration of government, whether in men or systems, and a declaration of defects, real or supposed, in the fundamental constitution of your country. The first may be cured in the individual by the motives of religion, virtue, honor, fear, shame, or interest. Men may be made to abandon also false systems, by ex-posing their absurdity or mischievous tendency to their own better thoughts, or to the contempt or indignation of the public; and after all, if they should exist, and exist uncorrected, they only disgrace individuals as fugitive opinions. But it is quite otherwise with the frame and constitution of the state: if that is disgraced, patriotism is destroyed in its very source. No man has ever willingly obeyed, much less was desirous of defending with his blood, a mischievous and absurd scheme of government. Our first, our dearest, most comprehensive relation, our country, is gone.

It suggests melancholy reflections, in consequence of the strange course we have long held, that we are now no longer quarrelling about the character, or about the conduct of men, or the tenor of measures, but we are grown out of humor with the English Constitution itself: this is become the object of the animosity of Englishmen. This Constitution in former days used to be the admiration and the envy of the world: it was the pattern for politicians, the theme of the eloquent, the meditation of the philosopher, in every part of the world. As to Englishmen, it was their pride, their consolation. By it they lived, for it they were ready to die. Its defects, if it had any, were partly covered by partiality, and partly borne by prudence. Now all its excellencies are forgot, its faults are now forcibly dragged into day, exaggerated by every artifice of representation. It is despised and rejected of men, and every device and invention of ingenuity or idleness set up in opposition or in preference to it. It is to this humor, and it is to the measures growing out of it, that I set myself (I hope not alone) in the most determined opposition . . . Never before did we at any time in this country meet upon the theory of our frame of government, to sit in judgment on the constitution of our country, to call it as a delinquent before us, and to accuse it of every defect and every vice; to see whether it, an object of our veneration, even our adoration, did or did not accord with a preconceived scheme in the minds of certain gentlemen. Cast your eyes on the journals of Parliament. It is for fear of losing the inestimable treasure we have that I do not venture to game it out of my hands for the vain hope of improving it. I look with filial reverence on the constitution of my country, and never will cut it in pieces, and put it into the kettle of any magician, in order to boil it, with the puddle of their compounds, into youth and vigor. On the contrary, I will drive away such pretenders; I will nurse its venerable age, and with lenient arts extend a parent's breath.

"RATHER GEORGE III OR IV THAN DR. PRIESTLEY"

A large number of the leaders of reform sentiment in England were religious dissenters—Unitarians, Presbyterians, and Baptists —who made up only seven percent of the population of England. In their efforts to repeal the Test and Corporation Acts, laws which denied government positions and university places to non-subscribers to the Church of England, the dissenters made frequent appeals to arguments of natural right and individual freedom. Burke was convinced that the leaders of this radical dissenting community, Rev. Richard Price and Rev. Joseph Priestley, were the vanguard of revolutionary upheaval in England. In the following excerpts from speeches made in Commons in the early 1790s, one sees Burke's angry response to the religious and political demands of the dissenters.

Speech on Mr. Fox's Motion to Repeal the Test Act (1790)

Abstract principles were what his clumsy apprehension could not grasp; he must have a principle embodied in some manner or other, and the conduct held upon it ascertained, before he could pretend to judge of its propriety and advantage in practice. But of all abstract principles, abstract principles of natural right which the dissenters rested on as their stronghold—were the most idle, because the most useless and the most dangerous to resort to. They superceeded society and broke asunder all those bonds which had formed the happiness of mankind for ages . . . If they were to go back abstractly to original rights, there would be an end of all society. Abstract principles of natural right had been long given up for the advantage of having, what was much better, society, which substituted wisdom and justice in the room of original right.

Speech on a Motion to Repeal Laws Making It a Crime to Hold Unitarian Views (1791)

Unitarians were associated for the express purpose of proselytism, aiming to collect a multitude sufficient by force and violence to overturn the church, and this concurrent with a design to subvert the state. The House ought not to wait till the conspirators, met to commemorate the fourteenth of July, shall seize the Tower of London and the magazines it contains, murder the governor and the Mayor of London, seize upon the King's person, drive out the House of Lords, occupy your gallery and thence as from an high tribunal, dictate to you . . .

Speech on Fox's Motion for Repeal of Certain Penal Statutes Respecting Religious Opinions (1792)

Let not both Houses of Parliament be led in triumph along with him (the King) and have law dictated to them by the Constitutional, the Revolution, and the Unitarian societies. These insect reptiles, whilst they go on only caballing and toasting, only fill us with disgust;

if they get above their natural size and increase the quantity, whilst they keep the quality of their venom, they become objects of the greatest terror. A spider in his natural size is only a spider ugly and loathsome, and his flimsy net is only fit for catching flies. But good God! Suppose a spider as large as an ox . . . What would they do if they had power commensurate to their malice. God forbid I ever should have a despotic master—but if I must, my choice is made, I will have Louis XVI rather than Monsieur Brissot or Chabot; rather George III or IV than Dr. Priestley . . . persons who would not load a tyrannous power by the poisoned talents of a vulgar low bred insolence.

4
The French Revolution

Burke was the most outspoken English critic of the French Revolution. All about him intellectual England thrilled at the news from France. Wordsworth wrote of how "Bliss was it that dawn to be alive." The revolution seemed to usher in a new age. Eventually, after the terror, many Englishmen like Wordsworth, Coleridge, Southey, and others soured on the Revolution and abandoned revolutionary (and often even reform) attitudes. Burke alone had criticized the Revolution from its outset, even breaking with his Whig colleagues—most dramatically with Charles James Fox—over the support of the new French regime. In 1790, before the terror, Burke rushed into print his Reflections on the Revolution in France, *prompted by a sermon preached by Richard Price. It was the catalyst for a furious debate in English letters, giving rise to answers from Paine, Godwin, Wollstonecraft and countless other tracts. In the* Reflections, *all the themes of Burke's conservatism come together. Here he develops most clearly and passionately his views on change, innovation, natural and prescriptive rights, speculative theorizing about politics, and the restricted role of reason. Here is most clearly demonstrated his aristocratic and antidemocratic preferences, as well as his reverence for prescriptive institutions and established religion.*

"YOU MIGHT HAVE REPAIRED THOSE WALLS"

The primary sin of the French revolutionaries was to tear down the building lock, stock, and barrel, to totally destroy the social fabric instead of repairing whatever the few abuses had damaged. There was much of value worth preserving in the French past, but the revolutionaries mindlessly destroyed everything. Equally shameful, Burke insists in the Reflections, *is that this was done in the name of novel, abstract, and inappropriate speculations about politics and society.*

You might, if you pleased, have profited of our example and have given to your recovered freedom a correspondent dignity. Your privileges, though discontinued, were not lost to memory. Your constitution, it is true, whilst you were out of possession, suffered waste and dilapidation; but you possessed in some parts the walls and, in all, the foundations of a noble and venerable castle. You might have repaired those walls; you might have built on those old foundations. Your constitution was suspended before it was perfected, but you had the elements of a constitution very nearly as good as could be wished. In your old states you possessed that variety of parts corresponding with the various descriptions of which your community was happily composed; you had all that combination and all that opposition of interests; you had that action and counteraction which, in the natural and in the political world, from the reciprocal struggle of discordant powers, draws out the harmony of the universe. These opposed and conflicting interests which you considered as so great a blemish in your old and in our present constitution interpose a salutary check to all precipitate resolutions. They render deliberation a matter, not of choice, but of necessity; they make all change a subject of *compromise,* which naturally begets moderation; they produce *temperaments* preventing the sore evil of harsh, crude, unqualified reformations and rendering all the headlong exertions of arbitrary power, in the few or in the many, forever impracticable. Through that diversity of members and interests, general liberty had as many securities as there were separate views in the several orders, whilst, by pressing down the whole by the weight of a real monarchy, the separate parts would have been prevented from warping, and starting from their allotted places.

You had all these advantages in your ancient states, but you chose to act as if you had never been molded into civil society and had everything to begin anew. You began ill, because you began by despising everything that belonged to you. You set up your trade without a capital. If the last generations of your country appeared without much luster in your eyes, you might have passed them by and derived your claims from a more early race of ancestors. Under a pious predilection for those ancestors, your imaginations would have realized in them a standard of virtue and wisdom beyond the vulgar practice of the hour; and you would have risen with the example to whose imitation you aspired. Respecting your forefathers, you would have been taught to respect yourselves. You would not have chosen to consider the French as a people of yesterday, as a nation of low-born servile wretches until the emancipating year of 1789. In order to furnish, at the expense of your honor, an excuse to your apologists here for several enormities of yours, you would not have been content to be represented as a gang of Maroon slaves suddenly broke loose from the house of bondage, and therefore to be pardoned for your abuse of the liberty to which you were not accustomed and ill fitted. Would it not, my worthy friend, have been wiser to have you thought, what I, for one, always thought you, a generous and gallant nation, long misled to your disadvantage by your high and romantic sentiments of fidelity, honor, and loyalty; that events had been unfavorable to you, but that you were not enslaved through any illiberal or servile disposition; that in your most devoted submission you were actuated by a principle of public spirit, and that it was your country you worshiped in the person of your king? Had you made it to be understood that in the delusion of this amiable error you had gone further than your wise ancestors, that you were resolved to resume your ancient privileges, whilst you preserved the spirit of your ancient and your recent loyalty and honor; or if, diffident of yourselves and not clearly discerning the almost obliterated constitution of your ancestors, you had looked to your neighbors in this land who had kept alive the ancient principles and models of the old common law of Europe meliorated and adapted to its present state —by following wise examples you would have given new examples of wisdom to the world. You would have rendered the cause of liberty venerable in the eyes of every worthy mind in every nation. You would have shamed despotism from the earth by showing that freedom was not only reconcilable, but, as when well disciplined it is, auxiliary to law. You would have had an unoppressive but a productive revenue. You would have had a flourishing commerce to feed it. You would have had a free constitution, a potent monarchy, a disciplined army, a reformed and venerated clergy, a mitigated but spirited nobility to lead your virtue, not to overlay it; you would have had a liberal order of commons to emulate and to recruit that nobility; you would have had a protected, satisfied, laborious, and obedient people, taught to seek and to recognize the happiness that is to be found by virtue in all conditions; in which consists the true moral equality of mankind, and not in that monstrous fiction which, by inspiring false ideas and vain expectations into men destined to travel in the obscure walk of laborious life, serves only to aggravate and embitter that real inequality which it never can remove, and which the order of civil life establishes as much for the benefit of those whom it must leave in a humble state as those whom it is able to exalt to a condition more splendid, but not more happy. You had a smooth and easy career of felicity and glory laid open to you, beyond anything recorded in the history of the world, but you have shown that difficulty is good for man.

Compute your gains: see what is got by those extravagant and presumptuous speculations which have taught your leaders to despise all their predecessors, and all their contemporaries, and even to despise themselves until the moment in which they become truly despicable. By following those false lights, France has bought undisguised calam-

ities at a higher price than any nation has purchased the most un-
equivocal blessings! France has bought poverty by crime! France has
not sacrificed her virtue to her interest, but she has abandoned her
interest, that she might prostitute her virtue. All other nations have
begun the fabric of a new government, or the reformation of an old,
by establishing originally or by enforcing with greater exactness some
rites or other of religion. All other people have laid the foundations
of civil freedom in severer manners and a system of a more austere and
masculine morality. France, when she let loose the reins of regal authority, doubled the license of a ferocious dissoluteness in manners
and of an insolent irreligion in opinions and practice, and has extended through all ranks of life, as if she were communicating some
privilege or laying open some secluded benefit, all the unhappy corruptions that usually were the disease of wealth and power. This is
one of the new principles of equality in France.

France, by the perfidy of her leaders, has utterly disgraced the tone
of lenient council in the cabinets of princes, and disarmed it of its
most potent topics. She has sanctified the dark, suspicious maxims of
tyrannous distrust, and taught kings to tremble at (what will hereafter
be called) the delusive plausibility of moral politicians. Sovereigns will
consider those who advise them to place an unlimited confidence in
their people as subverters of their thrones, as traitors who aim at their
destruction by leading their easy good-nature, under specious pre-
tenses, to admit combinations of bold and faithless men into a par-
ticipation of their power. This alone (if there were nothing else) is an
irreparable calamity to you and to mankind. Remember that your parliament of Paris told your king that, in calling the states together, he
had nothing to fear but the prodigal excess of their zeal in providing
for the support of the throne. It is right that these men should hide
their heads. It is right that they should bear their part in the ruin
which their counsel has brought on their sovereign and their country.
Such sanguine declarations tend to lull authority asleep, to encourage
it rashly to engage in perilous adventures of untried policy; to neglect
those provisions, preparations, and precautions which distinguish benevolence from imbecility, and without which no man can answer for
the salutary effect of any abstract plan of government or of freedom.
For want of these, they have seen the medicine of the state corrupted
into its poison. They have seen the French rebel against a mild and
lawful monarch with more fury, outrage, and insult than ever any
people has been known to rise against the most illegal usurper or the
most sanguinary tyrant. Their resistance was made to concession, their
revolt was from protection, their blow was aimed at a hand holding
out graces, favors, and immunities.

This was unnatural. The rest is in order. They have found their punishment in their success: laws overturned; tribunals subverted; industry without vigor; commerce expiring; the revenue unpaid, yet the people impoverished; a church pillaged, and a state not relieved; civil and military anarchy made the constitution of the kingdom; everything human and divine sacrificed to the idol of public credit, and national bankruptcy the consequence; and, to crown all, the paper securities of new, precarious, tottering power, the discredited paper securities of impoverished fraud and beggared rapine, held out as a currency for the support of an empire in lieu of the two great recognized species [i.e. gold and silver] that represent the lasting, conventional credit of mankind, which disappeared and hid themselves in the earth from whence they came, when the principle of property, whose creatures and representatives they are, was systematically subverted.

Were all these dreadful things necessary? Were they the inevitable results of the desperate struggle of determined patriots, compelled to wade through blood and tumult to the quiet shore of a tranquil and prosperous liberty? No! nothing like it. The fresh ruins of France, which shock our feelings wherever we can turn our eyes, are not the devastation of civil war; they are the sad but instructive monuments of rash and ignorant counsel in time of profound peace. They are the display of inconsiderate and presumptuous, because unresisted and irresistible, authority. The persons who have thus squandered away the precious treasure of their crimes, the persons who have made this prodigal and wild waste of public evils (the last stake reserved for the ultimate ransom of the state) have met in their progress with little or rather with no opposition at all. Their whole march was more like a triumphal procession than the progress of a war. Their pioneers have gone before them and demolished and laid everything level at their feet. Not one drop of *their* blood have they shed in the cause of the country they have ruined. They have made no sacrifices to their projects of greater consequence than their shoebuckles, whilst they were imprisoning their king, murdering their fellow citizens, and bathing in tears and plunging in poverty and distress thousands of worthy men and worthy families. Their cruelty has not even been the base result of fear. It has been the effect of their sense of perfect safety, in authorizing treasons, robberies, rapes, assassinations, slaughters, and burnings throughout their harassed land. But the cause of all was plain from the beginning.

"THEY HAVE THE 'RIGHTS OF MAN' "

The Reflections *singles out as an example of the misguided reliance on abstraction the revolutionary doctrine of the rights of man. Such metaphysical notions, Burke contends, have no place in politics, which is better guided by prudence and long*

*experience. True government is based on convention and de-
signed to provide a restraint on the passions, not to legitimize
independence and unlimited freedom. Society and human nature
are complex; the simplicity of abstract arguments of natural right
in no way corresponds to the intricacies of reality.*

It is no wonder, therefore, that with these ideas of everything in
their constitution and government at home, either in church or state,
as illegitimate and usurped, or at best as a vain mockery, they look
abroad with an eager and passionate enthusiasm. Whilst they are
possessed by these notions, it is vain to talk to them of the practice of
their ancestors, the fundamental laws of their country, the fixed form
of a constitution whose merits are confirmed by the solid test of long
experience and an increasing public strength and national prosperity.
They despise experience as the wisdom of unlettered men; and as for
the rest, they have wrought underground a mine that will blow up, at
one grand explosion, all examples of antiquity, all precedents, charters,
and acts of parliament. They have "the rights of men." Against these
there can be no prescription, against these no agreement is binding;
these admit no temperament and no compromise; anything withheld
from their full demand is so much of fraud and injustice. Against
these their rights of men let no government look for security in the
length of its continuance, or in the justice and lenity of its administration. The objections of these speculatists, if its forms do not quadrate
with their theories, are as valid against such an old and beneficent
government as against the most violent tyranny or the greenest usurpation. They are always at issue with governments, not on a question of
abuse, but a question of competency and a question of title. I have
nothing to say to the clumsy subtilty of their political metaphysics . . .
Far am I from denying in theory, full as far is my heart from with-
holding in practice (if I were of power to give or to withhold) the *real*
rights of men. In denying their false claims of right, I do not mean
to injure those which are real, and are such as their pretended rights
would totally destroy. If civil society be made for the advantage of
man, all the advantages for which it is made become his right. It is an
institution of beneficence; and law itself is only beneficence acting by
a rule. Men have a right to live by that rule; they have a right to do
justice, as between their fellows, whether their fellows are in public
function or in ordinary occupation. They have a right to the fruits of
their industry and to the means of making their industry fruitful.
They have a right to the acquisitions of their parents, to the nourish-
ment and improvement of their offspring, to instruction in life, and
to consolation in death. Whatever each man can separately do, with-

out trespassing upon others, he has a right to do for himself; and he has a right to a fair portion of all which society, with all its combinations of skill and force, can do in his favor. In this partnership all men have equal rights, but not to equal things. He that has but five shillings in the partnership has as good a right to it as he that has five hundred pounds has to his larger proportion. But he has not a right to an equal dividend in the product of the joint stock; and as to the share of power, authority, and direction which each individual ought to have in the management of the state, that I must deny to be amongst the direct original rights of man in civil society, for I have in my contemplation the civil social man, and no other. It is a thing to be settled by convention.

If civil society be the offspring of convention, that convention must be its law. That convention must limit and modify all the descriptions of constitution which are formed under it. Every sort of legislative, judicial, or executory power are its creatures. They can have no being in any other state of things; and how can any man claim under the conventions of civil society rights which do not so much as suppose its existence—rights which are absolutely repugnant to it? One of the first motives to civil society, and which becomes one of its fundamental rules, is *that no man should be judge in his own cause.* By this each person has at once divested himself of the first fundamental right of uncovenanted man, that is, to judge for himself and to assert his own cause. He abdicates all right to be his own governor. He inclusively, in a great measure, abandons the right of self-defense, the first law of nature. Men cannot enjoy the rights of an uncivil and of a civil state together. That he may obtain justice, he gives up his right of determining what it is in points the most essential to him. That he may secure some liberty, he makes a surrender in trust of the whole of it.

Government is not made in virtue of natural rights, which may and do exist in total independence of it, and exist in much greater clearness and in a much greater degree of abstract perfection; but their abstract perfection is their practical defect. By having a right to everything they want everything. Government is a contrivance of human wisdom to provide for human *wants.* Men have a right that these wants should be provided for by this wisdom. Among these wants is to be reckoned the want, out of civil society, of a sufficient restraint upon their passions. Society requires not only that the passions of individuals should be subjected, but that even in the mass and body, as well as in the individuals, the inclinations of men should frequently be thwarted, their will controlled, and their passions brought into subjection. This can only be done *by a power out of themselves,* and not, in the exercise of its function, subject to that will and to those passions which it is its office to bridle and subdue. In this sense the restraints on men, as well as their liberties, are to be reckoned among their rights. But as the liberties and the restrictions vary with times and circumstances and admit to infinite modifications, they cannot be settled upon any abstract rule; and nothing is so foolish as to discuss them upon that principle.

The moment you abate anything from the full rights of men, each to govern himself, and suffer any artificial, positive limitation upon those rights, from that moment the whole organization of government becomes a consideration of convenience. This it is which makes the constitution of a state and the due distribution of its powers a matter of the most delicate and complicated skill. It requires a deep knowledge of human nature and human necessities, and of the things which facilitate or obstruct the various ends which are to be pursued by the mechanism of civil institutions. The state is to have recruits to its strength, and remedies to its distempers. What is the use of discussing a man's abstract right to food or medicine? The question is upon the method of procuring and administering them. In that deliberation I shall always advise to call in the aid of the farmer and the physician rather than the professor of metaphysics.

The science of constructing a commonwealth, or renovating it, or reforming it, is, like every other experimental science, not to be taught a priori. Nor is it a short experience that can instruct us in that practical science, because the real effects of moral causes are not always immediate; but that which in the first instance is prejudicial may be excellent in its remoter operation, and its excellence may arise even from the ill effects it produces in the beginning. The reverse also happens: and very plausible schemes, with very pleasing commencements, have often shameful and lamentable conclusions. In states there are often some obscure and almost latent causes, things which appear at first view of little moment, on which a very great part of its prosperity or adversity may most essentially depend. The science of government being therefore so practical in itself and intended for such practical purposes—a matter which requires experience, and even more experience than any person can gain in his whole life, however sagacious and observing he may be—it is with infinite caution that any man ought to venture upon pulling down an edifice which has answered in any tolerable degree for ages the common purposes of society, or on building it up again without having models and patterns of approved utility before his eyes.

These metaphysic rights entering into common life, like rays of light which pierce into a dense medium, are by the laws of nature refracted from their straight line. Indeed, in the gross and complicated mass of human passions and concerns the primitive rights of men undergo such a variety of refractions and reflections that it becomes absurd to talk of them as if they continued in the simplicity of their original direction. The nature of man is intricate; the objects of society are of the greatest possible complexity; and, therefore, no simple disposition or direction of power can be suitable either to man's nature or to the quality of his affairs. When I hear the simplicity of contrivance aimed at and boasted of in any new political constitutions, I am at no loss to decide that the artificers are grossly ignorant of their trade or totally negligent of their duty. The simple governments are fundamentally defective, to say no worse of them. If you were to contemplate society in but one point of view, all these simple modes of polity are infinitely captivating. In effect each would answer its single end much more perfectly than the more complex is able to attain all its complex purposes. But it is better that the whole should be imperfectly and anomalously answered than that, while some parts are provided for with great exactness, others might be totally neglected or perhaps materially injured by the overcare of a favorite member.

The pretended rights of these theorists are all extremes; and in proportion as they are metaphysically true, they are morally and politically false. The rights of men are in a sort of *middle,* incapable of definition, but not impossible to be discerned. The rights of men in governments are their advantages; and these are often in balances between differences of good, in compromises sometimes between good and evil, and sometimes between evil and evil. Political reason is a computing principle: adding, subtracting, multiplying, and dividing, morally and not metaphysically, or mathematically, true moral denominations.

By these theorists the right of the people is almost always sophistically confounded with their power. The body of the community, whenever it can come to act, can meet with no effectual resistance; but till power and right are the same, the whole body of them has no right inconsistent with virtue, and the first of all virtues, prudence. Men have no right to what is not reasonable and to what is not for their benefit.

"THE AGE OF CHIVALRY IS GONE"

The proper principles around which society and government are to be organized, according to Burke, are prescription and prejudice. Institutions and ideas that have survived are essentially what most effectively provide the necessary restraint on evil passions. Since man's reason is limited, he should submit instinctively to prescriptive institutions, to ancient ideas and prejudices. The aristocracy with the monarchy at its apex is one of the most important such institutions inherited from the past. In the following excerpt from the Reflections, *Burke laments the sad fate of the French nobility, epitomized here by the brutal treatment of the Queen. In almost lyrical terms, Burke siezes upon this as*

symptomatic of the passing of an age and the arrival of the new
liberal-capitalist world. No longer is society ordered in ranks of
privilege and status; now all are considered equal. Kings are but
men and queens but women!

Yielding to reasons, at least as forcible as those which were so
delicately urged in the compliment on the new year, the king of
France will probably endeavor to forget these events and that compliment. But history, who keeps a durable record of all our acts and
exercises her awful censure over the proceedings of all sorts of sovereigns, will not forget either those events or the era of this liberal refinement in the intercourse of mankind. History will record that on
the morning of the 6th of October, 1789, the king and queen of France,
after a day of confusion, alarm, dismay, and slaughter, lay down, under the pledged security of public faith, to indulge nature in a few
hours of respite and troubled, melancholy repose. From this sleep the
queen was first startled by the sentinel at her door, who cried out to
her to save herself by flight—that this was the last proof of fidelity he
could give—that they were upon him, and he was dead. Instantly he
was cut down. A band of cruel ruffians and assassins, reeking with his
blood, rushed into the chamber of the queen and pierced with a hundred strokes of bayonets and poniards the bed, from whence this
persecuted woman had but just time to fly almost naked, and, through
ways unknown to the murderers, had escaped to seek refuge at the feet
of a king and husband not secure of his own life for a moment.

This king, to say no more of him, and this queen, and their infant
children (who once would have been the pride and hope of a great
and generous people) were then forced to abandon the sanctuary of
the most splendid palace in the world, which they left swimming in
blood, polluted by massacre and strewed with scattered limbs and
mutilated carcasses. Thence they were conducted into the capital of
their kingdom.

Two had been selected from the unprovoked, unresisted, promiscu-
ous slaughter, which was made of the gentlemen of birth and family
who composed the king's body guard. These two gentlemen, with all
the parade of an execution of justice, were cruelly and publicly
dragged to the block and beheaded in the great court of the palace.
Their heads were stuck upon spears and led the procession, whilst the
royal captives who followed in the train were slowly moved along,
amidst the horrid yells, and shrilling screams, and frantic dances, and
infamous contumelies, and all the unutterable abominations of the
furies of hell in the abused shape of the vilest of women.

After they had been made to taste, drop by drop, more than the
bitterness of death in the slow torture of a journey of twelve miles,

protracted to six hours, they were, under a guard composed of those very soldiers who had thus conducted them through this famous triumph, lodged in one of the old palaces of Paris now converted into a bastille for kings . . .

Although this work of our new light and knowledge did not go to the length that in all probability it was intended it should be carried, yet I must think that such treatment of any human creatures must be shocking to any but those who are made for accomplishing revolutions. But I cannot stop here. Influenced by the inborn feelings of my nature, and not being illuminated by a single ray of this new-sprung modern light, I confess to you, Sir, that the exalted rank of the persons suffering, and particularly the sex, the beauty, and the amiable qualities of the descendant of so many kings and emperors, with the tender age of royal infants, insensible only through infancy and innocence of the cruel outrages to which their parents were exposed, instead of being a subject of exultation, adds not a little to any sensibility on that most melancholy occasion. . . .

It is now sixteen or seventeen years since I saw the queen of France, then the dauphiness, at Versailles, and surely never lighted on this orb, which she hardly seemed to touch, a more delightful vision. I saw her just above the horizon, decorating and cheering the elevated sphere she just began to move in—glittering like the morning star, full of life and splendor and joy. Oh! what a revolution! and what a heart must I have to contemplate without emotion that elevation and that fall! Little did I dream when she added titles of veneration to those of enthusiastic, distant, respectful love, that she should ever be obliged to carry the sharp antidote against disgrace concealed in that bosom, little did I dream that I should have lived to see such disasters fallen upon her in a nation of gallant men, in a nation of men of honor and of cavaliers. I thought ten thousand swords must have leaped from their scabbards to avenge even a look that threatened her with insult. But the age of chivalry is gone. That of sophisters, economists, and calculators has succeeded, and the glory of Europe is extinguished forever. Never, never more shall we behold that generous loyalty to rank and sex, that proud submission, that dignified obedience, that subordination of the heart which kept alive, even in servitude itself, the spirit of an exalted freedom. The unbought grace of life, the cheap defense of nations, the nurse of manly sentiment and heroic enterprise, is gone! It is gone—that sensibility of principle, that charity of honor which felt a stain like a wound, which inspired courage whilst it mitigated ferocity, which ennobled whatever it touched, and under which vice itself lost half its evil by losing all its grossness.

This mixed system of opinion and sentiment had its origin in the ancient chivalry; and the principle, though varied in its appearance by the varying state of human affairs, subsisted and influenced through a long succession of generations even to the time we live in. If it should ever be totally extinguished, the loss I fear will be great. It is this which has given its character to modern Europe. It is this which has distinguished it under all its forms of government, and distinguished it to its advantage, from the states of Asia and possibly from those states which flourished in the most brilliant periods of the antique world. It was this which, without confounding ranks, had produced a noble equality and handed it down through all the gradations of social life. It was this opinion which mitigated kings into companions and raised private men to be fellows with kings. Without force or opposition, it subdued the fierceness of pride and power, it obliged sovereigns to submit to the soft collar of social esteem, compelled stern authority to submit to elegance, and gave a dominating vanquisher of laws to be subdued by manners.

But now all is to be changed. All the pleasing illusions which made power gentle and obedience liberal, which harmonized the different shades of life, and which, by a bland assimilation, incorporated into politics the sentiments which beautify and soften private society, are to be dissolved by this new conquering empire of light and reason. All the decent drapery of life is to be rudely torn off. All the super-added ideas, furnished from the wardrobe of a moral imagination, which the heart owns and the understanding ratifies, as necessary to cover the defects of our naked, shivering nature, and to raise it to dignity in our own estimation, are to be exploded, as a ridiculous, absurd, and antiquated fashion.

On this scheme of things, a king is but a man, a queen is but a woman, a woman is but an animal—and an animal not of the highest order. All homage paid to the sex in general as such, and without distinct views, is to be regarded as romance and folly. Regicide, and parricide, and sacrilege are but fictions of superstition, corrupting jurisprudence by destroying its simplicity. The murder of a king, or a queen, or a bishop, or a father, are only common homicide; and if the people are by any chance or in any way gainers by it, a sort of homicide much the most pardonable, and into which we ought not to make too severe a scrutiny.

On the scheme of this barbarous philosophy, which is the offspring of cold hearts and muddy understandings, and which is as void of solid wisdom as it is destitute of all taste and elegance, laws are to be supported only by their own terrors, and by the concern which each individual may find in them from his own private speculations or can spare to them from his own private interests. In the groves of *their* academy, at the end of every vista, you see nothing but the gallows. Nothing is left which engages the affections on the part of the commonwealth. On the principles of this mechanic philosophy, our institutions can never be embodied, if I may use the expression, in persons so as to create in us love, veneration, admiration, or attachment. But that sort of reason which banishes the affections is incapable of filling their place. These public affections, combined with manners, are required sometimes as supplements, sometimes as correctives, always as aids to law. . . .

But power, of some kind or other, will survive the shock in which manners and opinions perish; and it will find other and worse means for its support. The usurpation which, in order to subvert ancient institutions, has destroyed ancient principles will hold power by arts similar to those by which it has acquired it. When the old feudal and chivalrous spirit of *fealty*, which, by freeing kings from fear, freed both kings and subjects from the precautions of tyranny, shall be extinct in the minds of men, plots and assassinations will be anticipated by preventive murder and preventive confiscation, and that long roll of grim and bloody maxims which form the political code of all power not standing on its own honor and the honor of those who are to obey it. Kings will be tyrants from policy when subjects are rebels from principle.

When ancient opinions and rules of life are taken away, the loss cannot possibly be estimated. From that moment we have no compass to govern us; nor can we know distinctly to what port we steer. Europe, undoubtedly, taken in a mass, was in a flourishing condition the day on which your revolution was completed. How much of that prosperous state was owing to the spirit of our old manners and opinions is not easy to say; but as such causes cannot be indifferent in their operation, we must presume that on the whole their operation was beneficial.

We are but too apt to consider things in the state in which we find them, without sufficiently adverting to the causes by which they have been produced and possibly may be upheld. Nothing is more certain than that our manners, our civilization, and all the good things which are connected with manners and with civilization have, in this European world of ours, depended for ages upon two principles and were, indeed, the result of both combined: I mean the spirit of a gentleman and the spirit of religion. The nobility and the clergy, the one by profession, the other by patronage, kept learning in existence, even in the midst of arms and confusions, and whilst governments were rather in their causes than formed. Learning paid back what it received to nobility and to priesthood, and paid it with usury, by enlarging their ideas and by furnishing their minds. Happy if they had all continued to know their indissoluble union and their proper place! Happy if learning, not debauched by ambition, had been satisfied to continue the instructor, and not aspired to be the master! Along with its natural protectors and guardians, learning will be cast into the mire and trodden down under the hoofs of a swinish multitude.

If, as I suspect, modern letters owe more than they are always willing to owe to ancient manners, so do other interests which we value full as much as they are worth. Even commerce and trade and manufacture, the gods of our economical politicians, are themselves perhaps but creatures, are themselves but effects which, as first causes, we choose to worship. They certainly grew under the same shade in which learning flourished. They, too, may decay with their natural protecting principles. With you, for the present at least, they all threaten to disappear together. Where trade and manufactures are wanting to a people, and the spirit of nobility and religion remains, sentiment supplies, and not always ill supplies, their place; but if commerce and the arts should be lost in an experiment to try how well a state may stand without these old fundamental principles, what sort of a thing must be a nation of gross, stupid, ferocious, and, at the same time, poor and sordid barbarians, destitute of religion, honor, or manly pride, possessing nothing at present, and hoping for nothing hereafter?

I wish you may not be going fast, and by the shortest cut, to that horrible and disgustful situation. Already there appears a poverty of conception, a coarseness, and a vulgarity in all the proceedings of the Assembly and of all their instructors. Their liberty is not liberal. Their science is presumptuous ignorance. Their humanity is savage and brutal.

It is not clear whether in England we learned those grand and decorous principles and manners, of which considerable traces yet remain, from you or whether you took them from us. But to you, I think, we trace them best. . . . France has always more or less influenced manners in England; and when your fountain is choked up and polluted, the stream will not run long, or not run clear, with us or perhaps with any nation. This gives all Europe, in my opinion, but too close and connected a concern in what is done in France. Excuse me, therefore, if I have dwelt too long on the atrocious spectacle of the 6th of October, 1789, or have given too much scope to the reflections which have arisen in my mind on occasion of the most important of all revolutions which may be dated from that day—I mean a revolution in sentiments, manners, and moral opinions. As things now stand, with everything respectable destroyed without us, and an attempt to destroy within us every principle of respect, one is almost forced to apologize for harboring the common feelings of men.

"IN ENGLAND, WE GIVE NO CREDIT TO THEM"

Against the sins of the French, Burke juxtaposes the virtuous English. They are a traditional people, respectful of their country's customs, respectful of rank and hierarchy, and respectful of religion. The English, far from rejecting ancient ideas, glory in

*them, well aware that left to his own devices man is weak and
irrational. He needs the comforting cloak of prejudice. In pas-
sages such as the following it is quite clear that Burke has England very much in mind as he writes the Reflections. His description of the English would be by no means shared by the good
Reverends Price and Priestley, nor, of course, by Tom Paine.*

In England, we give no credit to them. We are generous enemies;
we are faithful allies. We spurn from us with disgust and indignation
the slanders of those who bring us their anecdotes with the attestation
of the flower-de-luce on their shoulder. We have Lord George Gordon
fast in Newgate; and neither his being a public proselyte to Judaism,
nor his having, in his zeal against Catholic priests and all sorts of ec-
clesiastics, raised a mob (excuse the term, it is still in use here) which
pulled down all our prisons, have preserved to him a liberty of which
he did not render himself worthy by a virtuous use of it. We have rebuilt Newgate and tenanted the mansion. We have prisons almost as
strong as the Bastille for those who dare to libel the queens of
France. . . .

Thanks to our sullen resistance to innovation, thanks to the cold
sluggishness of our national character, we still bear the stamp of our
forefathers. We have not (as I conceive) lost the generosity and dignity
of thinking of the fourteenth century, nor as yet have we subtilized
ourselves into savages. We are not the converts of Rousseau; we are
not the disciples of Voltaire; Helvetius has made no progress amongst
us. Atheists are not our preachers; madmen are not our lawgivers. We
know that *we* have made no discoveries, and we think that no discoveries are to be made, in morality, nor many in the great principles
of government, nor in the ideas of liberty, which were understood
long before we were born, altogether as well as they will be after the
grave has heaped its mold upon our presumption and the silent tomb
shall have imposed its law on our pert loquacity. In England we have
not yet been completely embowelled of our natural entrails; we still
feel within us, and we cherish and cultivate, those inbred sentiments
which are the faithful guardians, the active monitors of our duty, the
true supporters of all liberal and manly morals. We have not been
drawn and trussed, in order that we may be filled, like stuffed birds in
a museum, with chaff and rags and paltry blurred shreds of paper
about the rights of men. We preserve the whole of our feelings still
native and entire, unsophisticated by pedantry and infidelity. We have
real hearts of flesh and blood beating in our bosoms. We fear God; we
look up with awe to kings, with affection to parliaments, with duty
to magistrates, with reverence to priests, and with respect to nobility.

Why? Because when such ideas are brought before our minds, it is *natural* to be so affected; because all other feelings are false and spurious and tend to corrupt our minds, to vitiate our primary morals, to render us unfit for rational liberty, and, by teaching us a servile, licentious, and abandoned insolence, to be our low sport for a few holidays, to make us perfectly fit for, and justly deserving of, slavery through the whole course of our lives.

You see, Sir, that in this enlightened age I am bold enough to confess that we are generally men of untaught feelings, that, instead of casting away all our old prejudices, we cherish them to a very considerable degree, and, to take more shame to ourselves, we cherish them because they are prejudices; and the longer they have lasted and the more generally they have prevailed, the more we cherish them. We are afraid to put men to live and trade each on his own private stock of reason, because we suspect that this stock in each man is small, and that the individuals would do better to avail themselves of the general bank and capital of nations and of ages. Many of our men of speculation, instead of exploding general prejudices, employ their sagacity to discover the latent wisdom which prevails in them. If they find what they seek, and they seldom fail, they think it more wise to continue the prejudice, with the reason involved, than to cast away the coat of prejudice and to leave nothing but the naked reason; because prejudice, with its reason, has a motive to give action to that reason, and an affection which will give it permanence. Prejudice is of ready application in the emergency; it previously engages the mind in a steady course of wisdom and virtue and does not leave the man hesitating in the moment of decision skeptical, puzzled, and unresolved. Prejudice renders a man's virtue his habit, and not a series of unconnected acts. Through just prejudice, his duty becomes a part of his nature.

Your literary men and your politicians, and so do the whole clan of the enlightened among us, essentially differ in these points. They have no respect for the wisdom of others, but they pay it off by a very full measure of confidence in their own. With them it is a sufficient motive to destroy an old scheme of things because it is an old one. As to the new, they are in no sort of fear with regard to the duration of a building run up in haste, because duration is no object to those who think little or nothing has been done before their time, and who place all their hopes in discovery. They conceive, very systematically, that all things which give perpetuity are mischievous, and therefore they are at inexpiable war with all establishments. They think that government may vary like modes of dress, and with as little ill effect; that there needs no principle of attachment, except a sense of present convenience, to any constitution of the state. They always speak as if they were of opinion that there is a singular species of compact between them and their magistrates which binds the magistrate, but which has nothing reciprocal in it, but that the majesty of the people has a right to dissolve it without any reason but its will. Their attachment to their country itself is only so far as it agrees with some of their fleeting projects; it begins and ends with that scheme of polity which falls in with their momentary opinion.

These doctrines, or rather sentiments, seem prevalent with your new statesmen. But they are wholly different from those on which we have always acted in this country.

I hear it is sometimes given out in France that what is doing among you is after the example of England. I beg leave to affirm that scarcely anything done with you has originated from the practice or the prevalent opinions of this people, either in the act or in the spirit of the proceeding. Let me add that we are as unwilling to learn these lessons from France as we are sure that we never taught them to that nation. The cabals here who take a sort of share of your transactions as yet consist of but a handful of people. If, unfortunately, by their intrigues, their sermons, their publications, and by a confidence derived from an expected union with the counsels and forces of the French nation, they should draw considerable numbers into their faction, and in consequence should seriously attempt anything here in imitation of what has been done with you, the event, I dare venture to prophesy, will be that, with some trouble to their country, they will soon accomplish their own destruction. This people refused to change their law in remote ages from respect to the infallibility of popes, and they will not now alter it from a pious implicit faith in the dogmatism of philosophers, though the former was armed with the anathema and crusade, and though the latter should act with the libel and the lamp-iron.

"RELIGION IS THE BASIS OF CIVIL SOCIETY"

The prejudice most fundamental to social order is religion, according to Burke, and one of the principal prescriptive institutions is the church. In the following passage from the Reflections, *Burke reveals the extent to which he sees society, religion, and the Church inextricably interwoven. Religious ideas and clerical institutions constitute the quintessence of an ordered hierarchical society mindful of and coming to terms with the basic limitations of human nature and man's reason.*

We know, and what is better, we feel inwardly, that religion is the basis of civil society and the source of all good and of all comfort. In England we are so convinced of this, that there is no rust of superstition with which the accumulated absurdity of the human mind might have crusted it over in the course of ages, that ninety-nine in a hundred of the people of England would not prefer to impiety. We shall never be such fools as to call in an enemy to the substance of any system to remove its corruptions, to supply its defects, or to perfect its construction. If our religious tenets should ever want a further elucidation, we shall not call on atheism to explain them. We shall not light up our temple from that unhallowed fire. It will be illuminated with other lights. It will be perfumed with other incense than the infectious stuff which is imported by the smugglers of adulterated metaphysics. If our ecclesiastical establishment should want a revision, it is not avarice or rapacity, public or private, that we shall employ for the audit, or receipt, or application of its consecrated revenue. Violently condemning neither the Greek nor the Armenian, nor, since heats are subsided, the Roman system of religion, we prefer the Protestant, not because we think it has less of the Christian religion in it, but because, in our judgment, it has more. We are Protestants, not from indifference, but from zeal.

We know, and it is our pride to know, that man is by his constitution a religious animal; that atheism is against, not only our reason, but our instincts; and that it cannot prevail long. But if, in the moment of riot and in a drunken delirium from the hot spirit drawn out of the alembic of hell, which in France is now so furiously boiling, we should uncover our nakedness by throwing off that Christian religion which has hitherto been our boast and comfort, and one great source of civilization amongst us and amongst many other nations, we are apprehensive (being well aware that the mind will not endure a void) that some uncouth, pernicious, and degrading superstition might take place of it.

For that reason, before we take from our establishment the natural, human means of estimation and give it up to contempt, as you have done, and in doing it have incurred the penalties you well deserve to suffer, we desire that some other may be presented to us in the place of it. We shall then form our judgment.

On these ideas, instead of quarrelling with establishments, as some do who have made a philosophy and a religion of their hostility to such institutions, we cleave closely to them. We are resolved to keep an established church, an established monarchy, an established aristocracy, and an established democracy, each in the degree it exists, and in no greater. I shall show you presently how much of each of these we possess.

It has been the misfortune (not, as these gentlemen think it, the glory) of this age that everything is to be discussed as if the constitution of our country were to be always a subject rather of altercation than enjoyment. For this reason, as well as for the satisfaction of those among you (if any such you have among you) who may wish to profit of examples, I venture to trouble you with a few thoughts upon each of these establishments. I do not think they were unwise in ancient Rome who, when they wished to new-model their laws, set commissioners to examine the best constituted republics within their reach.

First, I beg leave to speak of our church establishment, which is the first of our prejudices, not a prejudice destitute of reason, but involving in it profound and extensive wisdom. I speak of it first. It is first and last and midst in our minds. For, taking ground on that religious system of which we are now in possession, we continue to act on the early received and uniformly continued sense of mankind. That sense not only, like a wise architect, has built up the august fabric of states, but, like a provident proprietor, to preserve the structure from profanation and ruin, as a sacred temple purged from all the impurities of fraud and violence and injustice and tyranny has solemnly and forever consecrated the commonwealth and all that officiate in it. This consecration is made that all who administer in the government of men, in which they stand in the person of God himself, should have high and worthy notions of their function and destination, that their hope should be full of immortality, that they should not look to the paltry pelf of the moment nor to the temporary and transient praise of the vulgar, but to a solid, permanent existence in the permanent part of their nature, and to a permanent fame and glory in the example they leave as a rich inheritance to the world.

Such sublime principles ought to be infused into persons of exalted situations, and religious establishments provided that may continually revive and enforce them. Every sort of moral, every sort of civil, every sort of politic institution, aiding the rational and natural ties that connect the human understanding and affections to the divine, are not more than necessary in order to build up that wonderful structure, Man, whose prerogative it is to be in a great degree a creature of his own making, and who, when made as he ought to be made, is destined to hold no trivial place in the creation. But whenever man is put over men, as the better nature ought ever to preside, in that case more particularly, he should as nearly as possible be approximated to his perfection.

The consecration of the state by a state religious establishment is necessary, also, to operate with a wholesale awe upon free citizens, because, in order to secure their freedom, they must enjoy some determinate portion of power. To them, therefore, a religion connected with the state, and with their duty toward it, becomes even more necessary than in such societies where the people, by the terms of their subjection, are confined to private sentiments and the management of their own family concerns. All persons possessing any portion of power ought to be strongly and awfully impressed with an idea that they act in trust, and that they are to account for their conduct in that trust to the one great Master, Author, and Founder of society.

"A PERFECT DEMOCRACY IS, THEREFORE, THE MOST SHAMELESS THING IN THE WORLD"

One of the greatest faults of the French, according to Burke, and of democracy in general, is the disregard for tradition. Both are preoccupied with the present. As they are oblivious to the past, so, too, they have no sense of organic responsibility to future generations. A democratic people, Burke insists in the Reflections, care as much for the continuity of the state as do flies of the summer; they will, at the urging of a sudden whim, rashly hack the constitution to pieces. They have no sense of society as a partnership between the living, the dead, and the yet to be born.

But where popular authority is absolute and unrestrained, the people have an infinitely greater, because a far better founded, confidence in their own power. They are themselves, in a great measure, their own instruments. They are nearer to their objects. Besides, they are less under responsibility to one of the greatest controlling powers on the earth, the sense of fame and estimation. The share of infamy that is likely to fall to the lot of each individual in public acts is small indeed, the operation of opinion being in the inverse ratio to the number of those who abuse power. Their own approbation of their own acts has to them the appearance of a public judgment in their favor. A perfect democracy is, therefore, the most shameless thing in the world. As it is the most shameless, it is also the most fearless. No man apprehends in his person that he can be made subject to punishment. Certainly the people at large never ought, for as all punishments are for example toward the conservation of the people at large, the people at large can never become the subject of punishment by any human hand. It is therefore of infinite importance that they should not be suffered to imagine that their will, any more than that of kings, is the standard of right and wrong. They ought to be persuaded that they are full as little entitled, and far less qualified with safety to themselves, to use any arbitrary power whatsoever; that therefore they are not under a false show of liberty, but in truth do exercise an unnatural, inverted domination, tyrannically to exact from those who officiate in the state not an entire devotion to their interest, which is their right, but an abject submission to their occasional will, extinguishing thereby in all those who serve them all moral principle, all sense of dignity, all use of judgment, and all consistency of character; whilst by the very same process they give themselves up a proper, a suitable, but a most contemptible prey to the servile ambition of popular sycophants or courtly flatterers.

When the people have emptied themselves of all the lust of selfish will, which without religion it is utterly impossible they ever should, when they are conscious that they exercise, and exercise perhaps in a higher link of the order of delegation, the power, which to be legitimate must be according to that eternal, immutable law in which will and reason are the same, they will be more careful how they place power in base and incapable hands. In their nomination to office, they will not appoint to the exercise of authority as to a pitiful job, but as to a holy function, not according to their sordid, selfish interest, nor to their wanton caprice, nor to their arbitrary will, but they will confer that power (which any man may well tremble to give or to receive) on those only in whom they may discern that predominant proportion of active virtue and wisdom, taken together and fitted to the charge, such as in the great and inevitable mixed mass of human imperfections and infirmities is to be found.

When they are habitually convinced that no evil can be acceptable, either in the act or the permission, to him whose essence is good, they will be better able to extirpate out of the minds of all magistrates, civil, ecclesiastical, or military, anything that bears the least resemblance to a proud and lawless domination.

But one of the first and most leading principles on which the commonwealth and the laws are consecrated is, lest the temporary possessors and life-renters in it, unmindful of what they have received from their ancestors or of what is due to their posterity, should act as if they were the entire masters, that they should not think it among their rights to cut off the entail or commit waste on the inheritance by destroying at their pleasure the whole original fabric of their society, hazarding to leave to those who come after them a ruin instead of an habitation—and teaching these successors as little to respect their contrivances as they had themselves respected the institutions of their forefathers. By this unprincipled facility of changing the state as often, and as much, and in as many ways as there are floating fancies or fashions, the whole chain and continuity of the commonwealth would be broken. No one generation could link with the other. Men would become little better than the flies of a summer.

And first of all, the science of jurisprudence, the pride of the human intellect, which with all its defects, redudancies, and errors is the collected reason of ages, combining the principles of original justice with the infinite variety of human concerns, as a heap of old exploded errors, would be no longer studied. Personal self-sufficiency and arrogance (the certain attendants upon all those who have never experienced a wisdom greater than their own) would usurp the tribunal. Of course, no certain laws, establishing invariable grounds of hope and fear, would keep the actions of men in a certain course or direct them to a certain end. Nothing stable in the modes of holding property or exercising function could form a solid ground on which any parent could speculate in the education of his offspring or in a choice for their future establishment in the world. No principles would be early worked into the habits. As soon as the most able instructor had completed his laborious course of institution, instead of sending forth his pupil, accomplished in a virtuous discipline, fitted to procure him attention and respect in his place in society, he would find everything altered, and that he had turned out a poor creature to the contempt and derision of the world, ignorant of the true grounds of estimation. Who would insure a tender and delicate sense of honor to beat almost with the first pulses of the heart when no man could know what would be the test of honor in a nation continually varying the standard of its coin? No part of life would retain its acquisitions. Barbarism with regard to science and literature, unskilfulness with regard to arts and manufactures, would infallibly succeed to the want of a steady education and settled principle; and thus the commonwealth itself would, in a few generations, crumble away, be disconnected into the dust and powder of individuality, and at length dispersed to all the winds of heaven.

To avoid, therefore, the evils of inconstancy and versatility, ten thousand times worse than those of obstinacy and the blindest prejudice, we have consecrated the state that no man should approach to look into its defects or corruptions but with due caution, that he should never dream of beginning its reformation by its subversion, that he should approach to the faults of the state as to the wounds of a father, with pious awe and trembling solicitude. By this wise prejudice we are taught to look with horror on those children of their country who are prompt rashly to hack that aged parent in pieces and put him into the kettle of magicians, in hopes that by their poisonous weeds and wild incantations they may regenerate the paternal constitution and renovate their father's life.

Society is indeed a contract. Subordinate contracts for objects of mere occasional interest may be dissolved at pleasure—but the state ought not to be considered as nothing better than a partnership agreement in a trade of pepper and coffee, calico, or tobacco, or some other such low concern, to be taken up for a little temporary interest, and to be dissolved by the fancy of the parties. It is to be looked on with other reverence, because it is not a partnership in things subservient only to the gross animal existence of a temporary and perishable nature. It is a partnership in all science; a partnership in all art; a partnership in every virtue and in all perfection. As the ends of such a partnership cannot be obtained in many generations, it becomes a partnership not only between those who are living, but between those who are living, those who are dead, and those who are to be born. Each contract of each particular state is but a clause in the great primeval contract of eternal society, linking the lower with the higher natures, connecting the visible and invisible world, according to a fixed compact sanctioned by the inviolable oath which holds all physical and all moral natures, each in their appointed place. This law is not subject to the will of those who by an obligation above them, and infinitely superior, are bound to submit their will to that law. The municipal corporations of that universal kingdom are not morally at liberty at their pleasure, and on their speculations of a contingent improvement, wholly to separate and tear asunder the bands of their subordinate community and to dissolve it into an unsocial, uncivil, unconnected chaos of elementary principles. It is the first and supreme necessity only, a necessity that is not chosen but chooses, a necessity paramount to deliberation, that admits no discussion and demands no evidence, which alone can justify a resort to anarchy. This necessity is no exception to the rule, because this necessity itself is a part, too, of that moral and physical disposition of things to which man must be obedient by consent or force; but if that which is only submission to necessity should be made the object of choice, the law is broken, nature is disobeyed, and the rebellious are outlawed, cast forth, and exiled from this world of reason, and order, and peace, and virtue, and fruitful penitence, into the antagonist world of madness, discord, vice, confusion, and unavailing sorrow.

"THE FRENCH SPIRIT OF PROSELYTISM"

In December 1791, Burke wrote his Thoughts on French Affairs, *which was a plea for England and all Europe to wage war on revolutionary France. In the following selection from this essay Burke describes the revolutionaries as a threat not only to traditional France, but to the entire civilized world as well. The joint effort of all Christian nations was required to meet and defeat its cancerous spread. In his evocation of a "free" world resisting the conspiratorial spread of subversive ideology, Burke used rhetoric that would be available to the many who rediscovered his message in the years after 1945. Note also in this passage Burke's acute sense of the social base of the Jacobin movement. The revolutionaries and their European supporters were not the poor, according to Burke, but the restless middle class.*

. . . There have been many internal revolutions in the government of countries, both as to persons and forms, in which the neighboring states have had little or no concern. Whatever the government might be with respect to those persons and those forms, the stationary interests of the nation concerned have most commonly influenced the new governments in the same manner in which they influenced the old; and the revolution, turning on matter of local grievance or of local accommodation, did not extend beyond its territory.

The present Revolution in France seems to me to be quite of another character and description, and to bear little resemblance or analogy to any of those which have been brought about in Europe upon principles merely political. *It is a revolution of doctrine and theoretic dogma.* It has a much greater resemblance to those changes which have been made upon religious grounds, in which a spirit of proselytism makes an essential part.

The last revolution of doctrine and theory which has happened in Europe is the Reformation. It is not for my purpose to take any notice here of the merits of that revolution, but to state one only of its effects.

That effect was *to introduce other interests into all countries than those which arise from their locality and natural circumstances.* The principle of the Reformation was such as, by its essence, could not be local or confined to the country in which it had its origin. For instance, the doctrine of "Justification by Faith or by Works," which was the original basis of the Reformation, could not have one of its alternatives true as to Germany and false as to every other country. Neither are questions of theoretic truth and falsehood governed by circumstances any more than by places. On that occasion, therefore, the spirit of proselytism expanded itself with great elasticity upon all sides: and great divisions were everywhere the result.

These divisions, however, in appearance merely dogmatic, soon became mixed with the political; and their effects were rendered much more intense from this combination. Europe was for a long time divided into two great factions, under the name of Catholic and Protestant, which not only often alienated state from state, but also divided almost every state within itself. The warm parties in each state were more affectionately attached to those of their own doctrinal interest in some other country than to their fellow-citizens or to their natural government, when they or either of them happened to be of a different persuasion. These factions, wherever they prevailed, if they did not absolutely destroy, at least weakened and distracted the locality of patriotism. The public affections came to have other motives and other ties.

It would be to repeat the history of the two last centuries to exemplify the effects of this revolution.

Although the principles to which it gave rise did not operate with a perfect regularity and constancy, they never wholly ceased to operate. Few wars were made, and few treaties were entered into, in which they did not come in for some part. They gave a color, a character, and direction to all the politics of Europe.

These principles of internal as well as external division and coalition are but just now extinguished. But they who will examine into the true character and genius of some late events must be satisfied that other sources of faction, combining parties among the inhabitants of different countries into one connection, are opened, and that from these sources are likely to arise effects full as important as those which had formerly arisen from the jarring interests of the religious sects. The intention of the several actors in the change in France is not a matter of doubt. It is very openly professed. . . .

The political dogma which, upon the new French system, is to unite the factions of different nations is this: "That the majority, told by the head, of the taxable people in every country is the perpetual, natural, unceasing, indefeasible sovereign; that this majority is perfectly master of the form as well as the administration of the state, and that the magistrates, under whatever names they are called, are only functionaries to obey the orders (general as laws or particular as decrees) which that majority may make; that this is the only natural government; that all others are tyranny and usurpation."

In order to reduce this dogma into practice, the republicans in France, and their associates in other countries, make it always their business, and often their public profession, to destroy all traces of ancient establishments, and to form a new commonwealth in each country, upon the basis of the French *Rights of Men*. On the principle of these rights, they mean to institute in every country, and as it were the germ of the whole, parochial governments, for the purpose of what they call equal representation. From them is to grow, by some media, a general council and representative of all the parochial governments. In that representative is to be vested the whole national power—totally abolishing hereditary name and office, leveling all conditions of men (except where money *must* make a difference), breaking all connection between territory and dignity, and abolishing every species of nobility, gentry, and church establishments: all their priests and all their magistrates being only creatures of election and pensioners at will.

Knowing how opposite a permanent landed interest is to that scheme, they have resolved, and it is the great drift of all their regulations, to reduce that description of men to a mere peasantry for the sustenance of the towns, and to place the true effective government in cities, among the tradesmen, bankers, and voluntary clubs of bold, presuming young persons: advocates, attorneys, notaries, managers of newspapers, and those cabals of literary men called academies. . . .

This system has very many partisans in every country in Europe, but particularly in England, where they are already formed into a body, comprehending most of the Dissenters of the three leading denominations. To these are readily aggregated all who are Dissenters in character, temper, and disposition, though not belonging to any of their congregations: that is, all the restless people who resemble them, of all ranks and all parties—Whigs, and even Tories; the whole race of half-bred speculators; all the atheists, deists, and Socinians; all those who hate the clergy and envy the nobility; a good many among the moneyed people; the East Indians almost to a man, who cannot bear to find that their present importance does not bear a proportion to their wealth. . . .

Formerly few, except the ambitious great or the desperate and indigent, were to be feared as instruments in revolutions. What has happened in France teaches us, with many other things, that there are more causes than have commonly been taken into our consideration by which government may be subverted. The moneyed men, merchants, principal tradesmen, and men of letters (hitherto generally thought the peaceable and even timid part of society) are the chief actors in the French Revolution. But the fact is that, as money increases and circulates, and as the circulation of news in politics and letters becomes more and more diffused, the persons who diffuse this money and this intelligence become more and more important. This was not long undiscovered. Views of ambition were in France, for the first time, presented to these classes of men: objects in the state, in the army, in the system of civil offices of every kind. Their eyes were dazzled with this new prospect. They were, as it were, electrified, and made to lose the natural spirit of their situation. A bribe, great without example in the history of the world, was held out to them—the whole government of a very large kingdom. . . .

What direction the French spirit of proselytism is likely to take, and in what order it is likely to prevail in the several parts of Europe, it is not easy to determine. The seeds are sown almost everywhere, chiefly by newspaper circulations, infinitely more efficacious and extensive than ever they were. And they are a more important instrument than generally is imagined. They are a part of the reading of all; they are the whole of the reading of the far greater number. There are thirty of them in Paris alone. The language diffuses them more widely than the English, though the English too are much read. The writers of these papers, indeed, for the greater part, are either unknown or in contempt, but they are like a battery, in which the stroke of any one ball produces no great effect, but the amount of continual repetition is decisive. Let us only suffer any person to tell us his story, morning and evening, but for one twelvemonth, and he will become our master.

All those countries in which several states are comprehended under some general geographical description, and loosely united by some federal constitution—countries of which the members are small, and greatly diversified in their forms of government, and in the titles by which they are held—these countries, as it might be well expected, are the principal objects of their hopes and machinations. . . .

As to Germany (in which, from their relation to the Emperor, I comprehend the Belgic Provinces), it appears to me to be, from several circumstances, internal and external, in a very critical situation; and the laws and liberties of the Empire are by no means secure from the contagion of the French doctrines and the effect of French intrigues, or from the use which two of the greater German powers may make of a general derangement to the general detriment. . . .

The Germanic body is a vast mass of heterogeneous states, held together by that heterogeneous body of old principles which formed the public law positive and doctrinal. The modern laws and liberties, which the new power in France proposes to introduce into Germany, and to support with all its force of intrigue and of arms, is of a very different nature, utterly irreconcilable with the first, and indeed fundamentally the reverse of it: I mean the *rights and liberties of the man,* the *droit de l'homme.* That this doctrine has made an amazing progress in Germany there cannot be a shadow of doubt. They are infected by it along the whole course of the Rhine, the Meuse, the Moselle, and in the greater part of Suabia and Franconia. It is particularly prevalent amongst all the lower people, churchmen and laity, in the dominions of the Ecclesiastical Electors. It is not easy to find or to conceive governments more mild and indulgent than these church sovereignties; but good government is as nothing when the rights of man take possession of the mind. Indeed, the loose rein held over the people in these provinces must be considered as one cause of the facility with which they lend themselves to any schemes of innovation, by inducing them to think lightly of their governments, and to judge of grievances, not by feeling, but by imagination.

It is in these electorates that the first impressions of France are likely to be made; and if they succeed, it is over with the Germanic body as it stands at present. A great revolution is preparing in Germany, and a revolution, in my opinion, likely to be more decisive upon the general fate of nations than that of France itself—other than as in France is to be found the first source of all the principles which are in any way likely to distinguish the troubles and convulsions of our age. If Europe does not conceive the independence and the equilibrium of the Empire to be in the very essence of the system of balanced power in Europe, and if the scheme of public law, or mass of laws, upon which that independence and equilibrium are founded, be of no leading consequence as they are preserved or destroyed, all the politics of Europe for more than two centuries have been miserably erroneous.

"ROUSSEAU IS THEIR CANON OF HOLY WRIT"

England finally went to war with France in 1793 along with most of the European powers. France did exceedingly well against this array of forces, and by late 1795, after the fall of Robespierre, Pitt's government made peace overtures to Paris. Negotiations dragged on. An angry Burke wrote four Letters on a Regicide Peace in 1796, opposing peace and urging a continuation of the holy war of Christian Europe against sinful France. In an interesting passage in these Letters Burke singled out one Frenchman as particularly responsible for the nightmare of the revolution and the war: Rousseau was the most pernicious among the "political men of letters," of "the literary Cabal" that brought forth the revolution. The malevolent tendencies of his political and educational writings led to social and political levelling, moral insensitivity, and cold irreligion. Against all this, Burke hoped England would continue to fight.

Besides the sure tokens which are given by the spirit of their particular arrangements, there are some characteristic lineaments in the general policy of your tumultuous despotism which, in my opinion, indicate, beyond a doubt, that no revolution whatsoever *in their disposition* is to be expected: I mean their scheme of educating the rising generation, the principles which they intend to instill and the sympathies which they wish to form in the mind at the season in which it is the most susceptible. Instead of forming their young minds to that docility, to that modesty, which are the grace and charm of youth, to an admiration of famous examples, and to an averseness to anything which approaches to pride, petulance, and self-conceit (distempers to which that time of life is of itself sufficiently liable), they artificially foment these evil dispositions, and even form them into springs of action. Nothing ought to be more weighed than the nature of books recommended by public authority. So recommended, they soon form the character of the age. Uncertain indeed is the efficacy, limited indeed is the extent, of a virtuous institution. But if education takes in *vice* as any part of its system, there is no doubt but that it will operate with abundant energy, and to an extent indefinite. The magistrate who in favor of freedom thinks himself obliged to suffer all sorts of publications is under a stricter duty than any other well to consider what sort of writers he shall authorize, and shall recommend by the strongest of all sanctions; that is, by public honors and rewards. He ought to be cautious how he recommends authors of mixed or ambiguous morality. He ought to be fearful of putting into the hands of youth writers indulgent to the peculiarities of their own complexion, lest they should teach the humors of the professor rather than the principles of the science. He ought, above all, to be cautious in recommending any writer who has carried marks of a deranged understanding: for where there is no sound reason, there can be no real virtue; and madness is ever vicious and malignant.

The Assembly proceeds on maxims the very reverse of these. The Assembly recommends to its youth a study of the bold experimenters in morality. Everybody knows that there is a great dispute amongst their leaders which of them is the best resemblance of Rousseau. In truth, they all resemble him. His blood they transfuse into their minds and into their manners. Him they study; him they meditate; him they turn over in all the time they can spare from the laborious mischief of the day or the debauches of the night. Rousseau is their canon of holy writ; in his life he is their canon of Polycletus; he is their standard figure of perfection. To this man and this writer, as a pattern to authors and to Frenchmen, the foundries of Paris are now running for statues, with the kettles of their poor and the bells of their churches. If an author had written like a great genius on geometry, though his practical and speculative morals were vicious in the extreme, it might appear that in voting the statue they honored only the geometrician. But Rousseau is a moralist or he is nothing. It is impossible, therefore, putting the circumstances together, to mistake their design in choosing the author with whom they have begun to recommend a course of studies.

Their great problem is to find a substitute for all the principles which hitherto have been employed to regulate the human will and action. They find dispositions in the mind of such force and quality as may fit men, far better than the old morality, for the purposes of such a state as theirs, and may go much further in supporting their power and destroying their enemies. They have therefore chosen a selfish, flattering, seductive, ostentatious vice, in the place of plain duty. True humility, the basis of the Christian system, is the low, but deep and firm foundation of all real virtue. But this, as very painful in the practice, and little imposing in the appearance, they have totally discarded. Their object is to merge all natural and all social sentiment in inordinate vanity. In a small degree, and conversant in little things, vanity is of little moment. When full-grown, it is the worst of vices, and the occasional mimic of them all. It makes the whole man false. It leaves nothing sincere or trustworthy about him. His best qualities are poisoned and perverted by it, and operate exactly as the worst. When your lords had many writers as immoral as the object of their statue (such as Voltaire and others), they chose Rousseau, because in him that peculiar vice which they wished to erect into ruling virtue was by far the most conspicuous.

We have had the great professor and founder of *the philosophy of vanity* in England. As I had good opportunities of knowing his proceedings almost from day to day, he left no doubt on my mind that he entertained no principle, either to influence his heart or to guide his understanding, but *vanity*. With this vice he was possessed to a degree little short of madness. It is from the same deranged, eccentric vanity that this, the insane Socrates of the National Assembly, was impelled to publish a mad confession of his mad faults, and to attempt a new sort of glory from bringing hardily to light the obscure and vulgar vices which we know may sometimes be blended with eminent talents. He has not observed on the nature of vanity who does not know that it is omnivorous; that it has no choice in its food; that it is fond to talk even of its own faults and vices, as what will excite surprise and draw attention, and what will pass at worst for openness and candor.

It was this abuse and perversion, which vanity makes even of hypocrisy, which has driven Rousseau to record a life not so much as checkered or spotted here and there with virtues, or even distinguished by a single good action. It is such a life he chooses to offer to the attention of mankind. It is such a life that, with a wild defiance, he flings in the face of his Creator, whom he acknowledges only to brave. Your Assembly, knowing how much more powerful example is found than precept, has chosen this man (by his own account without a single virtue) for a model. To him they erect their first statue. From him they commence their series of honors and distinctions.

It is that new-invented virtue which your masters canonize that led their moral hero constantly to exhaust the stores of his powerful rhetoric in the expression of universal benevolence, whilst his heart was incapable of harboring one spark of common parental affection. Benevolence to the whole species, and want of feeling for every individual with whom the professors come in contact, form the character of the new philosophy. Setting up for an unsocial independence, this their hero of vanity refuses the just price of common labor, as well as the tribute which opulence owes to genius, and which, when paid, honors the giver and the receiver; and then he pleads his beggary as an excuse for his crimes. He melts with tenderness for those only who touch him by the remotest relation, and then, without one natural pang, casts away, as a sort of offal and excrement, the spawn of his disgustful amours, and sends his children to the hospital of foundlings. The bear loves, licks, and forms her young: but bears are not philosophers. Vanity, however, finds its account in reversing the train of our natural feelings. Thousands admire the sentimental writer; the affectionate father is hardly known in his parish.

Under this philosophic instructor in *the ethics of vanity*, they have attempted in France a regeneration of the moral constitution of man. Statesmen like your present rulers exist by everything which is spurious, fictitious, and false; by everything which takes the man from his house and sets him on a stage; which makes him up an artificial creature, with painted, theatric sentiments, fit to be seen by the glare of candlelight, and formed to be contemplated at a due distance. Vanity is too apt to prevail in all of us, and in all countries. To the improvement of Frenchmen, it seems not absolutely necessary that it should be taught upon system. But it is plain that the present rebellion was its legitimate offspring, and it is piously fed by that rebellion with a daily dole.

If the system of institution recommended by the Assembly is false and theatric, it is because their system of government is of the same character. To that, and to that alone, it is strictly conformable. To understand either, we must connect the morals with the politics of the legislators. Your practical philosophers, systematic in everything, have wisely begun at the source. As the relation between parents and children is the first among the elements of vulgar, natural morality, they erect statues to a wild, ferocious, low-minded, hard-hearted father, of fine general feelings—a lover of his kind, but a hater of his kindred. Your masters reject the duties of this vulgar relation, as contrary to liberty, as not founded in the social compact, and not binding according to the rights of men; because the relation is not, of course, the result of *free election*—never so on the side of the children, not always on the part of the parents.

. . . Through this same instructor, by whom they corrupt the morals, they corrupt the taste. Taste and elegance, though they are reckoned only among the smaller and secondary morals, yet are of no mean importance in the regulation of life. A moral taste is not of force to turn vice into virtue; but it recommends virtue with something like the blandishments of pleasure, and it infinitely abates the evils of vice. Rousseau, a writer of great force and vivacity, is totally destitute of taste in any sense of the word. Your masters, who are his scholars, conceive that all refinement has an aristocratic character. The last age had exhausted all its powers in giving a grace and nobleness to our natural appetites, and in raising them into a higher class and order than seemed justly to belong to them. Through Rousseau, your masters are resolved to destroy these aristocratic prejudices. The passion called love has so general and powerful an influence, it makes so much of the entertainment, and indeed so much the occupation, of that part of life which decides the character forever, that the mode and the principles on which it engages the sympathy and strikes the imagination become of the utmost importance to the morals and manners of every society. Your rulers were well aware of this; and in their system of changing your manners to accommodate them to their politics, they found nothing so convenient as Rousseau. Through him they teach men to love after the fashion of philosophers: that is, they teach to men, to Frenchmen, a love without gallantry—a love without anything of that fine flower of youthfulness and gentility which places it, if not among the virtues, among the ornaments of life. Instead of this passion, naturally allied to grace and manners, they infuse into their youth an unfashioned, indelicate, sour, gloomy, ferocious medley of pedantry and lewdness—of metaphysical speculations blended with the coarsest sensuality. . . .

I am certain that the writings of Rousseau lead directly to this kind of shameful evil. I have often wondered how he comes to be so much more admired and followed on the Continent than he is here. Perhaps a secret charm in the language may have its share in this extraordinary difference. We certainly perceive, and to a degree we feel, in this writer a style glowing, animated, enthusiastic, at the same time that we find it lax, diffuse, and not in the best taste of composition; all the members of the piece being pretty equally labored and expanded, without any due selection or subordination of parts. He is generally too much on the stretch, and his manner has little variety. We cannot rest upon any of his works, though they contain observations which occasionally discover a considerable insight into human nature. But his doctrines, on the whole, are so inapplicable to real life and manners that we never dream of drawing from them any rule for laws or conduct, or for fortifying or illustrating anything by a reference to his opinions. . . .

Perhaps bold speculations are more acceptable because more new to you than to us, who have been long since satiated with them. We continue, as in the two last ages, to read, more generally than I believe is now done on the Continent, the authors of sound antiquity. These occupy our minds; they give us another taste and turn; and will not suffer us to be more than transiently amused with paradoxical morality. It is not that I consider this writer as wholly destitute of just notions. Amongst his irregularities, it must be reckoned that he is sometimes moral, and moral in a very sublime strain. But the *general spirit and tendency* of his works is mischievous—and the more mischievous for this mixture; for perfect depravity of sentiment is not reconcilable with eloquence; and the mind (though corruptible, not complexionally vicious) would reject and throw off with disgust a lesson of pure and unmixed evil. These writers make even virtue a pander to vice.

However, I less consider the author than the system of the Assembly in perverting morality through his means. This I confess makes me nearly despair of any attempt upon the minds of their followers, through reason, honor, or conscience. The great object of your tyrants is to destroy the gentlemen of France; and for that purpose they destroy, to the best of their power, all the effect of those relations which may render considerable men powerful or even safe. To destroy that order, they vitiate the whole community. . . . They propagate principles by which every servant may think it, if not his duty, at least his privilege, to betray his master. By these principles, every considerable father of a family loses the sanctuary of his house. . . . They destroy all the tranquillity and security of domestic life: turning the asylum of the house into a gloomy prison, where the father of the family must drag out a miserable existence, endangered in proportion to the apparent means of his safety; where he is worse than solitary in a crowd of domestics, and more apprehensive from his servants and inmates than from the hired, bloodthirsty mob without doors who are ready to pull him to the *lanterne*.

It is thus, and for the same end, that they endeavor to destroy that tribunal of conscience which exists independently of edicts and decrees. Your despots govern by terror. They know that he who fears God fears nothing else; and therefore they eradicate from the mind, through their Voltaire, their Helvétius, and the rest of that infamous gang, that only sort of fear which generates true courage. . . .

5
Principles of Society
and Social Change

In the course of his many pamphlets, speeches, essays, and letters, Burke often addressed himself to important areas of social theory. To be sure, his reflex was, as we have seen, to stick to the specific historical issue before him, to eschew general or abstract discussions unrelated to the concrete event. Still, he would, on occasion, enter the realm of speculative social thought. In this section Burke speaks on law, on authority, on economic principles, and on the dynamics of change. What one hears is predominantly the language of Burke the great conservative, but occasionally there can be heard other less expected voices.

"THOSE PRINCIPLES OF ORIGINAL JUSTICE"

Burke was a consistent champion of the Irish Catholic case in the British Parliament. His mother had been a Catholic, he was born and schooled in Ireland, he had kinsmen still living there, and he felt very strongly the injustice of English and Protestant rule. The heart of this oppressive system were the "Popery Laws," strict penal codes that discriminated against Catholics in all features of Irish life—commercial, political, and even familial. Burke attacked these laws in parliamentary speeches and in his correspondence. On one occasion, he condemned them in terms of their violation of higher law, of natural and original principles of justice. These legal reflections on the Irish question were written early in his career but published only after his death as the Tract on the Popery Laws. *In the* Tract, *one finds Burke firmly in the natural law tradition, insisting that the Catholics are victims of unjust laws. But the general discussion reveals him to be in the tradition of Cicero and Aquinas, for whom natural law is only a rational or divine limit to human action; not in the tradition of Locke or Paine, for whom natural law is also the source of positive natural rights.*

But if we could suppose that such a ratification was made, not virtually, but actually, by the people, not representatively, but even collectively, still it would be null and void. They have no right to make a law prejudicial to the whole community, even though the delinquents in making such an act should be themselves the chief sufferers by it; because it would be made against the principle of a superior law, which it is not in the power of any community, or of the whole race of man, to alter,—I mean the will of Him who gave us our nature, and in giving impressed an invariable law upon it. It would be hard to point out any error more truly subversive of all the order and beauty, of all the peace and happiness of human society, than the position, that any body of men have a right to make what laws they please,—or that laws can derive any authority from their institution merely, and independent of the quality of the subject-matter. No arguments of policy, reason of state, or preservation of the constitution can be pleaded in favor of such a practice. They may, indeed, impeach the frame of that constitution, but can never touch this immovable principle. This seems to be, indeed, the doctrine which Hobbes broached in the last century, and which was then so frequently and so ably refuted. Cicero exclaims with the utmost indignation and contempt against such a notion: he considers it not only as unworthy of a philosopher, but of an illiterate peasant; that of all things this was the most truly absurd, to fancy that the rule of justice was to be taken from the constitutions of commonwealths, or that laws derived their authority from the statutes of the people, the edicts of princes, or the decrees of judges. If it be admitted that it is not the black-letter and the king's arms that makes the law, we are to look for it elsewhere.

In reality there are two, and only two, foundations of law; and they are both of them conditions without which nothing can give it any force: I mean equity and utility. With respect to the former, it grows out of the great rule of equality, which is grounded upon our common nature, and which Philo, with propriety and beauty, calls the mother of justice. All human laws are, properly speaking, only declaratory; they may alter the mode and application, but have no power over the substance of original justice. The other foundation of law, which is utility, must be understood, not of partial or limited, but of general and public utility, connected in the same manner with, and derived directly from, our rational nature: for any other utility may be the utility of a robber, but cannot be that of a citizen,—the interest of the domestic enemy, and not that of a member of the commonwealth. This present equality can never be the foundation of statutes which create an artificial difference between men, as the laws before us do, in order to induce a consequential inequality in the distribution of justice. Law is a mode of human action respecting society, and must be governed by the same rules of equity which govern every private action. . . .

If any proposition can be clear in itself, it is this: that a law which shuts out from all secure and valuable property the bulk of the people cannot be made for the utility of the party so excluded. This, therefore, is not the utility which Tully mentions. But if it were true (as it is not) that the real interest of any part of the community could be separated from the happiness of the rest, still it would afford no just foundation for a statute providing exclusively for that interest at the expense of the other; because it would be repugnant to the essence of law, which requires that it be made as much as possible for the benefit of the whole. If this principle be denied or evaded, what ground have we left to reason on? We must at once make a total change in all our ideas, and look for a new definition of law. Where to find it I confess myself at a loss. . . .

I am sensible that these principles, in their abstract light, will not be very strenuously opposed. Reason is never inconvenient, but when it comes to be applied. Mere general truths interfere very little with the passions. They can, until they are roused by a troublesome application, rest in great tranquillity, side by side with tempers and proceedings the most directly opposite to them. Men want to be reminded, who do not want to be taught; because those original ideas of rectitude, to which the mind is compelled to assent when they are proposed, are not always as present to it as they ought to be. When people are gone, if not into a denial, at least into a sort of oblivion of those ideas, when they know them only as barren speculations, and not as practical motives for conduct, it will be proper to press, as well as to offer them to the understanding; and when one is attacked by prejudices which aim to intrude themselves into the place of law, what is left for us but to vouch and call to warranty those principles of original justice from whence alone our title to everything valuable in society is derived? Can it be thought to arise from a superfluous, vain parade of displaying general and uncontroverted maxims, that we should revert at this time to the first principles of law, when we have directly under our consideration a whole body of statutes, which, I say, are so many contradictions, which their advocates allow to be so many exceptions from those very principles? Take them in the most favorable light, every exception from the original and fixed rule of equality and justice ought surely to be very well authorized in the reason of their deviation, and very rare in their use. For, if they should grow to be frequent, in what would they differ from an abrogation of the rule itself? By becoming thus frequent, they might even go further, and, establishing themselves into a principle, convert the rule into the exception. It cannot be dissembled that this is not at all remote from the case before us, where the great body of the people are excluded from all valuable property,—where the greatest and most ordinary benefits of society are conferred as privileges, and not enjoyed on the footing of common rights.

"HAVING DISPOSED AND MARSHALLED US BY A DIVINE TACTIC"

In 1791, Burke wrote an essay to justify his break with Fox and the other Whigs over the question of the French Revolution. Burke insisted that he had not changed but had remained true to old Whig principles, whereas Fox and the supporters of the French had succumbed to new and dangerous views. This Appeal from the New to the Old Whigs *contains one of Burke's longest discussions of old-Whig notions. He deals with the role of the people, the social contract, the necessity of hierarchy, and the role of aristocracy. In this long selection from the* Appeal, *the conservative implications of Burke's natural-law thinking are clear. Burke's thought on natural law emphasizes duties and not rights, principally the duty to maintain social order and to accept one's God-given place. One must accept subordination and privilege as givens, not subject to change. Burke is critical of the voluntaristic conceptions of liberal thinkers in which men are conceived of as individuals entering and leaving civil society at will. Much more congenial to Burke is the view that government emerges from the general acceptance of a natural governing aristocracy.*

The factions now so busy amongst us, in order to divest men of all love for their country, and to remove from their minds all duty with regard to the state, endeavor to propagate an opinion, that the *people,* in forming their commonwealth, have by no means parted with their power over it. This is an impregnable citadel, to which these gentlemen retreat, whenever they are pushed by the battery of laws and usages and positive conventions. Indeed, it is such, and of so great force, that all they have done in defending their outworks is so much time and labor thrown away. Discuss any of their schemes, their answer is, It is the act of the *people,* and that is sufficient. Are we to deny to a *majority* of the people the right of altering even the whole frame of their society, if such should be their pleasure? They may change it, say they, from a monarchy to a republic to-day, and to-morrow back again from a republic to a monarchy; and so backward and forward as often as they like. They are masters of the commonwealth, because in substance they are themselves the commonwealth. The French Revolution, say they, was the act of the majority of the people; and if the majority of any other people, the people of England, for instance, wish to make the same change, they have the same right.

Just the same, undoubtedly. That is, none at all. Neither the few nor the many have a right to act merely by their will, in any matter connected with duty, trust, engagement, or obligation. The Constitution of a country being once settled upon some compact, tacit or expressed, there is no power existing of force to alter it, without the breach of the covenant, or the consent of all the parties. Such is the nature of a contract. And the votes of a majority of the people, whatever their infamous flatterers may teach in order to corrupt their minds, cannot alter the moral any more than they can alter the physical essence of things. The people are not to be taught to think lightly of their engagements to their governors; else they teach governors to think lightly of their engagements towards them. In that kind of game, in the end, the people are sure to be losers. To flatter them into a contempt of faith, truth, and justice is to ruin them; for in these virtues consists their whole safety. To flatter any man, or any part of mankind, in any description, by asserting that in engagements he or they are free, whilst any other human creature is bound, is ultimately to vest the rule of morality in the pleasure of those who ought to be rigidly submitted to it,—to subject the sovereign reason of the world to the caprices of weak and giddy men.

But, as no one of us men can dispense with public or private faith, or with any other tie of moral obligation, so neither can any number of us. The number engaged in crimes, instead of turning them into laudable acts, only augments the quantity and intensity of the guilt. I am well aware that men love to hear of their power, but have an extreme disrelish to be told of their duty. This is of course; because every duty is a limitation of some power. Indeed, arbitrary power is so much to the depraved taste of the vulgar, of the vulgar of every description, that almost all the dissensions which lacerate the commonwealth are not concerning the manner in which it is to be exercised, but concerning the hands in which it is to be placed. Somewhere they are resolved to have it. Whether they desire it to be vested in the many or the few depends with most men upon the chance which they imagine they themselves may have of partaking in the exercise of that arbitrary sway, in the one mode or in the other.

It is not necessary to teach men to thirst after power. But it is very expedient that by moral instruction they should be taught, and by their civil constitutions they should be compelled, to put many restrictions upon the immoderate exercise of it, and the inordinate desire. The best method of obtaining these two great points forms the important, but at the same time the difficult problem to the true statesman. He thinks of the place in which political power is to be lodged with no other attention than as it may render the more or the less practicable its salutary restraint and its prudent direction. For this reason, no legislator, at any period of the world, has willingly placed the seat of active power in the hands of the multitude; because there it admits of no control, no regulation, no steady direction whatsoever. The people are the natural control on authority; but to exercise and to control together is contradictory and impossible.

As the exorbitant exercise of power cannot, under popular sway, be effectually restrained, the other great object of political arrangement, the means of abating an excessive desire of it, is in such a state still worse provided for. The democratic commonwealth is the foodful nurse of ambition. Under the other forms it meets with many restraints. Whenever, in states which have had a democratic basis, the legislators have endeavored to put restraints upon ambition, their methods were as violent as in the end they were ineffectual,—as violent, indeed, as any the most jealous despotism could invent. The ostracism could not very long save itself, and much less the state which it was meant to guard, from the attempts of ambition,—one of the natural, inbred, incurable distempers of a powerful democracy.

But to return from this short digression,—which, however, is not wholly foreign to the question of the effect of the will of the majority upon the form or the existence of their society. I cannot too often recommend it to the serious consideration of all men who think civil society to be within the province of moral jurisdiction, that, if we owe to it any duty, it is not subject to our will. Duties are not voluntary. Duty and will are even contradictory terms. Now, though civil society might be at first a voluntary act, (which in many cases it undoubtedly was,) its continuance is under a permanent standing covenant, coexisting with the society; and it attaches upon every individual of that society, without any formal act of his own. This is warranted by the general practice, arising out of the general sense of mankind. Men without their choice derive benefits from that association; without their choice they are subjected to duties in consequence of these benefits; and without their choice they enter into a virtual obligation as binding as any that is actual. Look through the whole of life and the whole system of duties. Much the strongest moral obligations are such as were never the results of our option. I allow, that, if no Supreme Ruler exists, wise to form, and potent to enforce, the moral law, there is no sanction to any contract, virtual or even actual, against the will of prevalent power. On that hypothesis, let any set of men be strong enough to set their duties at defiance, and they cease to be duties any longer. . . .

Taking it for granted that I do not write to the disciples of the Parisian philosophy, I may assume that the awful Author of our being is the Author of our place in the order of existence,—and that, having disposed and marshalled us by a divine tactic, not according to our will, but according to His, He has in and by that disposition virtually subjected us to act the part which belongs to the place assigned us. We have obligations to mankind at large, which are not in consequence of any special voluntary pact. They arise from the relation of man to man, and the relation of man to God, which relations are not matters of choice. On the contrary, the force of all the pacts which we enter into with any particular person or number of persons amongst mankind depends upon those prior obligations. In some cases the subordinate relations are voluntary, in others they are necessary,—but the duties are all compulsive. When we marry, the choice is voluntary, but the duties are not matter of choice: they are dictated by the nature of the situation. Dark and inscrutable are the ways by which we come into the world. The instincts which give rise to this mysterious process of Nature are not of our making. But out of physical causes, unknown to us, perhaps unknowable, arise moral duties, which, as we are able perfectly to comprehend, we are bound indispensably to perform. Parents may not be consenting to their moral relation; but, consenting or not, they are bound to a long train of burdensome duties towards those with whom they have never made a convention of any sort. Children are not consenting to their relation; but their relation, without their actual consent, binds them to its duties,—or rather it implies their consent, because the presumed consent of every rational creature is in unison with the predisposed order of things. Men come in that manner into a community with the social state of their parents, endowed with all the benefits, loaded with all the duties of their situation. If the social ties and ligaments, spun out of those physical relations which are the elements of the commonwealth, in most cases begin, and always continue, independently of our will, so, without any stipulation on our own part, are we bound by that relation called our country, which comprehends (as it has been well said) "all the charities of all." Nor are we left without powerful instincts to make this duty as dear and grateful to us as it is awful and coercive. Our country is not a thing of mere physical locality. It consists, in a great measure, in the ancient order into which we are born. We may have the same geographical situation, but another country; as we may have the same country in another soil. The place that determines our duty to our country is a social, civil relation. . . .

[I am] convinced that neither . . . [I], nor any man, or number of men, have a right (except what necessity, which is out of and above all rule, rather imposes than bestows) to free themselves from that primary engagement into which every man born into a community as much contracts by his being born into it as he contracts an obligation to certain parents by his having been derived from their bodies. . . .

Amongst these nice, and therefore dangerous points of casuistry, may be reckoned the question so much agitated in the present hour,

—Whether, after the people have discharged themselves of their original power by an habitual delegation, no occasion can possibly occur which may justify the resumption of it? This question, in this latitude, is very hard to affirm or deny: but I am satisfied that no occasion can justify such a resumption, which would not equally authorize a dispensation with any other moral duty, perhaps with all of them together. However, if in general it be not easy to determine concerning the lawfulness of such devious proceedings, which must be ever on the edge of crimes, it is far from difficult to foresee the perilous consequences of the resuscitation of such a power in the people. The practical consequences of any political tenet go a great way in deciding upon its value. Political problems do not primarily concern truth or falsehood. They relate to good or evil. What in the result is likely to produce evil is politically false; that which is productive of good, politically true.

Believing it, therefore, a question at least arduous in the theory, and in the practice very critical, it would become us to ascertain as well as we can what form it is that our incantations are about to call up from darkness and the sleep of ages. When the supreme authority of the people is in question, before we attempt to extend or to confine it, we ought to fix in our minds, with some degree of distinctness, an idea of what it is we mean, when we say, the PEOPLE.

In a state of *rude* Nature there is no such thing as a people. A number of men in themselves have no collective capacity. The idea of a people is the idea of a corporation. It is wholly artificial, and made, like all other legal fictions, by common agreement. What the particular nature of that agreement was is collected from the form into which the particular society has been cast. Any other is not *their* covenant. When men, therefore, break up the original compact or agreement which gives its corporate form and capacity to a state, they are no longer a people,—they have no longer a corporate existence, —they have no longer a legal coactive force to bind within, nor a claim to be recognized abroad. They are a number of vague, loose individuals, and nothing more. With them all is to begin again. Alas! they little know how many a weary step is to be taken before they can form themselves into a mass which has a true politic personality.

We hear much, from men who have not acquired their hardiness of assertion from the profundity of their thinking, about the omnipotence of a *majority,* in such a dissolution of an ancient society as hath taken place in France. But amongst men so disbanded there can be no such thing as majority or minority, or power in any one person to bind another. The power of acting by a majority, which the gentlemen theorists seem to assume so readily, after they have violated the contract out of which it has arisen, (if at all it existed,) must be grounded

on two assumptions: first, that of an incorporation produced by unanimity; and secondly, an unanimous agreement that the act of a mere
majority (say of one) shall pass with them and with others as the act
of the whole.

We are so little affected by things which are habitual, that we consider this idea of the decision of a *majority* as if it were a law of our
original nature. But such constructive whole, residing in a part only,
is one of the most violent fictions of positive law that ever has been
or can be made on the principles of artificial incorporation. Out of
civil society Nature knows nothing of it; nor are men, even when
arranged according to civil order, otherwise than by very long train-
ing, brought at all to submit to it. The mind is brought far more
easily to acquiesce in the proceedings of one man, or a few, who act
under a general procuration for the state, than in the vote of a vic-
torious majority in councils in which every man has his share in the
deliberation. For there the beaten party are exasperated and soured
by the previous contention, and mortified by the conclusive defeat.
This mode of decision, where wills may be so nearly equal, where,
according to circumstances, the smaller number may be the stronger
force, and where apparent reason may be all upon one side, and on
the other little else than impetuous appetite,—all this must be the
result of a very particular and special convention, confirmed afterwards by long habits of obedience, by a sort of discipline in society,
and by a strong hand, vested with stationary, permanent power to
enforce this sort of constructive general will. What organ it is that
shall declare the corporate mind is so much a matter of positive arrangement, that several states, for the validity of several of their acts,
have required a proportion of voices much greater than that of a mere
majority. These proportions are so entirely governed by convention
that in some cases the minority decides. The laws in many countries
to *condemn* require more than a mere majority; less than an equal
number to *acquit*. In our judicial trials we require unanimity either
to condemn or to absolve. In some incorporations one man speaks for
the whole; in others, a few. Until the other day, in the Constitution
of Poland unanimity was required to give validity to any act of their
great national council or diet. This approaches much more nearly to
rude Nature than the institutions of any other country. Such, indeed,
every commonwealth must be, without a positive law to recognize in
a certain number the will of the entire body.

If men dissolve their ancient incorporation in order to regenerate
their community, in that state of things each man has a right, if he
pleases, to remain an individual. Any number of individuals, who can
agree upon it, have an undoubted right to form themselves into a
state apart and wholly independent. If any of these is forced into the

fellowship of another, this is conquest and not compact. On every principle which supposes society to be in virtue of a free covenant, this compulsive incorporation must be null and void. . . .

As in the abstract it is perfectly clear, that, out of a state of civil society, majority and minority are relations which can have no existence, and that, in civil society, its own specific conventions in each corporation determine what it is that constitutes the people, so as to make their act the signification of the general will,—to come to particulars, it is equally clear that neither in France nor in England has the original or any subsequent compact of the state, expressed or implied, constituted *a majority of men, told by the head,* to be the acting people of their several communities. And I see as little of policy or utility as there is of right, in laying down a principle that a majority of men told by the head are to be considered as the people, and that as such their will is to be law. What policy can there be found in arrangements made in defiance of every political principle? To enable men to act with the weight and character of a people, and to answer the ends for which they are incorporated into that capacity, we must suppose them (by means immediate or consequential) to be in that state of habitual social discipline in which the wiser, the more expert, and the more opulent conduct, and by conducting enlighten and protect, the weaker, the less knowing, and the less provided with the goods of fortune. When the multitude are not under this discipline, they can scarcely be said to be in civil society. Give once a certain constitution of things which produces a variety of conditions and circumstances in a state, and there is in Nature and reason a principle which, for their own benefit, postpones, not the interest, but the judgment, of those who are *numero plures,* to those who are *virtute et honore majores.* Numbers in a state (supposing, which is not the case in France, that a state does exist) are always of consideration,—but they are not the whole consideration. . . .

A true natural aristocracy is not a separate interest in the state, or separable from it. It is an essential integrant part of any large body rightly constituted. It is formed out of a class of legitimate presumptions, which, taken as generalities, must be admitted for actual truths. To be bred in a place of estimation; to see nothing low and sordid from one's infancy; to be taught to respect one's self; to be habituated to the censorial inspection of the public eye; to look early to public opinion; to stand upon such elevated ground as to be enabled to take a large view of the wide-spread and infinitely diversified combinations of men and affairs in a large society; to have leisure to read, to reflect, to converse; to be enabled to draw the court and attention of the wise and learned, wherever they are to be found; to be habituated in armies to command and to obey; to be taught to despise danger in the pursuit of honor and duty; to be formed to the greatest degree of vigilance, foresight, and circumspection, in a state of things in which no fault is committed with impunity and the slightest mistakes draw on the most ruinous consequences; to be led to a guarded and regulated conduct, from a sense that you are considered as an instructor of your fellow-citizens in their highest concerns, and that you act as a reconciler between God and man; to be employed as an administrator of law and justice, and to be thereby amongst the first benefactors to mankind; to be a professor of high science, or of liberal and ingenuous art; to be amongst rich traders, who from their success are presumed to have sharp and vigorous understandings, and to possess the virtues of diligence, order, constancy, and regularity, and to have cultivated an habitual regard to commutative justice: these are the circumstances of men that form what I should call a *natural* aristocracy, without which there is no nation.

The state of civil society which necessarily generates this aristocracy is a state of Nature,—and much more truly so than a savage and incoherent mode of life. For man is by nature reasonable; and he is never perfectly in his natural state, but when he is placed where reason may be best cultivated and most predominates. Art is man's nature. We are as much, at least, in a state of Nature in formed manhood as in immature and helpless infancy. Men, qualified in the manner I have just described, form in Nature, as she operates in the common modification of society, the leading, guiding, and governing part. It is the soul to the body, without which the man does not exist. To give, therefore, no more importance, in the social order, to such descriptions of men than that of so many units is a horrible usurpation.

When great multitudes act together, under that discipline of Nature, I recognize the PEOPLE. I acknowledge something that perhaps equals, and ought always to guide, the sovereignty of convention. In all things the voice of this grand chorus of national harmony ought to have a mighty and decisive influence. But when you disturb this harmony,—when you break up this beautiful order, this array of truth and Nature, as well as of habit and prejudice,—when you separate the common sort of men from their proper chieftains, so as to form them into an adverse army,—I no longer know that venerable object called the people in such a disbanded race of deserters and vagabonds. For a while they may be terrible, indeed,—but in such a manner as wild beasts are terrible. The mind owes to them no sort of submission. They are, as they have always been reputed, rebels. They may lawfully be fought with, and brought under, whenever an advantage offers. Those who attempt by outrage and violence to deprive men of any advantage which they hold under the laws, and to destroy the natural order of life, proclaim war against them.

"TO PROVIDE FOR US IN OUR NECESSITIES IS NOT THE POWER OF GOVERNMENT"

The conservatism of his political principles notwithstanding, on matters of economics Burke was in full agreement with what was emerging in his own day as liberal orthodoxy. This aspect of Burke's writings—his advocacy of a laissez-faire economy—is often overlooked. One of the earliest converts to the liberal teachings of Adam Smith, Burke never adhered to the older Tory view of paternalist state intervention in economic life or the later Tory protectionist policy. In 1795, as scarcity and famine beset England, Burke wrote an essay, Thoughts and Details on Scarcity, *in which he advised Pitt on dealing with the economic woes caused in part by the war effort. As this section from the* Thoughts *makes clear, Burke advised against government interference with the natural laws of price and wage.*

To provide for us in our necessities is not in the power of government. It would be a vain presumption in statesmen to think they can do it. The people maintain them, and not they the people. It is in the power of government to prevent much evil; it can do very little positive good in this, or perhaps in anything else. It is not only so of the state and statesman, but of all the classes and descriptions of the rich: they are the pensioners of the poor, and are maintained by their superfluity. They are under an absolute, hereditary, and indefeasible dependence on those who labor and are miscalled the poor.

The laboring people are only poor because they are numerous. Numbers in their nature imply poverty. In a fair distribution among a vast multitude none can have much. That class of dependent pensioners called the rich is so extremely small, that, if all their throats were cut, and a distribution made of all they consume in a year, it would not give a bit of bread and cheese for one night's supper to those who labor, and who in reality feed both the pensioners and themselves.

But the throats of the rich ought not to be cut, nor their magazines plundered; because, in their persons, they are trustees for those who labor, and their hoards are the banking-houses of these latter. Whether they mean it or not, they do, in effect, execute their trust,—some with more, some with less fidelity and judgment. But, on the whole, the duty is performed, and everything returns, deducting some very trifling commission and discount, to the place from whence it arose. When the poor rise to destroy the rich, they act as wisely for their own purposes as when they burn mills and throw corn into the river to make bread cheap.

When I say that we of the people ought to be informed, inclusively I say we ought not to be flattered; flattery is the reverse of instruction. The *poor* in that case would be rendered as improvident as the rich, which would not be at all good for them.

Nothing can be so base and so wicked as the political canting language, "the laboring *poor*." Let compassion be shown in action,—the more, the better,—according to every man's ability; but let there be no lamentation of their condition. It is no relief to their miserable circumstances; it is only an insult to their miserable understandings. It arises from a total want of charity or a total want of thought. Want of one kind was never relieved by want of any other kind. Patience, labor, sobriety, frugality, and religion should be recommended to them; all the rest is downright *fraud*. It is horrible to call them "the *once happy* laborer."

Whether what may be called the moral or philosophical happiness of the laborious classes is increased or not, I cannot say. The seat of that species of happiness is in the mind; and there are few data to ascertain the comparative state of the mind at any two periods. Philosophical happiness is to want little. Civil or vulgar happiness is to want much and to enjoy much. . . .

Labor is a commodity like every other, and rises or falls according to the demand. This is in the nature of things; however, the nature of things has provided for their necessities. . . .

When a man cannot live and maintain his family by the natural hire of his labor, ought it not to be raised by authority?

On this head I must be allowed to submit what my opinions have ever been, and somewhat at large.

And, first, I premise that labor is, as I have already intimated, a commodity, and, as such, an article of trade. If I am right in this notion, then labor must be subject to all the laws and principles of trade, and not to regulations foreign to them, and that may be totally inconsistent with those principles and those laws. When any commodity is carried to market, it is not the necessity of the vendor, but the necessity of the purchaser, that raises the price. The extreme want of the seller has rather (by the nature of things with which we shall in vain contend) the direct contrary operation. If the goods at market are beyond the demand, they fall in their value; if below it, they rise. The impossibility of the subsistence of a man who carries his labor to a market is totally beside the question, in this way of viewing it. The only question is, *What* is it worth to the buyer?

But if authority comes in and forces the buyer to a price, what is this in the case (say) of a farmer who buys the labor of ten or twelve laboring men, and three or four handicrafts,—what is it but to make an arbitrary division of his property among them?

The whole of his gains (I say it with the most certain conviction) never do amount anything like in value to what he pays to his laborers and artificers; so that a very small advance upon what *one* man pays to *many* may absorb the whole of what he possesses, and amount to an actual partition of all his substance among them. A perfect equality will, indeed, be produced,—that is to say, equal want, equal wretchedness, equal beggary, and, on the part of the partitioners, a woeful, helpless, and desperate disappointment. Such is the event of all compulsory equalizations. They pull down what is above; they never raise what is below; and they depress high and low together beneath the level of what was originally the lowest.

If a commodity is raised by authority above what it will yield with a profit to the buyer, that commodity will be the less dealt in. If a second blundering interposition be used to correct the blunder of the first and an attempt is made to force the purchase of the commodity, (of labor, for instance,) the one of these two things must happen: either that the forced buyer is ruined, or the price of the product of the labor in that proportion is raised. Then the wheel turns round, and the evil complained of falls with aggravated weight on the complainant. The price of corn, which is the result of the expense of all the operations of husbandry taken together, and for some time combined, will rise on the laborer, considered as a consumer. The very best will be, that he remains where he was. But if the price of the corn should not compensate the price of labor, what is far more to be feared, the most serious evil, the very destruction of agriculture itself, is to be apprehended. . . .

A greater and more ruinous mistake cannot be fallen into than that the trades of agriculture and grazing can be conducted upon any other than the common principles of commerce: namely, that the producer should be permitted, and even expected, to look to all possible profit which without fraud or violence he can make; to turn plenty or scarcity to the best advantage he can; to keep back or to bring forward his commodities at his pleasure; to account to no one for his stock or for his gain. On any other terms he is the slave of the consumer: and that he should be so is of no benefit to the consumer. No slave was ever so beneficial to the master as a freeman that deals with him on an equal footing by convention, formed on the rules and principles of contending interests and compromised advantages. The consumer, if he were suffered, would in the end always be the dupe of his own tyranny and injustice. The landed gentleman is never to forget that the farmer is his representative. . . .

I beseech the government (which I take in the largest sense of the word, comprehending the two Houses of Parliament) seriously to consider that years of scarcity or plenty do not come alternately or at short intervals, but in pretty long cycles and irregularly, and consequently that we cannot assure ourselves, if we take a wrong measure, from the temporary necessities of one season, but that the next, and probably more, will drive us to the continuance of it; so that, in my opinion, there is no way of preventing this evil, which goes to the destruction of all our agriculture, and of that part of our internal commerce which touches our agriculture the most nearly, as well as the safety and very being of government, but manfully to resist the very first idea, speculative or practical, that it is within the competence of government, taken as government, or even of the rich, as rich, to supply to the poor those necessaries which it has pleased the Divine Providence for a while to withhold from them. We, the people, ought to be made sensible that it is not in breaking the laws of commerce, which are the laws of Nature, and consequently the laws of God, that we are to place our hope of softening the Divine displeasure to remove any calamity under which we suffer or which hangs over us. . . .

It is one of the finest problems in legislation, and what has often engaged my thoughts whilst I followed that profession,—What the state ought to take upon itself to direct by the public wisdom, and what it ought to leave, with as little interference as possible, to individual discretion. Nothing, certainly, can be laid down on the subject that will not admit of exceptions,—many permanent, some occasional. But the clearest line of distinction which I could draw, whilst I had my chalk to draw any line, was this: that the state ought to confine itself to what regards the state or the creatures of the state: namely, the exterior establishment of its religion; its magistracy; its revenue; its military force by sea and land; the corporations that owe their existence to its fiat; in a word, to everything that is *truly and properly* public,—to the public peace, to the public safety, to the public prosperity. In its preventive police it ought to be sparing of its efforts, and to employ means, rather few, unfrequent, and strong, than many, and frequent, and, of course, as they multiply their puny politic race and dwindle, small and feeble. Statesmen who know themselves will, with the dignity which belongs to wisdom, proceed only in this the superior orb and first mover of their duty, steadily, vigilantly, severely, courageously: whatever remains will, in a manner, provide for itself. But as they descend from the state to a province, from a province to a parish, and from a parish to a private house, they go on accelerated in their fall. They *cannot* do the lower duty; and in proportion as they try it, they will certainly fail in the higher. They ought to know the different departments of things,—what belongs to laws, and what manners alone can regulate. To these great politicians may give a leaning, but they cannot give a law.

"A BLIND AND FURIOUS SPIRIT OF INNOVATION"

It is in Burke's constant concern with the dynamics of change that his career as a statesman and his theoretical writings meet. He was engaged in a lifelong effort to distinguish among change, innovation, and reform, as these selections below indicate. Although adamantly opposed to whatever he considered abrupt and disruptive change, he did not oppose reform which maintained continuity with the past. This is quite apparent in the first selection below, which is taken from Burke's famous speech of 1780 calling for the reform of the King's finances and household. He is very careful to justify the action as a necessary and "timely" reform. The second excerpt is from a letter to an Irish friend in 1792 in which Burke indicates their common abhorrence of the hated system of popish laws; but he also makes quite clear that his Irish cohorts must respect the inner dynamics of change and "proceed by degrees." The third and fourth selections are written in Burke's last years. In a letter to a friend, in 1795, he tells of his prophetic mission in being called to warn England against a zealous spirit of innovation that masqueraded as reform. Written the year before his death, his Letter to a Noble Lord *defends Burke against, among other things, the charge of inconsistently approving reform and change early in his career and turning against it in his later years. He does this by once again seeking to distinguish between innovation and timely reform.*

Speech on the Plan for Economical Reform (1780)

If there is any one eminent criterion which above all the rest distinguishes a wise government from an administration weak and improvident, it is this: "well to know the best time and manner of yielding what it is impossible to keep." There have been, Sir, and there are, many who choose to chicane with their situation rather than be instructed by it. Those gentlemen argue against every desire of reformation upon the principles of a criminal prosecution. It is enough for them to justify their adherence to a pernicious system that it is not of their contrivance—that it is an inheritance of absurdity, derived to them from their ancestors—that they can make out a long and unbroken pedigree of mismanagers that have gone before them. They are proud of the antiquity of their house; and they defend their errors as if they were defending their inheritance, afraid of derogating from their nobility, and carefully avoiding a sort of blot in their scutcheon, which they think would degrade them forever.

It was thus that the unfortunate Charles the First defended himself on the practice of the Stuart who went before him, and of all the Tudors. His partisans might have gone to the Plantagenets. They might have found bad examples enough, both abroad and at home, that could have shown an ancient and illustrious descent. But there is a time when men will not suffer bad things because their ancestors have suffered worse. . . .

. . . I do most seriously put it to administration to consider the wisdom of a timely reform. Early reformations are amicable arrangements with a friend in power; late reformations are terms imposed upon a conquered enemy. Early reformations are made in cool blood; late reformations are made under a state of inflamation. In that state of things the people behold in government nothing that is respectable. They see the abuse, and they will see nothing else. They fall into the temper of a furious populace provoked at the disorder of a house of ill-fame; they never attempt to correct or regulate; they go to work by the shortest way: they abate the nuisance, they pull down the house.

This is my opinion with regard to the true interest of government. But as it is the interest of government that reformation should be early, it is the interest of the people that it should be temperate. It is their interest because a temperate reform is permanent, and because it has a principle of growth. Whenever we improve, it is right to leave room for a further improvement. It is right to consider, to look about us, to examine the effect of what we have done. Then we can proceed with confidence, because we can proceed with intelligence. Whereas in hot reformations, in what men more zealous than considerate call *making clear work,* the whole is generally so crude, so harsh, so indigested, mixed with so much imprudence and so much injustice, so contrary to the whole course of human nature and human institutions, that the very people who are most eager for it are among the first to grow disgusted at what they have done. Then some part of the abdicated grievance is recalled from its exile in order to become a corrective of the correction. Then the abuse assumes all the credit and popularity of a reform. The very idea of purity and disinterestedness in politics falls into disrepute, and is considered as a vision of hot and inexperienced men; and thus disorders become incurable, not by the virulence of their own quality, but by the unapt and violent nature of the remedies. A great part, therefore, of my idea of reform is meant to operate gradually: some benefits will come at a nearer, some at a more remote period. We must no more make haste to be rich by parsimony than by intemperate acquisition.

Letter to Sir Hercules Langrishe (1792)

You hated the old system as early as I did. Your first juvenile lance was broken against that giant. I think you were even the first who attacked the grim phantom. You have an exceeding good understanding, very good humour, and the best heart in the world. The dictates of that temper and that heart, as well as the policy pointed out by that understanding, led you to abhor the old code. You abhorred it, as I did, for its vicious perfection. For I must do it justice: it was a complete system, full of coherence and consistency; well digested and well composed in all its parts. It was a machine of wise and elaborate contrivance; and as well fitted for the oppression, impoverishment and degradation of a people, and the debasement in them, of human nature itself, as ever proceeded from the perverted ingenuity of man. It is a thing humiliating enough, that we are doubtful of the effect of the medicines we compound. We are sure of our poisons. My opinion ever was (in which I heartily agreed with those that admired the old code) that it was so constructed, that if there was once a breach in any essential part of it; the ruin of the whole, or nearly of the whole, was, at some time or other, a certainty. For that reason I honour, and shall for ever honour and love you, and those who first caused it to stagger, crack, and gape.—Others may finish; the beginners have the glory; and, take what part you please at this hour, (I think you will take the best) your first services will never be forgotten by a grateful country . . . There is another advantage in taking up this business singly and by an arrangement for the single object. It is that you may proceed by degrees. We must all obey the great law of change. It is the most powerful law of Nature, and the means perhaps of its conservation. All we can do, and that human wisdom can do, is to provide that the change shall proceed by insensible degrees. This has all the benefits which may be in change, without any of the inconveniences of mutation. Everything is provided for as it arrives. This mode will, on the one hand, prevent the unfixing old interests at once: a thing which is apt to breed a black and sullen discontent in those who are at once dispossessed of all their influence and consideration. This gradual course, on the other side, will prevent men long under depression from being intoxicated with a large draught of new power, which they always abuse with a licentious insolence. But, wishing, as I do, the change to be gradual and cautious, I would, in my first steps, lean rather to the side of enlargement than restriction.

Letter to William Elliot (1795)

I wished to warn the people against the greatest of all evils,—a blind and furious spirit of innovation, under the name of reform. I was, indeed, well aware that power rarely reforms itself. So it is, undoubtedly, when all is quiet about it. But I was in hopes that provident fear might prevent fruitless penitence. I trusted that danger might produce at least circumspection. I flattered myself, in a moment like this, that nothing would be added to make authority top-heavy,

—that the very moment of an earthquake would not be the time chosen for adding a story to our houses. I hoped to see the surest of all reforms, perhaps the only sure reform,—the ceasing to do ill. In the mean time I wished to the people the wisdom of knowing how to tolerate a condition which none of their efforts can render much more than tolerable. It was a condition, however, in which everything was to be found that could enable them to live to Nature, and, if so they pleased, to live to virtue and to honor.

Letter to a Noble Lord (1796)

I knew that there is a manifest, marked distinction, which ill men with ill designs, or weak men incapable of any design, will constantly be confounding,—that is, a marked distinction between change and reformation. The former alters the substance of the objects themselves, and gets rid of all their essential good as well as of all the accidental evil annexed to them. Change is novelty; and whether it is to operate any one of the effects of reformation at all, or whether it may not contradict the very principle upon which reformation is desired, cannot be certainly known beforehand. Reform is not a change in the substance or in the primary modification of the object, but a direct application of a remedy to the grievance complained of. So far as that is removed, all is sure. It stops there; and if it fails, the substance which underwent the operation, at the very worst, is but where it was.

All this, in effect, I think, but am not sure, I have said elsewhere. It cannot at this time be too often repeated, line upon line, precept upon precept, until it comes into the currency of a proverb,—*To innovate is not to reform.* The French revolutionists complained of everything; they refused to reform anything; and they left nothing, no, nothing at all, *unchanged.* The consequences are *before* us,—not in remote history, not in future prognostication: they are about us; they are upon us. They shake the public security; they menace private enjoyment. They dwarf the growth of the young; they break the quiet of the old. If we travel, they stop our way. They infest us in town; they pursue us to the country. Our business is interrupted, our repose is troubled, our pleasures are saddened, our very studies are poisoned and perverted, and knowledge is rendered worse than ignorance, by the enormous evils of this dreadful innovation. . . .

It was, then, not my love, but my hatred to innovation, that produced my plan of reform. Without troubling myself with the exactness of the logical diagram, I considered them as things substantially opposite. It was to prevent that evil, that I proposed the measures which his Grace is pleased, and I am not sorry he is pleased, to recall to my recollection. I had (what I hope that noble Duke will remember in all his operations) a state to preserve, as well as a state to reform. I had a people to gratify, but not to inflame or to mislead. I do not claim half the credit for what I did as for what I prevented from being done. In that situation of the public mind, I did not undertake, as was then proposed, to new-model the House of Commons or the House of Lords, or to change the authority under which any officer of the crown acted, who was suffered at all to exist. Crown, lords, commons, judicial system, system of administration, existed as they had existed before, and in the mode and manner in which they had always existed. My measures were, what I then truly stated them to the House to be, in their intent, healing and mediatorial. A complaint was made of too much influence in the House of Commons: I reduced it in both Houses; and I gave my reasons, article by article, for every reduction, and showed why I thought it safe for the service of the state. I heaved the lead every inch of way I made. A disposition to expense was complained of: to that I opposed, not mere retrenchment, but a system of economy, which would make a random expense, without plan or foresight, in future, not easily practicable. I proceeded upon principles of research to put me in possession of my matter, on principles of method to regulate it, and on principles in the human mind and in civil affairs to secure and perpetuate the operation. I conceived nothing arbitrarily, nor proposed anything to be done by the will and pleasure of others or my own,—but by reason, and by reason only. I have ever abhorred, since the first dawn of my understanding to this its obscure twilight, all the operations of opinion, fancy, inclination, and will, in the affairs of government, where only a sovereign reason, paramount to all forms of legislation and administration, should dictate. Government is made for the very purpose of opposing that reason to will and to caprice, in the reformers or in the reformed, in the governors or in the governed, in kings, in senates, or in people.

PART TWO

BURKE VIEWED BY HIS CONTEMPORARIES

6

Character and Achievements

> Burke came to Parliament at the relatively late age of thirty-six, but he still had a public career that spanned nearly forty years. In the course of that long career, his actions and writings were noted by virtually all the political, social, and literary leaders of English life. This section sets out some of their responses, appreciative and critical, to this Irish politician–statesman in their midst.

"YOUNG MR. BURK [sic]"

> For an outsider recently arrived in England, Burke made his way quickly. The establishment took to him immediately, some thinking he was destined for literary fame, others dazzled by his grasp of "affairs."

Horace Walpole, 1761

. . . I dined with your secretary [William Gerald Hamilton] yesterday; there were Garrick and a young Mr. Burk [sic], who wrote a book in the style of Lord Bolinbroke [sic] that was much admired. He is a sensible man, but has not worn off his authorism yet—and thinks there is nothing so charming as writers and to be one—he will know better one of these days.

Mrs. Montagu, a Leader of Fashionable Bluestocking Society, 1759

I shall send you a treatise on the Sublime and Beautiful, by Mr. Burke, a friend of mine; I do not know that you will always subscribe to his system, but I think you will find him an elegant and ingenious writer. He is far from the pert pedantry and assuming ignorance of modern witlings; but in conversation and writing, an ingenious and ingenuous man, modest and delicate, and on great and serious subjects full of that respect and veneration which a good mind and a great one is sure to feel.

Dr. Markham to the Duchess of Queensbury, September 25, 1759 [1]

As a literary man he [Burke] may be not quite unknown to you. He is the author of a piece which imposed on the world as Lord Bolingbroke's, called, "The Advantages of Natural Society," and of a very ingenious book published last year, called, "A Treatise on the Sublime and Beautiful." I must further say of him, that his chief application has been to the knowledge of public business, and our commercial interests, that he seems to have a most extensive knowledge, with extraordinary talents for business, and to want nothing but ground to stand upon to do his country very important services. Mr. Wood, the under secretary, has some knowledge of him, and will, I am persuaded, do ample justice to his abilities and character. As for myself, as far as my testimony may serve him, I shall freely venture it on all occasions; as I value him not only for his learning and talents, but as being, in all points of character, a most amiable and most respectable man.

"HIS IRISH ACCENT"

From the accounts of his contemporaries one has a glimpse of Burke's personality and domestic life, including the rather large tribe of Burkes with whose fortunes he was, according to many, overly concerned.

Wraxhall's Memoirs, London, 1815.
An Account by a Leading Diarist of the Period.

In his [Burke's] dress and exterior he was not less negligent than Fox: but, the spirit of party did not blend with the colour of his apparel: and he rarely or never came to the House in blue and Buff. Burke constantly wore spectacles. His enunciation was vehement, rapid and never checked by any embarrassment: for his ideas outran his powers of utterance and he drew from an exhaustless source. But, his Irish accent, which was as strong as if he had never quitted the banks of the Shannon, diminished to the ear, the enchanting effect of his

---

[1] On Burke's being recommended for the consulship of Madrid. Burke did not receive the job.

eloquence on the mind . . . His personal qualities of temper and disposition, by no means corresponded with his intellectual endowments. Throughout his general manner and deportment in Parliament, there was something petulant, impatient, and at times almost intractable, which greatly obscured the lustre of his talents. His very features, and the undulating motions of his head, were eloquently expressive of this irritability, which on some occasions seemed to approach towards alienation of mind. Even his friends could not always induce him to listen to reason and remonstrance, though they sometimes held him down in his seat, by the skirts of his coat, in order to prevent the ebullitions of his anger or indignation. Gentle, mild, and amenable to argument in private society, of which he formed the delight and the ornament, he was often intemperate, and even violent in Parliament. Fox, however irritated, never forgot that he was a chief. Burke, in his most sublime flights, was only a partizan . . . Burke retired from the discharge of his parliamentary functions exhausted, chagrined, and often irritated; to repair immediately to his family, or to the duties and avocations of domestic life. Fox, always fresh, and never more alert than after a long debate, only quitted the House, in order to drive to Brooke's.

Mrs. Montagu, on Visiting Burke at His Estate at Beaconsfield, 1771

Mr. Burke is an industrious farmer, a polite husband, a kind master, a charitable neighbour and a most excellent companion; the demons who hover about Westminster do not extend their influence as far as the villa . . . How delightfully did we spend our hours with farmer Burke! The busy statesman is all placidness and tranquility in retirment. I dare say Demosthenes at his villa was all sweetness and gentleness after he had uttered a Philippick.

Sir Gilbert Elliot, a Minor Political Figure, 1793

Burke has now got such a train after him as would sink anybody but himself: his son, who is quite *nauseated* by all mankind; his brother, who is liked better than his son, but is rather oppressive with animal spirits and brogue; and his cousin, Will Burke, who is just returned unexpectedly from India, as much ruined as when he went many years ago, and who is a fresh charge on any prospects of power Burke may ever have. Mrs. Burke has in her train Miss French, the most perfect *She Paddy* that ever was caught. Notwithstanding these disadvantages, Burke is in himself a sort of *power* in the state. It is even not too much to say that he is a sort of *power* in *Europe,* though totally without any of those means, or the smallest share in them. Mirabeau said, like a true Frenchman, but with some truth at one time, *"Ma tête aussi est une Puissance."* The same sort of thing is almost true of Burke, who does not, however, say it of himself.

"GREATEST AND MOST BRILLIANT PARTS OF ANY PERSON"

In this section, the entire span of Burke's career and general achievements are favorably assessed by some of his contemporaries. Included in these statements of praise is the judgement of one of Burke's most persistent critics, the anarchist philosopher, William Godwin.

Arthur Young, Distinguished Writer on Agriculture and Society, 1796

Burke is the man who I hold to possess the greatest and most brilliant parts of any person of the age in which he lived, whose conversation has often fascinated me; whose eloquence has charmed; whose writings have delighted and instructed the world; and whose name will without question descend to the latest posterity.

William Wilberforce, Whig Moralist and Political and Religious Reformer, 1788

He [Burke] was a great man—I never could understand how he grew to be at one time so entirely neglected. In part undoubtedly it was, like Mackintosh afterwards, he was above his audience. He had come late into Parliament, and had time to lay in vast stores of knowledge. The field from which he drew his illustrations was magnificent. Like the fabled object of the fairy's favours, whenever he opened his mouth pearls and diamonds dropped from him.

Fanny Burney, Authoress and Bluestocking, on Hearing of Burke's Death, 1797

How sincerely I sympathise in all you say of that truly great man! That his enemies say he was not perfect is nothing compared with his immense superiority over almost all those who are merely exempted from his peculiar defects. That he was upright in heart, even where he acted wrong; I do truly believe . . . he asserted nothing he had not persuaded himself to be true, from Mr. Hasting's being the most rapacious of villains, to the King's being incurably insane . . . Though free from all little vanity, high above envy, and glowing with zeal to exalt talents and merit in others he had, I believe, a consciousness of his own greatness, that shut out those occasional and useful self-doubts which keep our judgement in order, by calling our motives and our passions to account.

William Godwin, 1797

While this sheet is in the press for the third impression, I receive the intelligence of the death of Burke, who was principally in the author's mind, while he penned the preceding sentences. In all that is most exalted in talents, I regard him as the inferior of no man that ever adorned the face of earth; and, in the long record of human genius, I can find for him very few equals. In subtlety of discrimination, in magnitude of conception, in sagacity and profoundness of judgment, he was never surpassed. But his characteristic excellencies were vividness and justness of painting, and that boundless wealth of imagination that adorned the most ungrateful subjects, and heightened the most interesting. Of this wealth he was too lavish; and, though it is impossible for the man of taste not to derive gratification from almost every one of his images and metaphors while it passes before him, yet their exuberance subtracts, in no inconsiderable degree, from that irresistibleness and rapidity of general effect, which is the highest excellence of composition. No impartial man can recall Burke to his mind, without confessing the grandeur and integrity of his feelings of morality, and being convinced that he was eminently both the patriot and the philanthropist. His excellencies however were somewhat tinctured with a vein of dark and saturnine temper; so that the same man strangely united a degree of the rude character of his native island, with an urbanity and a susceptibility of the kinder affections, that have rarely been paralleled. But his principal defect consisted in this; that the false estimate as to the things entitled to our deference and admiration, which could alone render the aristocracy with whom he lived, unjust to his worth, in some degree infected his own mind. He therefore sought wealth and plunged in expence, instead of cultivating the simplicity of independence; and he entangled himself with a petty combination of political men, instead of reserving his illustrious talents unwarped, for the advancement of intellect, and the service of mankind. He has unfortunately left us a memorable example, of the power of a corrupt system of government, to undermine and divert from their genuine purposes, the noblest faculties that have yet been exhibited to the observation of the world.

Charles James Fox, Whig Parliamentary Leader Who Split with Burke on the Latter's Repudiation of the French Revolution in 1790

Such is my sense of the judgment of my right honourable friend, [Burke] such my knowledge of his principles, such the value which I set upon them, and such the estimation in which I hold his friendship, that if I were to put all the political information which I have learnt from books, all which I have gained from science, and all which any knowledge of the world and its affairs has taught me, into one scale, and the improvement which I have derived from my right honourable friend's instruction and conversation were placed in the other, I should be at a loss to decide to which to give the preference.

"A DAMNED WRONGHEADED FELLOW"

In this section we have some negative assessments of Burke's career and achievements. Occasionally, as with Fox, these are from men who were of two minds. A recurring criticism of Burke, illustrated here, was the allegation of inconsistency in the positions taken in his long career.

Samuel Rogers, Writer, 1804

Fox once said to me that "Burke was a most impracticable person, a most unmanageable colleague,—that he never would support any measure, however convinced he might be in his heart of its utility, if it had been first proposed by another." And he once used these very words, "After all, Burke was a damned wrongheaded fellow, through his whole life jealous and obstinate."

The Reverend J. Smith, Dissenting Minister, 1790

The history of Mr. Burke is really a curiosity of its kind. We have seen him at one time directing the most virulent invectives against the person of his sovereign; at another, with all his mother's softness, weeping at the remembrance of his generous virtue; at one time presenting the shield of his eloquence to guard the grossest peculation from public justice; at another, exerting the whole strength of his faculties to expose it to the vengeance of his country. To the extent and brilliancy of his genius every man of taste will pay a tribute of applause; but what are we to think of his wisdom? Or, has he not hazarded something infinitely more important than the character of his understanding? His imagination has given him an unlimited command over the most beautiful images, both in nature and in art; but deficient in those powers which should direct the operation, and control the excursions of fancy, though his eloquence has sometimes arrested the attention of the house, it has seldom been heard with conviction;—the coruscations (sic) of lightning may please by their novelty, their splendour, and their beauty, but the steady light of heaven guards us from danger, and conducts us on our way.

The Critical Review, 1790

The truth is, that brilliant as are Mr. Burke's abilities, they are untempered with (what alone stamps a value on the endowments of the mind) judgment. The dupe of his imagination or his passions, he despises arrangement or logical precision. He loses himself in a wilderness of words and figures. For want of temper and cool reflexion, he is an old statesman without the benefit of experience; an universal scholar without methodical science. We are far from wishing to be understood, that there are no traits of a fine understanding in the speeches or the writings of our author; on the contrary they occasionally abound in new, deep, and even judicious reflexions. But we fear it must be confessed that he is but seldom correct and consistent.

7
In Parliament

"OUR FRIEND MR. BURKE SPOKE DIVINELY"

Although known today primarily for the content and quality of his prose, to most of his contemporaries Burke's fame rested on his singular skills in the House of Commons. He was widely known for his abilities as a practicing politician, for his grasp of complicated commercial and economic matters. More than this, however, his reputation rested on his fame as an orator—the greatest of speakers in the House of Commons.

Duke of Grafton, Prime Minister, 1766

On thinking over the House of Commons, it appears that the ability among the leaders will be at least divided, if not drawn up against the well-wishers to administration; though the numbers of the voters will be clear. Those who have undertaken the weighty affairs of government are in duty called upon to facilitate, by honourable means, its success. If the discontented are not in some measure broken into, I do see a strong phalanx of able personages, who will give full employment, by the business they will raise up. Among those, whom I should wish, and Mr. Conway also wishes, to see support him is Mr. Burke, the readiest man upon all points perhaps in the whole House . . . I cannot help saying, that I look upon it, that he [Burke] is a most material man to gain, and one on whom the throughest dependence may be given, where an obligation is owned.

Adam Smith, 1779

Burke is the only man I ever knew who thinks on economic subjects exactly as I do without any previous communication having passed between us.

Mrs. Montagu, 1766

The stamp act was repeal'd by a majority of one hundred and eight, and our friend Mr. Burke spoke divinely, yes' divinely, don't misunderstand me, and report he spoke as well as mortal man could do,

I tell you he spoke better. The great commoner [Pitt] praised him highly in the Senate, and all people join in the chorus. Indeed Mr. Burke has every day acquired great praise but yesterday crown'd all.

Fanny Burney, on Hearing Burke's Speech at the Trial of Warren Hastings, 1788

All I had heard of his [Burke's] eloquence, and all I had conceived of his great abilities, was more than answered by his performance. Nervous, clear and striking was almost all that he uttered: the main business, indeed, of his coming forth was frequently neglected, and not seldom wholly lost; but his excursions were so fanciful, so entertaining, and so ingenious, that no miscellaneous hearer, like myself, could blame them. It is true he was unequal, but his inequality produced an effect which, in so long a speech, was perhaps preferable to greater consistency, since, though it lost attention in its falling off, it recovered it with additional energy by some ascent unexpected and wonderful. When he narrated he was easy, flowing, and natural; when he declaimed, energetic, warm, and brilliant.

Edward Gibbon, Member of Parliament, Historian, Author of *Decline and Fall of the Roman Empire,* 1786

I can never forget the delight with which that diffusive and ingenious orator was heard by all sides of the House, and even by those whose existence he proscribed. The Lords of trade blushed at their own insignificancy, and Mr. Eden's appeal to the two thousand five hundred volumes of our reports served only to excite a general laugh. I take this opportunity of certifying the correctness of Mr. Burke's printed speeches, which I have heard and read.

Wraxall's *Memoirs,* 1815

Burke, rising with evident marks of strong emotion, delivered an oration which lasted nearly five hours; and which neither Demosthenes nor Tully could have excelled in energy, eloquence, or animation. I speak with perfect impartiality, as I by no means coincided in opinion with Burke, whose prejudices and animosities almost always blinded his judgment, or obscured his superior intelligence. But, even when he most failed in producing conviction, he excited not less admiration for his resplendent talents . . .

Nature had bestowed on him [Burke] a boundless imagination, aided by a memory of equal strength and tenacity. His fancy was so vivid, that it seemed to light up by its own powers, and to burn without consuming the aliment on which it fed: sometimes bearing him away to ideal scenes created by his own exuberant mind, but from which he always returned to the subject of debate; descending from his most aerial fights by a gentle and imperceptible gradation, till he again touched the ground. Learning waited on him like a handmaid, presenting to his choice, all that Antiquity had culled or invented, most elucidatory of the topic under discussion. He always seemed to be oppressed under the load and variety of his intellectual treasures, of which he frequently scattered portions with a lavish hand, to inattentive, impatient, hungry and sleepy hearers, undeserving of such presents. Nor did he desist, though warned by clamorous vociferation of the House, to restrain or to abbreviate his speeches.

Rev. John Erskine, 1779

The speeches the world has of yours have been and shall continue to be my only school for public speaking. I have repeated them daily aloud and have endeavoured (tho' Heaven knows with faint success) to catch at that animation and splendour of diction which give argument a projectile force impossible to be described but which all men feel who hear or read Mr. Burke.

James Boswell, Writer, 1770

It was a great feast to me, who had never heard him before. It was astonishing how all kinds of figures of speech crowded upon him. He was like a man in an Orchard where boughs loaded with fruit hung around him, and he pulled apples as fast as he pleased and pelted the ministry. It seemed to me however that his Oratory rather tended to distinguish himself than assist his cause. There was amusement instead of persuasion. It was like the exhibition of a favourite Actor. But I would have been exceedingly happy to be him.

"HE SPOKE TOO OFTEN"

Some of his contemporaries were less than dazzled by his performance, and even questioned his parliamentary abilities. Once again there are some who could well be of two minds on Burke's merits.

Samuel Johnson, 1770

Speaking of Burke, he said, "It was commonly observed, he spoke too often in Parliament; but nobody could say he did not speak well, though too frequently and too familiarly. . . .

"But," said I, "they represent him [Burke] as actually mad."

"Sir," said he, "if a Man will appear extravagant as he does, and cry, can he wonder that he is represented as Mad?"

Charles James Fox, 1794

Burke's eloquence . . . rather injures his reputation, it is a veil over his wisdom; remove his eloquence, reduce his language, withdraw his images, and you will find that he is more wise than eloquent.

Richard B. Sheridan, Playwright and Whig Politician, 1793

Mr. Burke, I don't mean to flatter, but when posterity reads one of your speeches in Parliament, it will be difficult to believe that you took so much pains, knowing with certainty that it could produce no effect, that not one vote would be gained by it.

8

The Response to English Radicalism

"HAD REASON TO DOUBT HIS JUDGMENT"

In the following selections, spokesmen of the Protestant dissenters comment about the lukewarm aid Burke gave to legislation that would have eased the restrictions placed on their religious and civic life by Parliament. Joseph Priestley, the radical political and religious leader, also comments on Burke's views on religious establishments. The final selection is from a leader of the radical movement, John Cartwright, commenting on Burke's critique of the reform efforts of 1782.

Thomas Lindsey, Dissenter Friend of Priestley, 1779

Mr. Burke spoke admirably well, kept close to the point, and with fewer digressions, than I ever knew him, made use of a great deal of plausible reasoning, not without some artifice, to show the unaccountable peevishness and pursuances of man's refusing to subscribe what they did believe; never attending to the just objections some minds might make to do it at the bidding of the civil magistrate. He also dwelt long, and with more reason, on the inconsistency of objecting to subscribe the scripture, at the command of the magistrate, and yet making no objection to the declaration against popery . . . I am persuaded that this gentleman gave a turn to the House and the Test is to be ascribed to him; not that I think he did not speak his own sentiments sincerely, but with all his knowledge and parts, he presumes he knows more than he does.

Mr. Shore, Dissenter Friend of Priestley, 1779

It is hard to believe a man of Mr. Burke's distinguished abilities can seriously think that the imposition of any religious subscription, even that to the scriptures, can add security to the state, or promote the interests and do honour to genuine Christianity. If not what solid argument can be made use of in favor of such a test? If Mr. Burke be sincere, he is a striking instance of the strength of early prejudice.

He is certainly a man of very shining parts and eminent acquirements; but I have frequently had reason to doubt his judgement, always in religion and often in civil debate.

Joseph Priestley, *Letters to the Right Honorable Edmund Burke,* 1791

What I have more particularly replied to, is what he has advanced on civil establishments of religion, which makes no small figure in his performance, and which appears to be a subject not generally understood.

It is with very sensible regret that I find Mr. Burke and myself on the two opposite sides of any important question, and especially that I must now no longer class him among the friends of what I deem to be the cause of liberty, civil or religious, after having, in a pleasing occasional intercourse of many years, considered him in this respectable light. In the course of his public life, he has been greatly befriended by the Dissenters, many of whom were enthusiastically attached to him; and we always imagined that he was one on whom we could depend, especially as he spoke in our favour in the business of subscription, and he made a common cause with us in zealously patronizing the liberty of America.

In America also, and indeed in every other part of the known world, except the southern part of this particular island, Mr. Burke sees all civil offices open to persons of all religious persuasions without distinction, and without any inconvenience having been known to arise from it; and yet here he joins with a bigotted clergy, in rigorously confining them to the members of the established church. But even this is not so extraordinary as his not scrupling to class all the enemies of establishments with cheats and hypocrites, as if our opinions were so palpably absurd, that no honest man could possibly entertain them . . . On these principles, the church, or the state, once established, must for ever remain the same. This is evidently the real scope of Mr. Burke's pamphlet, the principles of it being, in fact, no other than those of passive obedience and non-resistance, peculiar to the Tories and the friends of arbitrary power, such as were echoed from the pulpits of all the high church party, in the reigns of the Stuarts, and of Queen Anne. Let them, however, be produced again, and let us see in what manner they will be treated by the good sense and spirit of Englishmen at the present day . . . Must we have no discussion concerning the nature, and influence, of the different kinds of religion, in order that, if we happen to have got a worse, we may relieve ourselves by substituting a better in its place? Must every thing once established be, for that reason only, for ever maintained? This is said, indeed, to be your maxim, openly avowed in the House of Commons, and, it is perfectly agreeable to every thing advanced in this publication. For you condemn the French National Assembly, for innovating in their religion, which is Catholic, as much as you could blame the English Parliament, for innovating in ours, which is Protestant. You condemn them for lowering the state of archbishops, bishops, and abbots, though they have improved that of the lower orders of the clergy; and therefore you would, no doubt, be equally offended at any diminution of the power of cardinals, or of the pope. We may therefore presume, that had you lived in Turkey, you would have been a mahometan, and in Thibet, a devout worshipper of the grand lama.

Your mind has been so dazzled with the fascinating idea of the majesty of the church (a phrase, I believe peculiar to yourself) that you have not been able to see any thing distinctly on the subject. You have not even dared to take a sufficiently near view of this very church of which you are so profound an admirer, but have only gazed at a humble distance, or have stood with your face towards it, but with your eyes reverently fixed on the ground. Thus awestruck, you have not had the courage to look up, or to look round you. You have not even been able to distinguish whether it was St. Paul's at London, St. Peter's at Rome, or the church of Sancta Sophia at Constantinople. For your description applies equally to them all. It seems to have been sufficient for you that it was not a conventicle.

As to every thing under this denomination, it has been your maxim, without any examination, to turn your back upon it. You would, no doubt, have done the same with respect to any place, in which Peter, or Paul, was permitted to preach; the christian religion being in their time, unfortunately, nothing more than a sect, taught in conventicles, and no where authorised by law. Had you lived at that time, you would, according to your general maxim, have "cherished your old" heathen "prejudices, because they were old," and have lived and died a humble worshipper of the Gods, and especially the Goddesses, of ancient Greece and Rome.

I the less wonder at this power of imagination and prejudice, and this stupefaction of all your rational faculties in matters of religion, as it is apparent that you have been under a similar suspension of your reason, and equally under the power of imagination, in your views of the principles of civil government. Such, Sir, is "your proud submission, and the subordination of your very heart," to princes, and nobles; such your devotion to rank and sex, in conjunction with your religious enthusiasm, that one might suspect that your book was composed after some solemn vigil, such as watching your arms at the shrine of the blessed virgin; after which you issued forth the champion, in form, of religion, of monarchy, and of the immaculate virtue of all handsome queens.

John Cartwright, *Give Us Our Rights*, London, 1782

As the subject of reforming the Commons House has so very lately engaged in no small degree the public attention, I should not in the year 1782, have attributed to Mr. Burke the doctrines he maintained on the subject in 1770, was there reason for supporting that time had materially changed them. Mr. Burke however in his letter of April 12, 1780, to a member of the Committee of Buckinghamshire, puts the matter still farther out of doubt. Considering that in 1770 he wrote a book, above 50 pages of which was a dissertation on "the nature and character" of the House of Commons, particularly with regard to "its spirit, and the purposes it was meant to answer in the constitution," in which he largely treats of its horrible corruption and the means of cure; considering also that, as he says, "He is now growing old; and has from his very early youth been conversant in reading, and thinking upon the subjects of our laws and constitution, as well as upon those of other times and countries;" and considering besides, his extraordinary learning and experience, and still more extraordinary abilities; considering, I say, all these particulars, it surely might not have been an unreasonable expectation, that when the tide of reformation had so strongly set in, he should have been prepared with the full means, formed into a complete plan of reform, and happy in the occasion of presenting it to the public. But after a lapse of so many years since he himself had shewn the necessity of such a plan, he hath it seems nothing further to offer on the subject, than what was contained in his Bill of Oeconomy, for the civil list expenditure, excepting some see-saw doubts and difficulties, and discouraging cautions, and a direct refusal to concur in the only measures which in the nature of things can possibly effect a reform. Ten long years had elapsed since the publication of his *Thoughts,* and ten such years for demonstrating the necessity of a reform as the nation had never before experienced, and yet with regard to a certain proposition in the line of reform he very calmly tells his friend, that, "Nothing ought to be hastily determined upon the subject;" that, "He cannot possibly give his vote for it, until he has considered it more fully; that, on the result of all his reading, thinking, experience and communication, he is not able to come to an immediate resolution in favour of a change in the ground work of our constitution; and that, he does dissent fully and directly from ANY RESOLUTION WHATSOEVER, on the subject of an alteration in the representation and election of the kingdom of this time."

But, notwithstanding all the above quotations, I do not, as I said before, at all despair but that Mr. Burke and the People's rights of election and representation, may yet in due time, and ere long, be reconciled: for really they are not so difficult of comprehension as to occasion any fears on that account; and although he may now and then shew a slight partiality for that slippery jade Discretion, yet he has often signalized himself as the warm friend of Justice.

Those who think it an undeniable proposition, that the present state of the representation and election of the kingdom, is the sole cause of the corruption of parliament, of the presumption of ministers; of the arbitrary power they exercise, and of every political evil now experienced by the English nation, must necessarily be somewhat surprised at Mr. Burke's language on the subject. And whether or not, until his opinions shall be changed, he is to be considered as a person to be particularly resorted to, for obtaining us a reform of parliament, is a question, Gentlemen, which it is very fit should be proposed to your serious consideration.

9
The "Reflections on the Revolution in France"

Burke's Reflections *was published in November, 1790. It set off a great debate among English intellectuals over the French Revolution. Whatever position would be taken in the next decade,* Reflections *served as the point of departure.*

"NEVER WAS THERE A WORK SO VALUABLE IN ITS KIND"

The establishment rallied to what they had long sought—a resounding defense of their privileges, and a clarion call for resistance to Jacobinism, to democracy and levelling in France, and, obviously of equal importance, to the potential of this in England.

William Windham, a Leader of Antirevolutionary Sentiment in the House of Commons, 1790

On Thursday I conceive it was, that a material incident happened —the arrival of Mr. Burke's pamphlet. Never was there, I suppose, a work so valuable in its kind, or that displayed powers of so extraordinary a nature. It is a work that may seem capable of overturning the National Assembly, and turning the stream of opinion throughout Europe. One would think, that the author of such a work, would be called to the government of his country, by the combined voice of every man in it. What shall be said of the state of things when it is remembered that the writer is a man decried, persecuted and proscribed; not being much valued, even by his own party, and by half the nation considered as little better than an ingenious madman!

George III, 1790

Burke's *Reflections* is a good book, a very good book; every gentleman ought to read it.

Mrs. Montagu, 1790

I hope before this time you are in full possession of Mr. Burke's admirable, excellent, incomparable pamphlet. I think it will do great service here in preventing confusion and rebellion; whether it can cure the evil already done in France it is difficult to say, for should it restore the Democrats to their senses, it cannot restore life to the murdered, nor property to the plundered, nor treat the wounds the state has received. It gives one great delight to see the fine talents employ'd to good and great purposes, and my pleasure was heightened by my long intimacy and friendship for Mr. Burke. If to his share some party frailties fall, read but his book and you'll forget them all.

Fanny Burney, 1790

I own myself entirely at Mrs. Montagu's opinion about Mr. Burke's book; it is the noblest, deepest, most animated and exalted work that I think I have ever read. I am charmed to hear its eloge from Mrs. Montagu; it is a tribute to its excellence which reflects high honour on her own candour, as she was one of those the most vehemently irritated against its author but a short time since. How can man, with all his inequalities, be so little resembling to himself at different periods as this man? He is in all ways a prodigy,—in fascinating talents and incomprehensible inconsistencies.

Edward Gibbon, 1791

Burke's book *Reflections* is a most admirable medicine against the French disease, which has made too much progress even in this happy country. I admire his eloquence, I approve his politics, I adore his chivalry, and I can forgive even his superstition. The primitive Church, which I have treated with some freedom, was itself at that time an innovation, and I was attached to the old Pagan establishment. The French spread so many lyes (sic) about the sentiments of the English nation that I wish the most considerable men of all parties and descriptions would join in some public act, declaring themselves, satisfied with and resolved to support our present constitution.

Horace Walpole, 1790

But the fatal blow has been at last given by Mr. Burke. His pamphlet [*Reflections . . .*] came out this sennight (sic), and is far superior to what was expected even by his warmest admirers. I have read it twice, and though of 350 pages, I wish I could repeat every page by heart. It is sublime, profound and gay. The wit and satire are equally brilliant, and the whole is wise, though in some points he goes too far —yet in general there is far less want of judgement than could be expected from him. If it could be translated, which from the wit and metaphors and allusions is almost impossible, I should think it would be a classic book in all countries, except in present France. To their tribunes it speaks daggers, though, unlike them, it uses none. Seven thousand copies have been taken off by the book-sellers already—and a new edition is preparing. I hope you will see it soon. . . .

Had I Mr. Burke's powers, I would have described her [the Queen of France] in his words. I like "the swords leaping out of their scabbards"—in short, I am not more charmed with his wit and eloquence, than with his enthusiasm. Every page shows how sincerely he is in earnest—a wondrous merit in a political pamphlet. All other party writers act zeal for the public, but it never seems to flow from the heart. That cordiality, like a phial of spirits, will preserve his book, when some of his doctrines have evaporated in fumes.

Sir Henry Dundas, a Leader of Antirevolutionary Sentiment in the House of Commons, 1791

Mr. Dundas admitted, that the French affairs at the beginning of the Revolution bore such an aspect that differences of opinion respecting them prevailed; it was reserved for the illuminated and comprehensive mind of Mr. Burke alone, to forsee what must be its fatal and necessary consequences.

Edward Tatham, Conservative Writer on Politics, 1791

Sir, To say how much I thank you for your *Reflections on the Revolution in France,* is very faintly to express the sense of obligation which I feel,—and which every one who loves his country and knows its interests, must feel, for that genuine and exalted patriotism which flows from your pen in so pure, so elegant, and so warm, a stream. The moral, the political, the historical, the classical learning you have brought together, and dedicated to the benefit of your own nation and to the well-being of others, do the highest credit to your understanding; and your zeal for the purity, the perfection, and the duration, of that excellent constitution in church and state, which is the basis of our public property and private happiness, confers equal honour upon your heart.

Your manly and animated politics, founded in philosophy and observation, and seasoned with that true honour and humanity which are the privilege of Englishmen, come out at important crises. Availing themselves of the confusion which prevails in a neighboring kingdom, they come out as an antidote to that slow poison, which has been so industriously administered, and insinuated with such consummate art into the veins of our countrymen, by a sect of phlegmatic politicians, who, whatever may be their views, whether they are deceived themselves or intend to deceive others, are without philosophy for their foundation, or experience for their guide; and who, I fear, have not too much honour and humanity for their companions. They come out at a time when a familiar poison has taken effect in a country

which is only separated from us by a narrow sea, and with which we
have an extensive intercourse; at a time when these innovators in
government are triumphing over the ruin of an ancient kingdom, to
which they flatter themselves they have been instrumental, without
knowing what new political chimera may spring out of its ashes; and
when, in the midst of their ignorant and malicious joy, they are point-
ing to the objects of their triumph, and labouring, with an infatuated
zeal, to persuade Englishmen, that their road to honour and happiness
lies in similar disgrace and ruin.

The Times, a Government Paper, November 30, 1790

It is but justice to Mr. Burke, to acknowledge that whatever may
be his conduct and sentiments relative to his party, he has shown in
his *Reflections on the Revolutions* (sic) *in France* a manly Constitutional spirit, not afraid to paint the miseries and errors of the misguided and interested politicians of France, and at the same time to
support the Constitution of this country against all those dark insidi-
ous minds who would wish to level it in a similar manner with the
French for the sake of their own selfish purposes. In doing this, Mr.
Burke has our praise, but what is to become in future of that *tria
juncta in Uno* (Mr. Fox, Mr. Burke, and Mr. Sheridan) who had hitherto so united in politics that nothing could shake or disunite them?
Mr. Fox and Mr. Sheridan both have avowed their approbation of the
National Assembly . . . It is therefore impossible, we think, that these
Gentlemen (differing so widely in sentiment) should ever draw to-
gether again in the team of Opposition.

Sir Gilbert Elliot, 1790

It is a book which I propose to read constantly and to make as much
my own as my faculties will allow . . . every man who is, or means
to be a Statesman nay every one who would desire only to be a good
citizen, must make it his first study and his *last* . . . Your book contains the fundamental elements of *all* political knowledge . . .

"IT IS IN GENERAL THOUGHT TO BE MADNESS"

*Although the establishment thrilled at its appearance, the Re-
flections also gave rise to much critical response. Some of these
have become lasting statements of political principle in their own
right.*

Charles James Fox, 1791

I have not read Burke's new pamphlet, but hear a very different
account of it from yours. It is in general thought to be madness, and

especially in those parts where he is for a general war, for the purpose of destroying the present government of France. There is a pamphlet by one Mackintosh, which I hear a great character of, though it is said to go too far in some respects, but I have not yet had time to read it.

James Mackintosh, *Vindicae Gallica*, 1791

He can cover the most ignominious retreat by a brilliant allusion. He can parade his arguments with masterly generalship, where they are strong. He can escape from an untenable position into a splendid declamation. He can sap the most impregnable conviction by pathos, and put to flight a host of syllogisms with a sneer. Absolved from the laws of vulgar method, he can advocate a group of magnificent horrors to make a breach in our hearts, through which the most indisciplined rabble of arguments may enter in triumph . . . But it is objected, these institutions might have been gradually reformed. The spirit of Freedom would have silently entered. The progressive wisdom of an enlightened nation would have remedied, in process of time, their defects, without convulsion. To this argument I confidently answer, that these institutions would have destroyed LIBERTY, before Liberty had corrected their SPIRIT. Power vegetates with more vigour after these gentle prunings. A slender reform amuses and lulls the people; the popular enthusiasm subsides, and the moment of effectual reform is irretrievably lost. No important political improvement was ever obtained in a period of tranquility. The corrupt interest of the Governors is so strong, and the cry of the people so feeble, that it were vain to expect it. If the effervescence of the popular mind is suffered to pass away without effect, it would be absurd to expect from languor what enthusiasm had not obtained. If radical reform is not, at such a moment, procured, all partial changes are evaded and defeated in the tranquility which succeeds. The gradual reform that arises from the presiding principle exhibited in the specious theory of Mr. Burke, is belied by the experience of all ages. Whatever excellence, whatever freedom is discoverable in Governments, has been infused into them by the shock of a revolution, and their subsequent progress has been only the accumulation of abuse. It is hence that the most enlightened politicians have recognized the necessity of frequently recalling Governments to their first principles; a truth equally suggested to the penetrating intellect of Machiavel, by his experience of the Florentine democracy, and by his research into the history of ancient Commonwealths.— Whatever is good ought to be pursued at the moment it is attainable. The public voice, irresistible in a period of convulsion, is contemned with impunity, when dictated by that lethargy into which nations are lulled by the tranquil course of their ordinary affairs. The ardour of reform languishes in unsupported tediousness. It perishes in an impotent struggle with adversaries, who receive new strength from the progress of the day. No hope of great political improvement (let us repeat it) is to be entertained from tranquility, for its natural operation is to strengthen all those who are interested in perpetuating abuse. The National Assembly seized the moment of eradicating the corruptions and abuses, which afflicted their country. Their reform was total, that it might be commensurate with the evil, and no part of it was delayed, because to spare an abuse at such a period was to consecrate it; because the enthusiasm which carries nations to such enterprises is short-lived, and the opportunity of reform, if once neglected, might be irrevocably fled.

Gazetteer and New Daily Advertiser, a Whig Paper, November 4, 1790

It is obvious to every reader of Mr. Burke, that in his argument on the *right of choice* in the people, which he refines upon so as totally to extinguish, he establishes a doctrine that would have kept England, and would keep the whole world in a state of villainage. If his principles had had weight on the public mind, at the time of the Reformation, they would have prevented the Reformation . . . They would equally in 1688, have prevented the glorious Revolution, which every true Whig will this day commemorate . . . And, what is personal to Mr. Burke, they ought to have made him an advocate for the American War.

> *Among the critics of Burke's* Reflections *were two radical women writers. Burke and Horace Walpole referred to Wollstonecraft and Macauley as the "Amazonian allies" of the Jacobins.*

Mary Wollstonecraft, 1791

Misery to reach your heart I perceive, must have its caps and bells; your tears are reserved, very naturally considering your character, for the declamation of the theater, or for the downfall of queens, whose rank throws a graceful veil over vices that degrade humanity; but the distress of many industrious mothers whose helpmates have been torn from them, and the hungry cry of the helpless babes, were vulgar sorrows that could not move your commiseration, though they might extort an alms.

Catherine Macauley, 1790

I have myself always considered the boasted birthright of an Englishman, as an arrogant pretension, built on a beggarly foundation. It is an arrogant pretension, because it intimates a kind of exclusion to the rest of mankind from the same privilege; and it is beggarly, because it rests our legitimate freedom on the alms of our princes. It is not my intention to make any formal comparison between the new constitution of France and the present existing constitution of England; or to presume to censure a government, from which an industrious people receive protection, and with which the large majority of the nation are entirely satisfied. Yet it may not be inexpedient to observe, that we cannot with any ground of reason or propriety, set up our own constitution as the model which all other nations ought implicitly to follow, unless we are certain that it bestows the greatest possible happiness on the people which in the nature of things any government can bestow. We ought to be certain, that this model will bear the most nice and critical examination. It ought to be void of any of those obvious, or more concealed causes, which produce perfect evils, and carry the mind to apprehensions of future mischiefs. We ought not at least to have had a national debt, swelled to a magnitude which terrifies even the most sanguine for its consequences. Our parliaments ought to have been eminently distinguished for their integrity, and a total independence of any corrupt influence; and no necessity ought to have existed in our affairs, which have obliged us to endure imposts which our ancestors would have rejected with horror, and resisted. If an Englishman sees any thing which is amiss in his own government, he ought not undoubtedly to look forward to any other remedy than those which the lenient hand of reformation will supply. But when the old vessel of a commonwealth is torn to pieces by the shocks it has sustained from contending parties; when the people, disdaining and rejecting all those fond opinions by which they have been enslaved to misery, assert their native right of forming a government for themselves; surely in such a case the builders are bound by no law of duty or reason to make use of these old materials in the structure of their new constitution, which they suppose to have been of an injurious tendency. The leaders of the French Revolution, and their followers, see none of those striking beauties in the old laws and rules of the Gothic institutions of Europe, which Mr. Burke does. They do not profess to have any of the spirit of antiquarians among them; and they have not perceived, in the experience of old or ancient times, a perfect harmony arising from oppression of interests; nor can they understand how such a combination can be formed as shall produce it. In such a view of things, they have chosen a simple rule for the model of their new structure, yet regulated with all that art and design which the experience of ages affords to the wisdom of man. They are accused of having entirely dismissed that useful guide experience from their councils, but they think they have made the best use of it; whether this opinion of theirs is founded in truth, time, and the future history of man, must evince.

A large number of replies to the Reflections *came from radical dissenters. Burke had, after all, accused them of leading the Jacobin cabal in England, and it was the sermon preached by the leading dissenting minister Richard Price which provoked Burke to write the* Reflections *in the first place.*

Thomas Cooper, a Leading Manchester Industrialist and Radical Dissenter, 1792

Such is Mr. Burke's description of his own Character. Boldly rejecting the shallow mask of Hypocrisy, he stands forward to the World the public professor of political Turpitude, the systematic opponent of every Species of Reform, and in love with the very Sinfulness of Sin. Other Offenders against the Rights of man and the Improvement of Society, have at least had the modesty to plead the common temptations, and palliate their offences by the common excuses; they have been led astray by the prevalence of example, by the love of riches, or the thirst of power; all have had their motives, extraneous to their crimes. But excuses suit not the high-minded iniquity of Mr. Burke's Politics, and he unblushingly obtrudes himself on the disgusted eye of the public, in all the nakedness and deformity of political Vice . . . Such is our Accuser; the professed opponent of the Rights of Man! May we never deserve his Panegyric.

Gilbert Wakefield, Dissenting Minister, 1795

With respect to Mr. Burke's renewed invectives on the French, they are virulent, they are furious, they are infernal, to the utmost capabilities of language. But, whether these torrent eruptions of outrageous zeal proclaim more loudly the powers of the head, or the perversities of the heart, is a problem beyond my materials of moral demonstration to resolve. To his vigour of conception, his comprehension and vivacity of thought, his energies of phrase, his accumulations of original and striking imagery, it is difficult to conjecture to fix a limit: but his acrimony, his phrenzies, his absurdities, his misrepresentations, and his inconsistencies have also no bounds . . . Surely, surely, Mr. Burke! it is less encroachment upon virtue, and the well-being of mankind, that one axe should be uncased for a few solitary victims of royal birth, than that myriads of swords should leap from the scabbards for the assassination of such multitudes of men.

William Belsham, Dissenting Writer on Politics, 1791

We all know that the English constitution supposes, and wisely supposes, that the King can do no wrong; and it is certain that no government can expressly authorize resistance against itself. Will Mr. Burke pretend that the Revolution in England was an event to be justified by an appeal to the forms of the constitution; which must necessarily regard resistance as rebellion? No; but the public safety required a deviation from forms. And how, in the name of common sense, with which the fine sense of Mr. Burke seems to have very little connection, is that deviation to be vindicated, but by resorting to the original and primary principles of government, as stated and defended by Dr. Price? Almost in the same breath, indeed, in which Dr. Price is impeached for inculcating treasonable doctrines, Mr. Burke himself admits that a tyrant may be deposed, and even punished, "provided it is done with dignity." But however dignified Mr. Burke's plan of resistance to tyranny might be, most assuredly in the execution of it, or "in reducing his principles to practice," he would not incur less personal risk from the penalties of the law than Dr. Price; so that his imperious scorn, which knows no distinction between a Cataline and a Cato, a Jack Cade and a Hampden, a Peters and a Price, may be with equal and retorted scorn repaid.

The Reverend Joseph Towers, Dissenting Minister, 1790

Burke's notion is that there is no other security for law and liberty, or no other claim to our rights, but what is merely grounded on the conduct, or the acquisition of our ancestors. He insists our rights come not from reason, or from nature, but from inheritance . . . In an age when men are led to scrutinize exactly into the nature of government, and to trace it to its first principles, he could lead them to the ideas of barbarous and gothic ages, and to ancient superstitions, which even the votaries of Popery now find it necessary to abandon . . . An appeal to the Rights of Man, if prosecuted to its natural and legitimate consequences, will give liberty to the whole human race; but an appeal to the Rights and privileges of ancestors, such rights as can be clearly and distinctly ascertained and proved, will give liberty only to a small part of the human species, and much of what is communicated will be necessarily defective and imperfect.

Joseph Priestley, 1791

You treat with ridicule the idea of the rights of men, and suppose that mankind, when once they have entered into a state of society, necessarily abandon all their proper natural rights, and thenceforth have only such as they derive from society. "As to the share of power," you say, "authority and direction, which each individual ought to have in the management of the state, that I must deny to be among the direct original rights of man in civil society; for I have in my contemplation the civil, social man, and no other. It is a thing to be settled by convention." . . .

It is one of the most curious paradoxes in this work of yours, which abounds with them, that the rights of men above-mentioned (called by you, "the pretended rights of the French theorists") "are all," you say, "extremes, and in proportion as they are metaphysically true, they are morally and politically false." Now by metaphysically true can only be meant strictly and properly true, and how this can be in any sense false, is to me incomprehensible. If the above-mentioned rights be the true, that is the just and reasonable rights of men, they ought to be provided for in all states, and all forms of government; and if they be not, the people have just cause to complain, and to look out for some mode of redress.

You strongly reprobate the doctrine of "kings being the choice of the people," a doctrine advanced, but not first advanced, by Dr. Price in his Revolution Sermon. "This doctrine," you say, "as applied to the prince now on the British throne, is either nonsense, and therefore neither true nor false, or it affirms a most unfounded, dangerous, illegal, and unconstitutional position. According to this spiritual doctor of politics, if his majesty does not owe his crown to the choice of his people, he is no lawful king."

On the same principle you equally reprobate the doctrine of "the king being the servant of the people," whereas the law, as you say, calls him "our sovereign lord the king." But since you allow that "kings are in one sense, undoubtedly, the servants of the people, because their power has no other rational end than that of the general advantage," it is evident that it is only Dr. Price's words that you quarrel with. Your ideas are, in fact, the very same with his, though you call his doctrine, not only unconstitutional, but seditious; adding that, "it is now publicly taught, avowed, and printed"; whereas it was taught, avowed, and even printed, before either you or Dr. Price were born . . .

If, as you expressly acknowledge, the only rational end of the power of a king is the general advantage, that is, the good of the people, must not the people be of course the judges whether they derive advantage from him and his government or not, that is, whether they be well or ill served by him? Though there is no express, there is, you must acknowledge, a virtual, compact between the king and the people. This, indeed, is particularly mentioned in the Act which implies the abdication of King James, though you say "it is too guarded and too circumstantial"; and what can this compact be, but a stipulation for protection etc. on the part of the king, and allegiance on the part of the people? If, therefore, instead of protection, they find oppression, certainly allegiance is no longer due. Hence, according to common sense and the principles of the Revolution, the right of a subject to resist a tyrant, and dethrone him; and what is this but, in other words, shocking as they may sound to your ears, dismissing, or cashiering, a bad servant as a person who had abused his trust . . . Your whole book, Sir, is little else than a vehicle for the same poison, inculcating, but inconsistently enough, a respect for princess, independent of their being originally the choice of the people as if they had some natural and indefensible right to reign over us, they being born to command, and we to obey; and then, whether the origin of this power be divine or have any other source independent of the people, it makes no longer difference to us.

With the superstitious respect for kings and the spirit of chivalry, which nothing but an age of extreme barbarism recommended and which civilization has banished, you seem to think that everything great and dignified has left us. "Never never more," you say, "shall we behold that generous loyalty to rank and sex, that proud submission, that dignified obedience, that subordination of the heart, that kept alive even in servitude itself the spirit of an exalted freedom. The unbought grace of life, the cheap defense of nations, the nurse of manly sentiment and heroic enterprise, is gone. It is gone; that sensibility of principle, that chastity of honour, which felt a stain like a wound, which inspired courage whilst it mitigated ferocity, which enobled whatever it touched, and under which vice itself lost half its evil, by losing all its grossness."

This is perhaps the most admired passage in your whole performance; but it appears to me that in a great pomp of words it contains but few ideas, and some of them inconsistent and absurd. So different also are men's feelings—from the difference, no doubt, of our educations and the different sentiments we voluntarily cherish through life —that a situation which gives you the idea of pride, gives me that of meanness. You are proud of what, in my opinion, you ought to be ashamed, the idolatry of a fellow creature, and the abasement of yourself. It discovers a disposition from which no "manly sentiment, or heroic enterprise" can be expected. I submit to a king, or to any other civil magistrate, because the good order of society requires it, but I feel no pride in that submission; and the "subordination of my heart" I reserve for character only, not for station. As a citizen, the object of my respect is the nation and the laws. The magistrates, by whatever name they are called, I respect only as the confidential servants of the nation, and the administrators of the laws.

These sentiments, just in themselves, and favouring of no superstition, appear to me to become men whom nature has made equal, and whose great object when formed into societies it should be to promote their common happiness. I am proud of feeling myself a man among men, and I leave it to you, Sir, to be "proud of your obedience, and to keep alive" as well as you can "in servitude itself the spirit of an exalted freedom." I think it much easier, at least, to be preserved out of a state of servitude than in it. You take much pains to gild your chains, but they are chains still.

> *One of Burke's most outspoken critics was John Thelwall, radical agitator, leader of the London Corresponding Society, the most active radical group in the 1790s. He attacked Burke weekly in his journal* The Tribune.

John Thelwall, *The Tribune*, 1795

In the same way argues that mirror of political orthodoxy Mr. Burke. For intolerance, religious or political, is the same in principle and must consequently appeal to the same mode of reasoning. If these enquiries, says he, in essence, at least, if not in words—if these enquiries are permitted to go on in the world—if political reformations are tolerated by the regular governments of Europe, from overthrowing the despotism of France, they will begin to reform the corruptions of rotten boroughs in Britain. From reforming the corruption of rotten boroughs, they will attack places and pensions; and from attacking places and pensions, they will proceed to grumble at enormous taxes. From grumbling at enormous taxes, they will attack the enchanted castle of the British Constitution itself, overthrow the venerable remains of feudal nechromacy, break down the magic tripos of ancestral inspiration; and hurl the great magician from his chair; throw all things into anarchy, and thence fall headlong into political perdition. The writing of his book was certainly one of the first active causes of the growth of democracy in this country. Discussion was no doubt considerably promoted by the immortal writings of Thomas Paine, Joel Barlow, Thomas Cooper of Manchester, James Mackintosh, and many other enlightened men, who took up the pen to vindicate the Revolution of France, little imagining that because they had thus vindicated the French revolution, persons in this country, some of whom had never read their books, were to be tried for high treason for that which they had written.

But however these books assisted, and undoubtedly they did very considerably assist the progress of the cause of Democracy, it is to be observed, that they owed their existence to the publication of Burke; and therefore we are to look upon him as the great father and first propagator of the principles of democracy in this country.

> *Without doubt, however, the most famous and most enduring reply to Burke's* Reflections *came from Tom Paine in his* Rights of Man.

Tom Paine, *Rights of Man*, 1791

Among the incivilities by which nations or individuals provoke and irritate each other, Mr. Burke's pamphlet on the French Revolution is an extraordinary instance. Neither the People of France, nor the National Assembly, were troubling themselves about the affairs of England, or the English Parliament; and why Mr. Burke should commence an unprovoked attack upon them, both in parliament and in public, is a conduct that cannot be pardoned on the score of manners, nor justified on that of policy.

There is scarcely an epithet of abuse to be found in the English language, with which Mr. Burke has not loaded the French Nation and the National Assembly. Everything which rancour, prejudice, ignorance, or knowledge could suggest, are poured forth in the copious fury of near four hundred pages. In the strain and on the plan Mr. Burke was writing, he might have written on to as many thousands. When the tongue or the pen is let loose in a frenzy of passion, it is the man, and not the subject, that becomes exhausted.

Hitherto Mr. Burke has been mistaken and disappointed in the opinions he had formed of the affairs of France; but such is the ingenuity of his hope, or the malignancy of his despair, that it furnishes him with new pretences to go on. There was a time when it was impossible to make Mr. Burke believe there would be any revolution in France. His opinion then was, that the French had neither spirit to undertake it, nor fortitude to support it; and now that there is one, he seeks an escape, by condemning it . . .

As Mr. Burke occasionally applies the poison drawn from his horrid principles, not only to the English nation, but to the French Revolution and the National Assembly, and charges that august, illuminated and illuminating body of men with the epithet of usurpers, I shall, sans ceremonie, place another system of principles in opposition to his. . . .

I am not contending for nor against any form of government, nor for nor against any party here or elsewhere. That which a whole nation chooses to do, it has a right to do. Mr. Burke says, No. Where then does the right exist? I am contending for the rights of the living, and against their being willed away, and controlled and contracted for, by the manuscript assumed authority of the dead; and Mr. Burke is contending the authority of the dead over the rights and freedom of the living. There was a time when kings disposed of their crowns by will upon their deathbeds, and consigned the people, like beasts of the field, to whatever successor they appointed. This is now so exploded as scarcely to be remembered, and so monstrous as hardly to be believed: But the parliamentary clauses upon which Mr. Burke builds his political church, are of the same nature . . .

We have seen (says Mr. Burke) "the French rebel against a mild and lawful Monarch, with more fury, outrage, and insult, than any people has been known to rise against the most illegal usurper, or the most sanguinary tyrant." This is one among a thousand other instances, in which Mr. Burke shows that he is ignorant of the springs and principles of the French Revolution.

It was not against Louis the XVIth, but against the despotic principles of the government, that the nation revolted. These principles had not their origin in him, but in the original establishment, many centuries back; and they were become too deeply rooted to be removed, and the augean stable of parasites and plunderers too abominably filthy to be cleansed by anything short of a complete and universal revolution. When it becomes necessary to do a thing, the whole heart and soul should go into the measure, or not attempt it. That crisis was then arrived, and there remained no choice but to act with determined vigour, or not to act at all. The king was known to be the friend of the nation, and this circumstance was favourable to the enterprise. Perhaps no man bred up in the style of an absolute King, ever possessed a heart so little disposed to the exercise of that species of power as the present King of France. But the principles of the government itself still remained the same. The Monarch and the Monarchy were distinct and separate things; and it was against the established despotism of the latter, and not against the person or principles of the former, that the revolt commenced, and the revolution has been carried.

Mr. Burke does not attend to the distinction between men and principles; and therefore, he does not see that a revolt may take place against the despotism of the latter, while there lies no charge of despotism against the former . . .

What Mr. Burke considers as a reproach to the French Revolution, (that of bringing it forward under a reign more mild than the preceding ones), is one of its highest honours. The revolutions that have taken place in other European countries have been excited by personal hatred. The rage was against the man, and he became the victim. But, in the instance of France, we see a revolution generated in the rational contemplation of the rights of man, and distinguishing from the beginning between persons and principles.

But Mr. Burke appears to have no idea of principles, when he is contemplating governments. "Ten years ago" (says he) "I could have felicitated France on her having a government without inquiring what the nature of that government was, or how it was administered." Is this the language of a rational man? Is it the language of a heart feeling as it ought to feel for the rights and happiness of the human race? On this ground, Mr. Burke must compliment all the governments in the world, while the victims who suffer under them, whether sold into slavery, or tortured out of existence, are wholly forgotten. It is power, and not principles, that Mr. Burke venerates; and under this abominable depravity, he is disqualified to judge between them. Thus much for his opinion as to the occasions of the French Revolution. I now proceed to other considerations.

I know a place in America called Point-no-Point; because as you proceed along the shore, gay and flowery as Mr. Burke's language, it continually recedes and presents itself at a distance before you; but when you have got as far as you can go, there is no point at all. Just thus it is with Mr. Burke's three hundred and fifty-six pages. It is therefore difficult to reply to him. But as the points he wishes to establish, may be inferred from what he abuses, it is in his paradoxes that we must look for his arguments.

As to the tragic paintings by which Mr. Burke has outraged his own imagination, and seeks to work upon that of his readers, they are very well calculated for theatrical representation, where facts are manufactured for the sake of show, and accommodated to produce, through the weakness of sympathy, a weeping effect. But Mr. Burke should recollect that he is writing History, and not Plays; and that his readers will expect truth, and not the spouting rant of high-toned exclamation.

When we see a man dramatically lamenting in a publication intended to be believed, that, "The age of chivalry is gone!" that "the glory of Europe is extinguished for ever!" that "The unbought grace of life" (If any one knows what it is), "the cheap defense of nations, the nurse of manly sentiment and heroic enterprise, is gone" and all this because the Quixote age of chivalry nonsense is gone, what opinion can we form of his judgement, or what regard can we pay to his facts? In the rhapsody of his imagination, he has discovered a world of windmills, and his sorrows are, that there are no Quixotes to attack them. But if the age of aristocracy, like that of chivalry, should fall, (and they had originally some connexion), Mr. Burke, the trumpeter of the Order, may continue his parody to the end, and finish with exclaiming, "Othello's occupation's gone" . . .

Through the whole of Mr. Burke's book I do not observe that the Bastille is mentioned more than once, and that with a kind of implication as if he were sorry it was pulled down, and wished it were built up again. "We have rebuilt Newgate" (says he), "and tenanted the mansion; and we have prisons almost as strong as the Bastille for those who dare to libel the Queens of France." . . . From his violence and his grief, his silence on some points, and his excess on others, it is difficult not to believe that Mr. Burke is sorry, extremely sorry, that arbitrary power, the power of the Pope, and the Bastille, are pulled down.

Not one glance of compassion, not one commiserating reflection, that I can find throughout his book, has he bestowed on those who lingered out the most wretched of lives, a life without hope, in the most miserable of prisons. It is painful to behold a man employing his talents to corrupt himself. Nature has been kinder to Mr. Burke than he is to her. He is not affected by the reality of distress touching his heart, but by the showy resemblance of it striking his imagination. He pities the plumage, but forgets the dying bird. Accustomed to kiss the aristocratical hand that hath purloined him from himself, he degenerates into a composition of art, and the genuine soul of nature forsakes him. His hero or his heroine must be a tragedy-victim expiring in show, and not the real prisoner of misery, sliding into death in the silence of a dungeon.

10

The View from America

"THE ROTTENNESS OF HIS MIND"

Despite his early efforts on behalf of the colonies, American sentiment in later years was not favorable to Burke. Even the more conservative statesman John Adams was critical. Joel Barlow, cited below, was an American active for a time in English and French radical politics.

Thomas Jefferson, 1791

The Revolution of France does not astonish me so much as the revolution of Mr. Burke. I wish I could believe the latter proceeded from as pure motives as the former. But what demonstration could scarcely have established before, less than the hints of Dr. Priestley and Mr. Paine establish firmly now. How mortifying that this evidence of the rottenness of his mind must oblige us now to ascribe to wicked motives those actions of his life which wore the mark of virtue and patriotism.

John Adams, 1813

Is it not laughable to hear Burke call Bolingbroke a superficial writer? . . . And in my opinion the epithet "superficial" belongs to you and your friend [Samuel] Johnson more than to him. I might say much more. But I believe Burke and Johnson to have been as political Christians, as Leo 10th.

Joel Barlow, *The Conspiracy*, 1793

Some of the author's friends in England, although they join with him in censuring the writings of Mr. Burke on the French Revolution, are of opinion that the picture here drawn of that writer is too highly coloured; or at least, that the censure is so severe as to lose the effect that it might otherwise produce . . . It may be proper to make some observations on the effect that has already followed from the writings of Mr. Burke. I speak not of what has taken place in England; where it is supposed that, contrary to his intentions and those of the government that set him at work, his malicious attack upon liberty has opened a discussion which cannot be closed until the whole system of despotism, which he meant to support, shall be overturned in that country. The present war with France is doubtless the last piece of delusion that a set of hereditary tyrants will ever be able to impose upon the people of England.

But this subject opens a field of contemplation far more serious and extensive on the continent of Europe; where, if Mr. Burke can view without horror the immensity of the mischiefs he has done, he will show himself worthy of much higher attributes of wickedness than have yet been ascribed to him. It is a painful task to traverse such a wide scene of slaughter and desolation as now involves the nations of Europe, and then to lay it all to the charge of a single individual; especially when we consider that individual as having, for a long time before, enjoyed the confidence of all good men, and having at last betrayed it from the worst and vilest motives; as he had established his previous reputation by speaking the language of liberty, and professing himself to be the friend of national felicity. But it is not from a transitory disgust at his detestible principles, it is from deliberate observation and mature conviction, that I state it as an historical fact, That the present war, with all its train of calamities, must be attributed almost exclusively to the pen of Mr. Burke.

There is a peculiar combination of circumstances which threw this power into his hands, and which ought to be duly considered, before we come to a decision on the subject. The people of England had enjoyed for several ages a much greater portion of liberty than any other people in Europe. This had raised them to a great degree of eminence in many respects. At the same time that it rendered them powerful as a nation, it made them sober, industrious and persevering, as individuals; it taught them to think and speak with a certain air of dignity, independence and precision, which was unknown in other countries. This circumstance could not fail to gain the admiration of foreigners, and to excite a perpetual emulation among themselves. England has therefore produced more than her proportion of the illustrious men of modern times, especially in politics and legislation, as these affairs came within the reach of a larger class of men in that country than in any other.

In a nation where there is an enormous civil list at the disposal of the crown, and a constitutional spirit of liberty kept alive in the people, we must necessarily expect to find two parties in the government. In such a case, as the king is sure to carry all the measures that he dares to propose, the party in favour of the people are called the opposition; and it being always a minority, it gives occasion for great exertion of talents, and is supposed to be the nurse of every public virtue. Such has been the composition of the English government ever since the last revolution. The opposition has been the school of great men; its principal disciples have been the apostles of liberty; and their exertions have made the British name respectable in every part of the world. Mr. Burke had been for many years at the head of this school; and from the brilliant talents he discovered in that conspicuous station, he rendered himself universally respected. His eloquence was of that flowery and figurative kind, which attracted great admiration in foreign countries; where it was viewed for the most part, though the medium of a translation; so that he was considered, at least in every country out of England, as the ablest advocate of liberty that then existed in Europe. Even kings and tyrants, who hated the cause, could not withhold their veneration from the man.

Under these impressions, their attention was called to the great event of the French revolution. It was a subject which they did not understand, a business in which they had no intention to interfere; as it was evidently no concern of theirs. But viewed as a speculative point, it is as natural for kings as for other persons to wait till they learn what great men have said, before they form their opinion. Mr. Burke did not suffer them to remain long in suspense; but, to enlighten their understandings and teach them how to judge, he came forward with his "Reflection on the Revolution in France;" where, in his quality of the political schoolmaster of his age, in his quality of the professed enemy of tyrants, the friend of the people, the most enlightened leader of the most enlightened nation in Europe, he tells them that this Revolution is an abominable usurpation of a gang of beggarly tyrants; that its principle is atheism and anarchy; that its instruments are murders, rapes, and plunders; that its object is to hunt down religion, overturn society, and deluge the world in blood. Then, in the whining cant of state-piety, and in the cowardly insolence of personal safety, he calls upon the principal sovereigns of Europe to unite in a general confederation, to march into France, to interfere in the affairs of an independent power, to make war with the principles which he himself had long laboured to support, to overturn the noblest monument of human wisdom, and blast the fairest hopes of public happiness that the world had ever seen.

Copies of his book were sent in great profusion by the courts of London and Paris to the other courts of Europe; it was read by all men of letters, and by all men of State, with an avidity inspired by the celebrity of the author and the magnitude of the subject; and it produced an effect which, in other circumstances, would have appeared almost miraculous; especially when we consider the intrinsic character of the work . . .

But this illustrious hypocrite possessed every advantage for deception. He palmed himself upon the world as a volunteer in the general cause of philanthropy. Giving himself up to the frenzy of an unbridled imagination, he conceives himself writing tragedy, without being confined to the obvious laws of fiction; and taking advantage of the recency of the events, and of the ignorance of those who were to read his rhapsodies, he peoples France with assassins, for the sake of raising a hue-and-cry against its peaceable inhabitants; he paints ideal murders, that they may be avenged by the reality of a wide extended slaughter; he transforms the mildest and most generous people in Europe into a nation of monsters and atheists; "heaping mountains upon mountains, and waging war with heaven," that he may interest the consciences of one part of his readers, and cloak the hypocrisy of another, to induce them both to renounce the character of men, while they avenge the cause of God.

Such was the first picture of the French Revolution presented at once to the eyes of all the men who held the reins of government in the several states of Europe; and such was the authority of the author by whom it was presented, that we are not to be astonished at the effect. The emigrant princes, and the agents of the court of the Thuilleries, who were then besieging the antichambers of ministers in every country, found a new source of impudence in this extraordinary work. They found their own invented fictions confirmed in their fullest latitude, and a rich variety of superadded falsehood, of which the most shameless sycophant of Louis or of Conde would have blushed to have been the author. With this book in their hands, it was easy to gain the ear of men already predisposed to listen to any project which might rivet the chains of their fellow creatures.

These arguments, detailed by proper agents, induced some of the principal sovereigns of Europe to agree to the treaty of Pilnitz; then the death of Leopold . . . unhappily removed the great obstacle to the execution of that treaty, and the war of Mr. Burke was let loose, with all the horrors he intended to excite. And what is the language proper to be used in describing the character of a man, who, in his situation, at his time of life, and for a pension of only fifteen hundred pounds a year, could sit down deliberately in his closet and call upon the powers of earth and hell to inflict such a weight of misery on the human race?

11

The Literary View

None of his contemporaries held neutral views about Burke. Occasionally the writers of his age uttered conflicting judgements, but they were never at a loss for clever words with which to describe their fellow clever man of words.

Boswell's *Life of Dr. Johnson*

1773

We talked of Mr. Burke—Dr. Johnson said, he had great variety of knowledge, store of imagery, copiousness of language. *Robertson.* "He has wit too." *Johnson.* "No, sir; he never succeeds there; 'tis low, 'tis conceit. I used to say Burke never once made a good joke. What I most envy Burke for is his being constantly the same. He is never what we call hum-drum; never unwilling to begin to talk, nor in haste to leave off. . . . Burke, sir, is such a man that if you met him for the first time in the street where you were stopped by a drove of oxen, and you and he stepped aside to take shelter but for five minutes, he'd talk to you in such a manner that, when you parted, you would say, this is an extraordinary man."

1773

Johnson. "No sir; I never heard Burke make a good joke in my life." *Boswell.* "But, sir, you will allow he is a hawk." *Dr. Johnson,* thinking that I meant this of his joking, said, "No, sir, he is not the hawk there. He is the beetle in the mire." I still adhered to my metaphor,—"But he soars as the hawk." *Johnson.* "Yes, sir; but he catches nothing." *McLeod* asked, what is the particular excellence of Burke's eloquence? *Johnson.* "Copiousness and fertility of allusion; a power of diversifying his matter by placing it in various relations. Burke has great information and great command of language; though, in my opinion, it has not in every respect the highest elegance." *Boswell.* "Do you think, sir, that Burke has read Cicero much?" *Johnson.* "I don't believe it, sir. Burke has great knowledge, great fluency of words, and great promptness of ideas, so that he can speak with great illustration on any subject that comes before him. He is neither like Cicero, nor like Demosthenes, nor like any one else, but speaks as well as he can."

March 20, 1776

I mentioned Mr. Burke. *Johnson.* "Yes, Burke is an extraordinary man. His stream of mind is perpetual." It is very pleasing for me to record that Johnson's high estimation of the talents of this gentleman was uniform from their early acquaintance. Sir Joshua Reynolds informs me, that when Mr. Burke was first elected a member of Parliament, and Sir John Hawkins expressed a wonder at his attaining a seat, Johnson said, "Now we who know Burke, know that he will be one of the first men in this country." And once, when Johnson was ill, and unable to exert himself as much as usual without fatigue, Mr. Burke having been mentioned, he said, "that fellow calls forth all my powers. Were I to see Burke now, it would kill me. So much was he accustomed to consider conversation as a contest, and such was his notion of Burke as an opponent."

1783

A man who is used to the applause of the House of Commons, has no wish for that of a private company. A man accustomed to throw for a thousand pounds, if set down to throw for sixpence, would not be at pains to count his dice. Burke's talk is the ebullition of his mind; he does not talk from a desire of distinction, but because his mind is full.

1784

Boswell: Mr. Burke has a constant stream of conversation: *Johnson:* "Yes, sir; if a man were to go by chance at the same time with Burke under a shed, to shun a shower, he would say—" this is an extraordinary man." If Burke should go into a stable to see his horse drest, the ostler would say—we have had an extraordinary man here . . . When Burke does not descend to be merry, his conversation is very superiour indeed. There is no proportion between the powers which he shews in serious talk and in jocularity. When he lets himself down to that, he is in the kennel.

Oliver Goldsmith, 1774

> Here lies our good Edmund, whose genius was such,
> We scarcely can praise it or blame it too much;
> Who, born for the universe, narrowed his mind,
> And to party gave up what was meant for mankind;
> Though fraught with all learning, yet straining his throat
> To persuade Tommy Townshend to give him a vote;
> Who, too deep for his hearers, still went on refining,

And thought of convincing, while they thought of dining;
Though equal to all things, for all things unfit;
Too nice for a statesman, too proud for a wit,
For a patriot too cool, for a drudge disobedient,
And too fond of the right to pursue the expedient.
In short, 'twas his fate, unemployed or in place, Sir,
To eat mutton cold, and cut blocks with a razor.

William Wordsworth, who by then had become a critic of the French Revolution, was kinder to Burke in 1799 than Goldsmith had been to the earlier Whig Burke.

William Wordsworth, *The Prelude*, 1799

Pass we . . .
        . . . to that great stage
Where senators, tongue-favoured men, perform,
Admired and envied. Oh! the beating heart,
When one among the prime of these rose up,—
One of whose name from childhood we had heard
Familiarly, a household term, like those,
The Bedfords, Glosters, Salisburys, of old
Whom the fifth Harry talks of. Silence! hush!
This is no trifler, no short-flighted wit,
No stammerer of a minute, painfully
Delivered. No! the Orator hath yoked
The hours, like young Aurora, to his car:
Thrice welcome Presence! how can patience ere
Grow weary of attending on a track
That kindles with such glory! All are charmed,
Astonished; like a hero in romance
He winds away his never-ending horn;
Words follow words, sense seems to follow sense:
What memory and what logic! till the strain,
Transcendent, superhuman as it seemed,
Grows tedious even in a young man's ear.

Genius of Burke! forgive the pen reduced
By specious wonders, and too slow to tell
Of what the ingenuous, what bewildered men,
Beginning to mistrust their boastful guides,
And wise men, willing to grow wiser, caught,
Rapt auditors! from thy most eloquent tongue—
Now mute, for ever mute in the cold grave

I see him,—old, but vigorous in age,—
Stand like an oak whose stag-horn branches start
Out of its leafy brow, the more to awe
The younger brethren of the grove. But some—
While he forewarns, denounces, launches forth,
Against all systems built on abstract rights,
Keen ridicule; the majesty proclaims
Of Institutes and Laws, hallowed by time;
Declares the vital power of social ties
Endeared by custom; and with high disdain,
Exploding against Theory, insists
Upon the allegiance to which men are born—
Some—say at once a forward multitude—
Murmur (for truth is hated, where not loved)
As the winds fret within the Aeolian cave,
Galled by their monarch's chain. The times were big
With ominous change, which, night by night, provoked
Keen struggles, and black clouds of passion raised;
But memorable moments intervened,
When Wisdom, like the Goddess from Jove's brain,
Broke forth in armour of resplendent words,
Startling the Synod. Could a youth, and one
In ancient story versed, whose breast had heaved
Under the weight of classic eloquence,
Sit, see, and hear, unthankful, uninspired?

Samuel Taylor Coleridge, who, like Wordsworth, had also moved from praise to condemnation of the French Revolution in the late 1790s, was more ambivalent about Burke than Wordsworth had been.

Samuel Taylor Coleridge

Table Talk, 1833

The very greatest writers write best when calm, and exerting themselves upon subjects uncompleted with party. Burke rarely shows all his powers, unless where he is in a passion. The French Revolution was alone a subject fit for him. We are not yet aware of all the consequences of that event. We are too near it. . . .

Burke was, indeed, a great man. No one ever read history so philosophically as he seems to have done. Yet, until he could associate his general principles with some sordid interest, panic of property, jacobinism, etc., he was a mere dinner bell. Hence you will find so many half truths in his speeches and writings. Nevertheless, let us heartily acknowledge his transcendant greatness. He would have been more influential if he had less surpassed his contemporaries as Fox and Pitt, men of much inferior minds in all respects.

The Friend, 1809

I do not mean, that this great man supported different principles at different eras of his political life. On the contrary, no man was ever more like himself. From his first published speech on the American colonies to his last posthumous tracts, we see the same man, the same doctrines, the same uniform wisdom of practical counsels, the same reasoning, and the same prejudices against all abstract grounds, against all deduction of practice from theory. The inconsistency to which I allude, is of a different kind: it is the want of congruity in the principles appealed to in different parts of the same work, it is an apparent versatility of the principle with the occasion. If his opponents are theorists, then everything is to be founded on prudence, on mere calculations of expediency; and every man is represented as acting according to the state of his own immediate self-interest. Are his opponents calculators? Then calculation itself is represented as a sort of crime. God has given us feelings, and we are to obey them; and the most absurd prejudices become venerable, to which these feelings have given consecration. I have not forgotten that Burke himself defended these half contradictions, on the pretext of balancing the too much on the one side by a too much on the other. But never can I believe, but that the straight line must needs be the nearest; and that where there is the most, and the most unalloyed truth, there will be the greatest and most permanent power of persuasion. But the fact was, that Burke in his public character found himself, as it were, in a Noah's ark, with a very few men and a great many beasts. He felt how much his immediate power was lessened by the very circumstance of his measureless superiority to those about him: he acted, therefore, under a perpetual system of compromise—a compromise of greatness with meanness; a compromise of comprehension with narrowness; a compromise of the philosopher (who armed with the twofold knowledge of history and the laws of spirit looked, as with a telescope, far around and into the far distance) with the mere men of business, or with yet coarser intellects, who handled a truth, which they were required to receive, as they would handle an ox, which they were desired to purchase.

The final comment by a contemporary of Burke is from the essayist and writer William Hazlitt. Though a political opponent of Burke, he feels obliged to praise Burke as a writer and speaker.

William Hazlitt, 1807

There is no single speech of Mr. Burke which can convey a satis-
factory idea of his powers of mind. To do him justice, it would be
necessary to quote all his works; the only specimen of Burke is, all
that he wrote. With respect to most other speakers, a specimen is
generally enough, or more than enough. When you are acquainted
with their manner, and see what proficiency they have made in the
mechanical exercise of their profession, with what facility they can
borrow a simile, or round a period, how dexterously they can argue,
and object, and rejoin, you are satisfied; there is no other difference
in their speeches than what arises from the difference of the subjects.
But this was not the case with Burke. He brought his subjects along
with him; he drew his materials from himself. The only limits which
circumscribed his variety were the stores of his own mind. His stock
of ideas did not consist of a few meagre facts, meagrely stated, of half
a dozen commonplaces tortured into a thousand different ways; but
his mine of wealth was a profound understanding, inexhaustible as
the human heart, and various as the sources of human nature. He
therefore enriched every subject to which he applied himself, and new
subjects were only the occasions of calling forth fresh powers of mind
which had not been before exerted. It would therefore be in vain to
look for the proof of his powers in any one of his speeches or writings;
they all contain some additional proof of power. In speaking of Burke,
then, I shall speak of the whole compass and circuit of his mind—not
of that small part or section of him which I have been able to give:
to do otherwise would be like the story of the man who put the brick
in his pocket, thinking to show it as the model of a house. I have been
able to manage pretty well with respect to all my other speakers, and
curtailed them down without remorse. It was easy to reduce them
within certain limits, to fix their spirit, and condense their variety; by
having a certain quantity given, you might infer all the rest; it was
only the same thing over again. But who can bind Proteus, or confine
the roving flight of genius?

Burke's writings are better than his speeches, and indeed his speeches
are writings. But he seemed to feel himself more at ease, to have a
fuller possession of his faculties in addressing the public than in addressing the House of Commons. Burke was raised into public life;
and he seems to have been prouder of this new dignity than became so
great a man. For this reason, most of his speeches have a sort of parliamentary preamble to them: he seems fond of coquetting with the
House of Commons, and is perpetually calling the Speaker out to
dance a minuet with him before he begins. There is also something
like an attempt to stimulate the superficial dullness of his hearers by
exciting their surprise, by running into extravagance, and he sometimes demeans himself by condescending to what may be considered

as bordering too much upon buffoonery, for the amusement of the company . . . The truth is, that he was out of his place in the House of Commons; he was eminently qualified to shine as a man of genius, as the instructor of mankind, as the brightest luminary of his age; but he had nothing in common with that motley crew of knights, citizens, and burgesses. He could not be said to be "native and endured unto that element." He was above it; and never appeared like himself but when, forgetful of the idle clamours of party, and of the little views of little men, he applied to his country and the enlightened judgement of mankind.

I am not going to make an idle panegyric on Burke (he has no need of it); but I cannot help looking upon him as the chief boast and ornament of the English House of Commons. What has been said of him is, I think, strictly true, that "he was the most eloquent man of his time: his wisdom was greater than this eloquence."

BURKE IN HISTORY

>   History has been good to Burke, as he was kind to it.
> He is seldom forgotten. As indicated in the introduction he was
> one thing for the nineteenth century and another for our own.
> To be sure, he was less the heroic figure for Victorian writers,
> but he was remembered, all the same, for his political career as
> a Whig statesman. Rather than parade excerpted evaluations and
> assessments of particular aspects of Burke and his colorful career
> from the nooks and crannies of scholarship, this section will be
> devoted solely to three diverse efforts to come to terms with
> Burke's overall achievement. These full-length articles are from
> the world of contemporary scholarship, and they agree that
> Burke's life, career, and writings were of great significance. They
> differ, however, on what that may have been. That they differ
> reflects in part their different orientation, for the selections are
> from the academic Right, Left, and Center, respectively.

12

Russell Kirk: Burke and the Philosophy of Prescription

>   Russell Kirk was one of the first scholarly figures of
> the American Right to "rediscover" Burke after World War II.
> In this piece, he makes the case for Burke as the paradigm con-
> servative, whose career and writings provide the conservative
> fountain out of which can be drawn the teachings of custom,
> tradition, prejudice, religion, prescription, and virtually anything
> else sacred to the conservative creed.[1]

[1] Reprinted from the *Journal of the History of Ideas, 14* (1953), 365–80, by permission of the editors and the author.

Conservatism, as a critically held system of ideas, is younger than equalitarianism and rationalism. For philosophical conservatism begins with Edmund Burke, who erected prescription and "prejudice"—by which he meant the supra-rational wisdom of the species—into a conscious and imaginative defense of the traditional ways of society.

> When the age of Miracles lay faded into the distance as an incredible tradition, and even the age of Conventionalities was not old; and Man's Existence had for long generations rested on mere formulas which were grown hollow by course of time; and it seemed as if no Reality any longer existed, but only Phantasms of realities and God's Universe were the work of the Tailor and the Upholsterer mainly, and men were buckram masks that went about becking and grimacing there,—on a sudden, the Earth yawns asunder, and amid Tartarean smoke, and glare of fierce brightness, rises Sansculottism, many-headed fire-breathing, and asks: What think you of *me?* Well may the buckram masks stay together, terror-struck; "into expressive well-concerted groups!"

Thus Carlyle on the events of 1789; his *French Revolution,* said Lord Acton, "delivered the English mind from the thraldom of Burke." Acton, by the way, would have hanged Robespierre and Burke on the same gallows, a judgment in this matter as philosophically representative of Liberal sentiment during the past century as its execution would have been abhorrent to Liberal practice. From Carlyle onward, a great part of the reflecting public maintained that the truth about the Revolution must lie somewhere between Burke and—why, Condorcet, if one must choose a name.

Throughout its century of ascendancy, indeed, Liberalism believed that Burke had erred woefully concerning the significance of the Deluge; Buckle went so far as to explain, in mournful pages, that Burke had gone mad in 1790.[2] But for all that, the intellectual defenses of the Revolution never recovered from the buffet Burke dealt them; Carlyle could not find it possible to share the ecstatic vision of Paine. Burke's *Reflections* had captured the imagination of a powerful section of the rising generation. His style "forked and playful as the lightning, crested like the serpent" (Hazlitt's description) had outshone the flame of Rousseau in the eyes of many a young man of mind and spirit; his great work had not only survived Paine's assault, but had eclipsed it. He had set the course for British conservatism, he had become a pattern for Continental theorists, and he had insinuated himself even into the rebellious soul of America. Buckram masks could not survive the Deluge which Burke himself proclaimed the revolution "most astonishing that has hitherto happened in the world." But Burke was other than buckram; nor did he belong to the age of Con-

2 Buckle, *History of Civilization in England,* I, 424–425.

ventionalities. He believed in the age of Miracles—the old age of Miracles, not the new. He lit a fire to stifle a fire.

For Burke provided the principles to refute the abstractions of the equalitarians. The task was not congenial to his nature. Even when he set himself doggedly to it, as in the *Reflections* and the *Appeal from the New Whigs,* he could hold himself to the abstract expression of general principles only for a few consecutive paragraphs. This present essay, intended to systematize Burke's opinions, might itself be anathema to him, since generalities separated from contingencies were in his eyes almost impious. Yet he perceived the necessity of opposing ideas with ideas, and by 1793 his tremendous countermine had effectually thwarted the sappers from the equalitarian school. "Nothing can be conceived more hard than the heart of a thoroughbred metaphysician," he had written. "It comes nearer to the cold malignity of a wicked spirit than to the frailty and passion of a man. It is like that of the principle of evil himself, incorporeal, pure, unmixed, dephlegmated, defecated evil." [3] In 1798, nevertheless, admiring Hazlitt was telling Southey that "Burke was a metaphysician, Mackintosh a mere logician." [4] By the clutch of circumstance, Burke had been compelled to enter the realm of the abstract, but he never went one foot further into that windy domain than exigency demanded: "I must see the things; I must see the men." Never was statesman more reluctant to turn political philosopher, but never, perhaps, was the metamorphosis more happy.

Edmund Burke was impelled to undertake the delineation of a system of general principles by his alarm at the rapidly swelling influence of three separate schools of thought: that of Rousseau, that of the *philosophes,* and that of the heritors of Locke. The hostility between Rousseau's romanticism and the rationalism of, say, Voltaire has been remarked often, and Burke was not unaware of it; he assaulted both camps, though generally sighting his heavy guns upon Rousseau. As for Locke and his successors, the great Whig orator could not well disavow the defender of the settlement of 1688; yet his fealty to Locke's politics is only nominal,[5] and he wholly disclaims or ignores Locke's psychology and metaphysics. That Burke represented the actual *sentiments* of the Whigs throughout their supremacy, the perspective of history certainly discloses; but the *theories* of the Whigs, so far as they are embodied in the works of Locke, passed to such diverse legatees as Rousseau in Geneva, Price in the Old Jewry, Fox in St. Stephen's, Jefferson at Monticello.

Numerous differences of opinion divided these several camps, of

[3] "Letter to a Noble Lord," *Works* (Bohn edition), V, 141.

[4] P. P. Howe, *The Life of William Hazlitt,* 60.

[5] See Alfred Cobban's chapter "Burke and the Heritage of Locke" in his *Edmund Burke and the Revolt against the Eighteenth Century.*

course; but the later followers of Locke were agreed that change they must have, and that *change* for them was very nearly a synonym for *reform*. One may go further, fixing upon a half-dozen points of doctrine concerning which they reached consensus—these:

> That God is a Being of a sort quite unlike Jehovah—at once incorporated in us, this God of the deists and of Rousseau, and yet infinitely distant.
>
> That abstract reason or imagination may be utilized not only to study, but to direct, the course of society.
>
> That man is naturally benevolent, generous, healthy-souled, but is corrupted by institutions.
>
> That mankind is struggling upward toward Elysium, is capable of infinite improvement, and should fix its gaze upon the future.
>
> That the aim of the reformer, intellectual and political, is emancipation—liberation from old creeds, old oaths, old establishments; that the man of the future is to rejoice in complete liberty, self-governing, self-satisfying.

To this catalogue of progressive philosophy, the Utilitarians and the Collectivists later submitted amendments; but it will serve for our present definition of that radical mind which Burke endeavored to discredit. Burke conceded his enemies not one premise. He began and ended his campaign upon the grand design of morality; for Burke, the whole of earthly reality was an expression of moral principle. This it is which lifts him so far above "political science" that many scholars have been unable to understand him; yet Burke remains, notwithstanding, so devoted to practicality that he leaves metaphysicians at a loss. It is wise to commence our view of Burke's reluctantly-produced system with an eye to his concept of the force which governs the universe. For him, the formulas upon which man's existence rested never had grown hollow.

"The Tory has always insisted that, if men would cultivate the individual virtues, social problems would take care of themselves." So Granville Hicks once wrote of Stevenson.[6] Extend the epithet "Tory" to "conservative," and the observation is sound enough. This is not the whole of Burke's opinion upon the ills of society, since no one knew better the power for good or evil that lies in establishments; but it is true that Burke saw politics as an exercise in morals and that a great part of conservative doctrine on this point comes out of Burke's dicta. To know the state, we must first know the ethical man—so Burke tells us.

"Rousseau is a moralist, or he is nothing." After delivering this judgment, Burke rises to an assault upon the Genevese so merciless

6 Hicks, *Figures of Transition*, 271–272.

that one is tempted to add the obvious quip. But Burke was in earnest. A false morality, Rousseau's, but a pretentious, in the view of the old Whig statesman: against it must be set a nobler. A new-forged morality was a monstrous imposture, and so Burke turned, as he always did, to prescription and precedent, to old materials ready to the true reformer's hand, in order to produce this opposing morality. The praise of humility was often on Burke's lips, and in his construction of a system of thought he showed himself a humble man. Disdaining a vain show of creation, he turned to Aristotle and Cicero, to the fathers of the Church, to Hooker and Milton, and put new warmth into their phrases, made their ideas flame above the revolutionary torches. And he poured in a catalyst of his own that transformed blind tradition into deliberate adherence to ancient values. Rejecting the concept of a world subject to impulse and appetite, he revealed a world always governed by strong and subtle purpose.

There is a God; and He is wise; and this world is His design; and man and the state are God's creations. Such is Burke's philosophical fundamental. These were ideas accepted without question in most ages, but obscured by the vanity of the eighteenth century. How is God's purpose revealed? Through the unrolling of history. And how do we know God's mind and will? Through the prejudices and traditions which milleniums of human experience with divine judgments have implanted in the mind of the race. What is our purpose in this world? Not to indulge our impulse, but to render our obedience to divine intent.

Now this view of the cosmos may be true, or it may be delusory; but it is not obscure, let alone incomprehensible. The enduring influence of latter-day rationalism and utilitarianism, nevertheless, has prevented a number of writers in our day, scholars in philosophy and politics, from understanding how a great statesman and man of letters could hold such a view. We have stated Burke's position in the simplest terms: he makes his own case in language at once more lucid and more lofty. For many hundreds of years, all thinking men held this position to be supported by truths undeniable. Yet even by friendly critics, the dread word "obscurantism" is applied to Burke's affection for a moral tradition that was venerable when Socrates undertook its defense. R. M. MacIver remarks with a species of indignation, "It was no service to our understanding when Burke enveloped once more in mystic obscurity the office of government and in the sphere of politics appealed once more against reason to tradition and religion." [7]

But is not this begging the question? The Age of Reason, Burke

[7] MacIver, *The Modern State,* 148.

protested with all his Irish fervor, was in reality an Age of Ignorance. If the basis of existence is genuinely divine will, limiting politics and ethics to a puny "reason" is an act of folly; it is this blindness to the effulgence of the burning bush, this deafness to the thunder above Sinai, this shrugging at *mene, mene, tekel, upharsin,* which Burke proclaimed a principal infatuation of the French "Enlightenment." Even Rousseau cried out against such overweening confidence in a reason which, though assertedly independent of providential guidance, proclaims its own infallibility. Here we are concerned with first principles, and Burke himself doubtless would have agreed that if the teleological arguments of Aristotle, Seneca, and the Schoolmen are rejected, there remains no means of converting the skeptic but revelation. To dismiss such postulates summarily, however, and resign man to an abstract "reason" (by which is generally meant analytic empiricism) was to Burke an act of intellectual impudence. For Burke's forceful imagination, there could be no suspension of judgment: either there was design, or there was chaos. If chaos is demonstrated, the fragile equalitarian doctrines and emancipating intentions of the revolutionaries had no significance; for in a world of chaos, only force and appetite are valid.

I allow, that if no supreme ruler exists, wise to form, and potent to enforce, the moral law, there is no sanction to any contract, virtual or even actual, against the will of prevalent power. On that hypothesis, let any set of men be strong enough to set their duties at defiance, and they cease to be duties any longer. We have but one appeal against irresistible power—

> *Si genus humanum et mortalia*
> *temnitis arma,*
> *At sperate Deos memores fandi*
> *atque nefandi.*

Taking it for granted that I do not write to the disciples of the Parisian philosophy, I may assume, that the awful Author of our Being is the Author of our place in the order of existence; and that having disposed and marshalled us by a divine tactic, not according to our will, but according to His, He has, in and by that disposition, virtually subjected us to act the part which belongs to the part assigned us. We have obligations to mankind at large, which are not in consequence of any special voluntary pact. They arise from the relation of man to man, and the relation of man to God, which relations are not a matter of choice. . . . When we marry, the choice is voluntary, but the duties are not matter of choice. . . . The instincts which give rise to this mysterious process of nature are not of our making. But out of physical causes, unknown to us, perhaps unknowable, arise moral duties, which, as we are able perfectly to comprehend, we are bound indispensably to perform.[8]

Was this aspect of the argument for Providence ever better expressed? If the sanction for human conduct be divine, the way of wisdom is comprehension of, and submission to, the divine injunction; if there be no such sanction, "reason," "enlightenment," "equality," and "natural justice" are so many figments of dreams, for men require neither knowledge nor charity in a world without purpose. MacCunn observes concerning Burke, "It seemed to him the sheet anchor of a true political faith that the whole great drama of national life should be reverently recognized as ordered by a Power to which past, present, and future are organically knit stages in one Divine plan." [9]

Polybius' contention that the ancients invented the myths of religion in order to shelter morality and property was repugnant to Burke. The arguments Burke advances to prove that society cannot subsist without divine sanction are so convincing that a skeptic might concede, "If there were no God, it would be necessary to invent one"; but this is inverting Burke's own conviction. His piety was fervent, and its source was innate conviction. A world away from that other great Whig, Locke, Burke frequently expounds the doctrine of innate ideas. For the rest, the great arguments of the Platonic tradition in behalf of a universe of purpose and order are implicit in his speeches and writings: the instinct toward perpetuation of the species; the conviction of conscience; the intimations of immortality; the awareness of immaterial soul. New proofs he does not attempt to introduce; a man always desperately busy, he leaves theology to the schools. We detect in him much of Doctor Johnson's exasperated, "Why, Sir, we *know* the will is free, and there's an end of it!" Christianity he believes established on foundations no one but the restless, the shallow, and the self-intoxicated would venture to assail; and the spectacle of Burke's great intellect thus convinced, his erudition supporting the common voice of centuries, his prudent, practical, reforming spirit submitting to the discipline of the Christian tradition, is as good a proof as any from the books of the Scholastics, perhaps, to attest the truth of Christianity. It is a Christian faith, Burke's, and also a Greek faith. Observe the Hellenic ring in this pronouncement:

> He who gave our nature to be perfected by our virtue, willed also the necessary means of its perfection. He willed therefore the state. He willed its connexion with the source and original archtype of all perfection. They who are convinced of this His will, which is the law of

[8] "Appeal from the New to the Old Whigs," *Works*, III, 79.
[9] John MacCunn, *The Political Philosophy of Burke*, 127.

laws, and the sovereign of sovereigns, cannot think it reprehensible that this our recognition of a signiory paramount, I had almost said this oblation of the state itself, as a worthy offering on the high altar of universal praise, should be performed as all public, solemn acts are performed, in buildings, in music, in decoration, in speech, in the dignity of persons, according to the customs of mankind taught by their nature; this is, with modest splendor and unassuming state, with mild majesty and sober pomp.[10]

Transcendent even of Christianity, Burke's piety; for he viewed with a corresponding reverence the rites of the Hindus and the Mohammedans: his fiercest indignation against Hastings was from the Governor-General's heavy-handed contempt for native religious ceremony.

Conceivably Burke's conservatism might stand of itself even though shorn of its religious buttresses. The doctrine of expediency in politics might suffice as an apology for a conservative order—and, indeed, seemed quite enough to such pupils of Burke as Sir James Fitzjames Stephen. But Burke himself found it impossible to envisage a social order worthy of respect from which the spirit of piety was absent. The state is a creation religiously consecrated, he tells us:

This consecration is made, that all who administer in the government of men, in which they stand in the person of God himself, should have high and worthy notions of their function and destination; that their hope should be full of immortality; that they should not look to the paltry pelf of the moment, nor to the temporary and transient praise of the vulgar, but to a solid, permanent existence, in the permanent part of their nature, and to a permanent fame and glory, in the example they leave as a rich inheritance to the world.[11]

Such consecration is necessary in a monarchy or an aristocracy—but even more necessary in a popular government:

The consecration of the state, by a state religious establishment, is necessary also to operate with a wholesome awe upon free citizens; because, in order to secure their freedom, they must enjoy some determinate portion of power. . . . All persons possessing any portion of power ought to be strongly and awfully impressed with an idea that they act in trust; and that they are to account for their conduct in that trust to the one great Master, Author, and Founder of society.[12]

To call such a faith "obscurantism" and "mysticism" illustrates the lexicographical Dark Age into which our time has been slipping. A

[10] "Reflections on the Revolution in France," *Works*, II, 370.
[11] *Ibid.*, 363–364.
[12] *Ibid.*, 365.

lofty faith, Burke's, but also a practical man's, linked to public honor and responsibility. The rationalist may believe such a man wrong, but the rationalist is confused if he calls him a "mystic." And Burke proceeds, by reference and aside throughout his political career and his writings, to make his creed still more a part of private and public life. If the state of the world is the consequence of God's design, we need to be cautious about our reformations; for though it may be God's will to use us as His instruments of alteration, yet we should first satisfy our consciences and our intellects on that point. Again, Burke tells us there is indeed a universal equality; but it is the equality of Christianity, moral equality, equality in the judgment of God; equality of any other sort we may be foolish, possibly impious, to seek. That shrewdest of Socialists, Sir Leonard Woolf, remarks this bond between Christianity and social conservatism:

> As soon as people began to believe that happiness was politically of supreme importance, that everyone had an equal right to happiness, or that government should aim at the greatest happiness of the greatest number, the conflict between political psychology and religious psychology began in their minds. Christianity envisages a framework for human society in which earthly miseries have a recognized, permanent, and honourable place. They are trials sent by Heaven to test and train us; as such, it is impious to repine against them.[13]

Burke would have taken up this gauntlet. Poverty, brutality, misfortune he did indeed view as portions of the eternal order of things; sin was a real and demonstrable fact; religion was the consolation for these ills, not the product of them. Religious faith made existence tolerable; vain ambition without pious restraint would fail of accomplishment and destroy the beauty of reverence.

Burke was well aware of the powerful conservative effect upon society of the church, and recommended to parliament a decent concern for the well-being of the Roman clergy in Ireland, that their influence might be for the preservation of order, not its subversion. In the years that followed the restoration, de Maistre and de Bonald were to adapt the concepts of Burke to French clerical conservatism and ultramontane theories.

True religion is not only identical with national spirit, in Burke's view; it rises superior to law, and is, indeed, the origin of all law. With Philo and Cicero, both of whom he quotes, Burke proclaims the doctrine of the *jus naturale*, the creation of the divine mind, of which the laws of man are but a manifestation. "All human laws are, properly speaking, only declaratory; they may alter the mode and applica-

13 Woolf, *After the Deluge*, 177.

tion, but have no power over the substance of original justice." [14] "Religion, to have any force on man's understandings, indeed to exist at all, must be supposed paramount to laws, and independent for its substance on any human institution. Else it would be the absurdest thing in the world; an acknowledged cheat." [15] The majority of the people "have no right to make a law prejudicial to the whole community, even though the delinquents in making such an act should be themselves the chief sufferers by it; because it would be made against the principle of a superior law, which it is not in the power of any community, or the whole race of man, to alter.—I mean the will of Him who gave us our nature, and in giving impressed an invariable law upon it. It would be hard to point out any error more truly subversive of all the order and beauty, of all the peace and happiness, of human society, than the position that any body of men have a right to make what laws they please; or that laws can derive any authority from their institution merely and independent of the quality of the subject-matter." [16]

By no means new, these concepts of the law; but powerfully presented, and that at a time when the world was infatuated with constitution-making, when Abbe Sièyes was drawing up organic documents wholesale. And these concepts are promulgated, too, by the spokesman of the Whigs, nominally the heritor of Locke the constitution-designer. America had just got fourteen new constitutions and was thinking of more. A man of strong conviction and original mind was required to find the basis of law in a transcendent plan, rather than in a neat parliamentary construction; and that man, paradoxically, was also the advocate of enlarged expediency as the guide to the conduct of affairs. But expediency, said Burke, always must yield to the dictates of right—the right which God teaches to man through the experience of the race.

Ours is a moral order, then, and our laws are representative of grander moral laws; the higher contentment is moral happiness, says Burke, and the cause of suffering is moral evil. Pride, ambition, avarice, revenge, lust, sedition, hypocrisy, ungoverned zeal, disorderly appetites—these vices are the true causes of the storms that trouble life. "Religion, morals, laws, prerogatives, privileges, liberties, rights of men, are the *pretexts*. The pretexts are always found in some specious appearance of a real good. You would not secure men from tyranny and sedition, by rooting out from the mind the principles to which these fraudulent principles apply? If you did, you would root out everything that is valuable in the human breast. . . . You would not cure the evil by resolving, that there should be no more monarchs,

[14] "Tracts on the Popery Laws," *Works*, VI, 22.
[15] *Ibid.*, 32–33.
[16] *Ibid.*, 21–22.

nor ministers of state, nor of the gospel; no interpreters of law; no general officers; no public councils. . . . Wise men will apply their remedies to vices, not to names." [17]

Nor can this moral order be altered by counting noses. "When we know, that the opinions of even the greatest multitudes are the standard of rectitude, I shall think myself obliged to make those opinions the masters of my conscience. But if it may be doubted whether Omnipotence itself is competent to alter the essential constitution of right and wrong, sure am I, that such *things,* as they and I, are possessed of no such power." [18]

This doctrine of the moral order, the realm of divine injunction, may appear to march with the bog of metaphysical abstraction so loathed by Burke himself. But the Whig orator would have thundered his retort upon the doubter. Surely as indulgence brings disgust, surely as violence is repaid in kind, just so certain is the operation of other causes and effects in the moral world; they are matters of observation, not of conjecture, Burke would have rejoined. The illustration of the principle he left to the preachers and essayists of the age. How is the nature of the moral world to be comprehended? How are we to guide ourselves within its bounds? By observance of tradition and prescription, says Burke.

"The reason first why we do admire those things which are greatest, and second those things which are ancientest, is because the one are the least distant from the infinite substance, the other from the infinite continuance, of God." [19] This was only a passing remark of Burke's, in a general conversation; but it holds the kernel of his philosophy of prescription.

What is the basis of authority in ethics, politics, public economy, law? Burke found it necessary to re-state for the eighteenth century the position of those who have faith in a permanent order of things. His answer, succinctly, was "Tradition tempered by expediency." The custom of mankind determines principles; expedience, its application. The contemner of abstraction was far from rejecting general principles and maxims; and his doctrine of divine purpose puts a gulf between his "expedience" and the expediency of the Machiavellians, just as it separates him from the geographical and historical determinism of his teacher Montesquieu and his pupil Taine.

Willfully or not, it was for a long time the fashion among the liberal admirers of Burke to look upon him as a sort of Benthamite, lauding his determination to deal with circumstances, not concepts;

17 "Reflections," *Works,* II, 412–413.
18 "Speech previous to the Election at Bristol," *Works,* II, 167.
19 Burke was quoting from Hooker's *Ecclesiastical Polity,* Book V, chapter 69.

Buckle is as enthusiastic about this side of Burke as he is indignant concerning the *Reflections*:

> We had, no doubt, other statesmen before him who denied the validity of general principles in politics; but their denial was only the happy guess of ignorance, and they rejected theories which they had never taken the pains to study. Burke rejected them because he knew them. It was his rare merit that, notwithstanding every inducement to rely upon his own generalizations, he resisted the temptation; that, though rich in all the varieties of political knowledge, he made his opinions subservient to the march of events; that he recognized as the object of government, not the preservation of particular institutions, nor the propagation of particular tenets, but the happiness of the people at large. . . . Burke was never weary of attacking the common argument that, because a country has long flourished under some particular custom, therefore the custom must be good.[20]

Curiously perverse here, Buckle, translating Burke's exceptions into Burke's rules. Above all else, Burke's philosophy has principle and prescription written upon the face of it; not these, but *abstraction* and *abuse*, does Burke attack. "I do not put abstract ideas wholly out of any question, because I well know that under that name I should dismiss principles; and that without the guide and light of sound, well-understood principles, all reasoning in politics, as in everything else, would be only a confused jumble of particular facts and details, without the means of drawing out any sort of theoretical or practical conclusion." [21]

Abstraction, no; principle, yes. To the first, the guide was knowledge of nature and history, the expressions of divine purpose; to the second, that prudence Burke extols as "the director, the regulator, the standard" of all the virtues. Expedience serves principle, never supplants it. For principle is our cognizance of the divine intent.

History, for Burke, was the gradual revelation of a Supreme design —often shadowy and subtle to our eyes, but quite resistless, wholly just. Burke stops far short of Hegel's mystical determinism, for his adherence to the doctrine of free will tells him that it is not arbitrary, unreasoning will, not material force or racial destiny, which make history, but rather human character and conduct. God makes history through the medium of human souls. It may become impious to resist the grand design, when once its character is irrefutably manifested; but a full comprehension of God's ends we are rarely vouchsafed. The statesman and the thinker must know more than history: they must know nature. Burke's "nature" is human nature, the revelation of universal and permanent principles through the study of mind and

20 Buckle, *The History of Civilization in England*, I, 424–425.
21 "Speech on the Petition of the Unitarians," *Works*, VI, 112–113.

soul—not the Romantics' half-pantheistic nature. The phrase "state of nature" was often irritating to Burke's accurate mind; "natural rights," as demanded by Rousseau and other equalitarians, he denied; but the usage of "nature" which was Cicero's is Burke's also. Know history and nature, and you may presume to guess at God's intent.

How has the human species collected and condensed the wisdom of its experience, the written part of which we call history? Chiefly through tradition, "prejudice," prescription—generally surer guides to conscience and conduct than books or speculation. Habit and custom may be the wisdom of unlettered men, but they come from the sound old heart of humanity.

> We are afraid to put men to live and trade each on his own private stock of reason; because we suspect that this stock in each man is small, and that the individuals would do better to avail themselves of the general bank and capital of nations and ages. Many of our men of speculation, instead of exploding general prejudices, employ their sagacity to discover the latent wisdom which prevails in them. If they find what they seek, and they seldom fail, they think it more wise to continue the prejudice, with the reason involved, than to cast away the coat of prejudice, and to leave nothing but the naked reason; because prejudice, with its reason, has a motive to give action to that reason, and an affection which will give it permanence.[22]

Without reverence, man will not serve God, and so will destroy himself; prejudice, prescription, and custom bring reverence.

They bring reverence, but they are not modes of action, of course. When society needs to act, it should resort to an expedience which is founded upon these traditions and habits of thought. "Expedience is that which is good for the community, and good for every individual in it." [23] These words of Burke's are not very different from the definitions of Hume or of Bentham; for that matter, one notes the similarity of this sentence to Rousseau's identification of individual happiness with the gratification of the General Will. But Burke meant something very unlike the several concepts of Hume and Bentham and Rousseau. His qualifying phrase really is his premise. The good of the individual, for Burke, is the *test* of expediency—not its consequence. When Burke thought of the "good of the community" he had in mind a spiritual good, an enduring good without the alloy of incidental and private deprivation. He was unyieldingly hostile to a vision of society composed of a satisfied majority and a submitting minority. The statesman who properly understands the functions of expedience, or prudence, will have for his model a society in which every man has his

[22] "Reflections," *Works,* II, 359.
[23] "Speech on the Reform of Representation," *Works,* VI, 149.

prerogatives, his accepted station, and his correspondent duties; tradition and prescription will have taught every man to recognize the justice of this order, and he will not merely acquiesce in the stability of social institutions, but will support them out of a sound prejudice. An intelligent exercise of expedience will save man from the anarchy of "natural right" and the presumption of "reason." Prescription as a guide for the great mass of mankind, tradition illuminated by expedience as a guide for the philosopher and the statesman who are shepherds of the mass of men: this combination is Burke's recipe for a society at once pious and vigorous.

Burke's praises of custom and traditional wisdom, ancient usage that is surer guarantee than statute, knowledge of the species that is beyond our own little intellects, are repeated in all his principal works. Of the persecution of Catholics, "You punish them for acting upon a principle which of all others is perhaps most necessary for preserving society, an implicit admiration and adherence to the establishments of their forefathers." [24] Again, "If prescription be once shaken, no species of property is secure, when it once becomes an object large enough to tempt the cupidity of indigent power." [25] The British Constitution itself is his best example of right established by custom:

> Our constitution is a prescriptive constitution; it is a constitution whose sole authority is that it has existed time out of mind. . . . Your king, your lords, your judges, your juries, grand and little, all are prescriptive; and what proves it is the dispute not yet concluded, and never near becoming so, when any of them first originated. Prescription is the most solid of all titles, not only to property, but, which is to secure that property, to government. They harmonize with each other, and give mutual aid to one another. It is accompanied with another ground of authority in the constitution of the human mind—presumption. It is a presumption in favour of any settled scheme of government against any untried project, that a nation has long existed and flourished under it. It is a far better presumption even of the *choice* of a nation, far better than any sudden and temporary arrangement by actual election.[26]

"Prejudice"—the half-intuitive knowledge that enables man to meet the problems of life without logic-chopping; "prescription"—the customary right which grows out of the implied conventions and compacts of many successive generations: employing these instruments, mankind manages to live together in some degree of amicability and freedom. They direct the individual conscience and the conscript fathers. Without them, society can be kept from destruction only by

[24] "Tracts on the Popery Laws," *Works*, VI, 32.
[25] "Reflections," *Works*, II, 422.
[26] "Speech on the Reform of Representation," *Works*, VI, 146.

force and a master. "Somewhere there must be a control upon will and appetite; and the less of it there is within, the more of it there must be without." For if prejudice and prescription be eradicated, only one peaceful instrument remains for preventing man from relapsing into that primitive natural state from which he has so painfully crept up through milleniums, and which existence Burke (in most matters at war with Hobbes) also knew to be "poor, nasty, brutish, and short." That surviving instrument is reasons. And Reason, the darling of the *philosophes,* seemed to Burke a poor weak servant. The mass of mankind Burke implies, reason hardly at all; deprived of folk-wisdom and folk-law, which are a part of prescription and prejudice, they can only troop after the demagogue, the charlatan, and the despot. The mass of mankind are not ignorant, but their knowledge is a kind of collective possession, the sum of the slow accretions of generations. This abandoned, they are thrown back upon their "own private stock of reason"; and that stock is very small, hopelessly inferior to the "general bank and capital of nations and of ages." Even the wisest and shrewdest of men are ridiculously conceited if they presume to set the products of their reason against the judgment of the centuries. It is possible, Burke concedes, that they may be right, and past humanity wrong; but the ordinary presumption is the other way; and in any case, it may be wiser to continue an old practice, even if it be the child of error, than to break radically with custom and run the risk of disturbing the body social merely to satisfy a doctrinaire affection for scientific precision. "You see, Sir, that in this enlightened age I am bold enough to confess, that we are generally men of untaught feelings; that instead of casting away all our old prejudices, we cherish them to a very considerable degree, and, to take more shame to ourselves, we cherish them because they are prejudices; and the longer they have lasted, and the more generally they have prevailed, the more we cherish them." [27]

Burke was not the first English philosopher to respect prejudice and prescription. Hume, for all his boldness, was aware of their social utility; and a writer whose ideas Burke generally disliked as much as Hume's, Chesterfield, praises prejudice nearly as eloquently as does Burke himself. In *The World,* Chesterfield has observed:

A prejudice is by no means (though generally thought so) an error; on the contrary, it may be a most unquestioned truth, though it be still a prejudice in those who, without any examination, take it upon trust and entertain it by habit. There are even some prejudices, founded upon error, which ought to be connived at, or perhaps encouraged; their effects being more beneficial to society than their detection can possibly be. . . . The bulk of mankind have neither leisure nor knowl-

27 "Reflections," *Works,* II, 359.

edge sufficient to reason right; why should they be taught to reason at all? Will not honest instinct prompt, and wholesome prejudices guide them, much better than half reasoning? [28]

Yet Burke's onslaught upon new-fangled Reason clashed with the great fashionable intellectual current of his time, with the whole principle of the Encyclopedia. Courage was required for such declarations in support of prejudice; in a lesser man, this stand would have been dismissed with scorn by the literate public. Burke, however, they could not scorn. It is some indication of the strength of Burke's belief in Christian humility that he, with his acute and far-ranging mind, could be the partisan of the instincts of the race against the assumptions of the man of genius.

Men are by appetite voracious and sanguinary, Burke thinks; they are held in check by this collective and immemorial wisdom we call morality, prejudice; reason alone never can bind them to their duties. Whenever the veneer of prejudice and prescription is cracked at any point, we are menaced by the danger that the crack may widen and lengthen, even to the annihilation of civilization. If men are discharged from reverence for custom and usage, they will treat this frail world as if it were their personal property, to be consumed for their immediate gratification; and thus they will destroy in their lust for enjoyment the property of future generations, of their own contemporaries, and indeed their very own capital:

> One of the first and most leading principles on which the common-wealth and the laws are consecrated, is lest the temporary possessors and life-renters in it, unmindful of what they have received from their ancestors, or of what is due to their posterity, should act as if they were the entire masters; that they should not think it among their rights to cut off the entail, or commit waste on the inheritance, by destroying at their pleasure the whole original fabric of their society; hazarding to leave to those who come after them a ruin instead of a habitation —and teaching these successors as little to respect their contrivances, as they had themselves respected the institutions of their forefathers. By this unprincipled facility of changing the state as often, and as much, and in as many ways, as there are floating fancies or fashions, the whole chain and continuity of the commonwealth would be broken. No one generation could link with another. Men would become little better than the flies of a summer.[29]

Prejudice and prescription, despite their great age—or perhaps because of it—are delicate growths, slow to rise, easy to injure, hardly possible to revive. The abstract metaphysician and fanatic reformer, intending to cleanse, may find he has scrubbed society clean away:

28 *The World,* No. 112.
29 "Reflections," *Works,* II, 366–367.

An ignorant man, who is not fool enough to meddle with his clock, is however sufficiently confident to think he can safely take to pieces, and put together at his pleasure, a moral machine of another guise, importance, and complexity, composed of far other wheels, and springs, and balances, and counteracting and co-operating powers. Men think little how immorally they act in rashly meddling with what they do not understand. Their delusive good intention is no sort of excuse for their presumption. They who truly mean well must be fearful of acting ill.[30]

Then is alteration of any sort undesirable? Do prejudice and prescription compel mankind to tread perpetually behind their ancestors? No, says Burke; change is inevitable; but let it come as the consequence of a need generally felt, not out of fine-spun abstractions. Both prejudice and prescription are altered by the newer experiences of humanity. This process should not be stifled, since it is a natural and providential means of prolonging life, quite like the physical renewal of the human body. But change should be considered as the manifestation of divine purpose, not simply as a mechanism for men to tinker with. The course of change is not truly a *conscious* process; some might call it a blind process. Our part is to patch and polish the old order of things, clothing ancient form with new substance, fitting recent experience and need into the pattern of the wisdom of our ancestors. We must try to distinguish between a profound, slow, natural alteration and some infatuation of the hour. Here again the instrument of expedience is required for the wise reconciliation of prescription with necessary alteration.

We must all obey the great law of change. It is the most powerful law of nature, and the means perhaps of its conservation. All we can do, and that human wisdom can do, is to provide that the change shall proceed by insensible degrees. This has all the benefits which may be in change, without any of the inconveniences of mutation. Everything is provided for as it arrives. This mode will, on the one hand prevent the unfixing old interests at once: a thing which is apt to breed a black and sullen discontent in those who are at once dispossessed of all their influence and consideration. This gradual course, on the other side, will prevent men, long under depression, from being intoxicated with a large draught of new power, which they always abuse with a licentious insolence.[31]

Prescription and prejudice are themselves subject to change, and the man who obstinately rejects even such innovations as are manifestly the improvements of Providence is as rash as the devotee of Reason.

[30] "Appeal from the New Whigs to the Old," *Works*, III, 111–112.
[31] "Letter to Sir Hercules Langrische on the Catholics" (1792), *Works*, III, 340.

Prescription and venerable precept never have received a more consistent and courageous defense than Burke's championship of the wisdom of our ancestors. Yet Burke has very little to say concerning the greatest social quandary of our time: once prescription and prejudice *are* violated, once the mass of mankind have been cast adrift, with only miscellaneous scraps of custom and tradition left to mingle with their private stock of reason, how is society to be kept from disintegration? "Burke was sincerely convinced that men's power of political reasoning was so utterly inadequate to their task," comments Graham Wallas, "that all his life long he urged the English nation to follow prescription, to obey, that is to say, on principle their habitual political impulses. But the deliberate following of prescription which Burke advocated was something different, because it was the result of choice, from the uncalculated loyalty of the past. Those who have eaten of the tree of knowledge cannot forget." [32]

"Prejudice renders a man's virtue his habit; and not a series of unconnected acts. Through just prejudice, his duty becomes a part of his nature"—thus Burke.[33] Can prejudice and prescription, once shattered, be restored? Wallas thinks not; and probably Burke would agree with him. Yet Wallas and other recent writers have come to agree with Burke that a private stock of reason is wholly inadequate to guide man and society. Perhaps Burke's confidence in the purposeful design of Providence would have prompted him to answer that out of the confusion of our century will be resolved a fresh set of prescriptions and prejudices remarkably like those his age knew; for prescription, he declared, has its true origin in the nature which God bestowed upon man.

[32] Wallas, *Human Nature in Politics* (4th ed., 1948), 182–183.
[33] "Reflections," *Works*, II, 359.

13
C. B. Macpherson:
Edmund Burke

Professor Macpherson of the University of Toronto is
a leading student of the history of political thought. He brings
to bear in that scholarship the intellectual perspective of the
Marxist left. In this piece he contends that Burke's laissez-faire
economics, with its nonintervening state and its acceptance of a
market economy, is by no means incompatible with his defense
of a hierarchical traditional order. Indeed, according to Macpher-
son, Burke's great achievement is to be the first to recognize that
the market economy requires class subordination in order to
work.[1]

Edmund Burke is at first sight ill-matched with Adam Smith.
Both indeed had copious minds; both had that mastery of the English
tongue which is so often to be found in Scottish and Irish writers; and
both, while addressing themselves to the highest questions of social
means and ends, had a strong historical and empirical sense. But their
paths are generally thought to have diverged widely. We know Adam
Smith as the great exponent of "the system of natural liberty," his
master work as the demonstration that if the whole business of producing a nation's wealth were left to the operation of the freely com-
petitive market the system would regulate itself, and would do so to
the greatest general benefit.

We know Burke, on the contrary, as the defender of the traditional
order, of prescription and custom, of inherited institutions and of
prejudice; the man whose scorn for "the age . . . of sophisters, economists and calculators" was unconcealed.[2] It was because the British
constitution embodied the collective wisdom of many generations that
it was the quintessence of political good:

1 Reprinted from the *Transactions of the Royal Society of Canada*, Vol. 53, Series
3, June 1959, Section 2, with the permission of the editors and the author.
2 *Reflections on the Revolution in France*, p. 83. (All page references for quotations from Burke are to the Oxford World's Classics edition of his writings.)

it has been the uniform policy of our constitution to claim and assert our liberties, as an *entailed inheritance* derived to us from our fore-fathers, and to be transmitted to our posterity; as an estate specially belonging to the people of this kingdom. . . . We have an inheritable crown; an inheritable peerage; and a House of Commons and a people inheriting privileges, franchises, and liberties, from a long line of an-cestors. This policy appears to me to be the result of profound reflec-tion; or rather the happy effect of following nature, which is wisdom without reflection, and above it. . . . the people of England well know, that the idea of inheritance furnishes a sure principle of con-servation, and a sure principle of transmission; without at all exclud-ing a principle of improvement. It leaves acquisition free; but it se-cures what it acquires. Whatever advantages are obtained by a state proceeding on these maxims, are locked fast as in a sort of family settlement; grasped as in a kind of mortmain for ever. By a constitu-tional policy, working after the pattern of nature, we receive, we hold, we transmit our government and our privileges, in the same manner in which we enjoy and transmit our property and our lives.[3]

Whatever may be thought of Burke's identification of "the pattern of nature" with the English law of entailed property, his veneration of inherited institutions is perfectly clear. He provides, indeed, for "improvement," but only such as would extend inherited benefits, never such as would challenge them.

His veneration of the inherited extended far beyond political insti-tutions. Civil society itself derived all its meaning and value from the organic relationships which had grown up within it. Burke did not reject the idea of a social contract, but he transformed it, now into something mysterious and transcendental, now into something his-torical and organic. He was willing that a social contract should be inferred, but he would allow it to be inferred only from a supposed divine and natural order, or from prescription. Everyone knows the splendid sentences in which Burke likens the state to a partnership:

Society is indeed a contract . . . but the state ought not to be con-sidered as nothing better than a partnership agreement in a trade of pepper and coffee, calico or tobacco, or some other such low concern. . . . It is a partnership in all science; a partnership in all art; a part-nership in every virtue and in all perfection. As the ends of such a partnership cannot be obtained in many generations, it becomes a partnership not only between those who are living, but between those who are living, those who are dead, and those who are to be born.

If this stretches the concept of partnership, it is at least quite compre-hensible. But Burke goes on, without pause, to subordinate this con-cept to an overriding transcendent contract:

3 *Ibid.,* pp. 35–6.

Each contract of each particular state is but a clause in the great primaeval contract of eternal society, linking the lower with the higher natures, connecting the visible and invisible world, according to a fixed compact sanctioned by the inviolable oath which holds all physical and all moral natures, each in their appointed place. This law is not subject to the will of those, who by an obligation above them, and infinitely superior, are bound to submit their will to that law.[4]

When Burke comes down to earth, we find that this natural law principle is essentially a principle of traditional subordination of ranks:

The idea of a people is the idea of a corporation. It is wholly artificial; and made like all other legal fictions by common agreement. What the particular nature of that agreement was, is collected from the form into which the particular society has been cast.[5]

And, we are told, it must always be cast in a mould of unequal ranks; otherwise, there is not a people, not a society:

To enable men to act with the weight and character of a people, and to answer the ends for which they are incorporated into that capacity, we must suppose them (by means immediate or consequential) to be in that state of habitual social discipline, in which the wiser, the more expert, and the more opulent conduct, and by conducting enlighten and protect the weaker, the less knowing, and the less provided with the goods of fortune. When the multitude are not under this discipline, they can scarcely be said to be in civil society.[6]

Society, in short, is an organism. It requires habitual social discipline. And that, Burke saw, requires an habitual social ethic; hence his praise of English moral prejudice: "We know," he said, writing to the French,

that *we* have made no discoveries, and we think that no discoveries are to be made, in morality; nor many in the great principles of government, nor in the ideas of liberty, which were understood long before we were born, altogether as well as they will be after the grave has heaped its mould upon our presumption. . . . Instead of casting away all our old prejudices, we cherish them to a very considerable degree, and . . . we cherish them because they are prejudices; and the longer they have lasted, and the more generally they have prevailed, the more we cherish them.[7]

---

[4] *Ibid.*, pp. 105–6.
[5] "Appeal from the New to the Old Whigs," *Works*, V, p. 96.
[6] *Ibid.*, p. 100.
[7] *Reflections*, pp. 94–5.

Habitual social discipline between ranks, an inherited morality embraced as prejudice—these are what is needed to hold any society together.

This is a far cry from accepting or advocating, in the eighteenth century, a market society; it seems rather to be a vehement defence of traditional social relations against the inroads of the market. But we have had so far only half the picture. When we examine Burke's economic ideas, and the explicit social assumptions on which he bases them, we find apparently another Burke, who outdoes Adam Smith in his insistence on the natural rightness and beneficence of pure market relations. This is the Burke to whom Adam Smith is reported to have said, after they had been discussing political economy, "that he was the only man who, without communication, thought on these topics exactly as he did." [8] When we have seen the extent of Burke's commitment to market principles, there can be no further question about his intellectual kinship with Adam Smith. But there will be a serious question of Burke's own consistency, which it will be the object of the rest of this paper to explore.

Burke wrote no general theoretical treatise on economics, any more than on politics, but his views are quite explicit in his writings on specific problems of economic policy, notably the *Thoughts and Details on Scarcity*, of 1795; and some of his assumptions were even more emphatically stated in the *Reflections on the Revolution in France* (1790).

The singular merit of the market economy—that it automatically turns private greed into general benefit—is stated in terms that allow no dissent: "the benign and wise Disposer of all things . . . obliges men, whether they will or not, in pursuing their own selfish interests, to connect the general good with their own individual success." [9] More specifically, he insists that the interests of the employer and the labourer "are always the same, and it is absolutely impossible that their free contracts can be onerous to either party." [10] Only the malignity and perversity of men could prevent them acknowledging these Divine arrangements.

The essential postulate of the self-regulating market economy is stated without qualification, and with full moral approval. "Labour

[8] Robert Bisset, *Life of Edmund Burke* (2nd ed., London, 1800), II, p. 429. Political economy was not just an acquisition of Burke's later years. He had applied himself to a search for its principles even before he entered Parliament (in 1766), where he was recognized as an expert on trade policy; and is said to have been "consulted, and the greatest deference was paid to his opinions, by Dr. Adam Smith, in the progress of the celebrated work on the Wealth of Nations." For this and other evidence see Donal Barrington, "Edmund Burke as an Economist," *Economica*, N.S. XXI, no. 83 (Aug., 1954).

[9] "Thoughts and Details on Scarcity," *Works*, VI, p. 9.

[10] *Ibid.*, p. 8.

is a commodity like every other, and rises or falls according to the demand." [11] Since labour is "an article of trade" it "must be subject to all the laws and principles of trade, and not to regulations foreign to them." [12] The market which settles the price of labour is, moreover, equitable and just. Even when it gives the labourer less than his necessary subsistence there is no case for relief by the state:

> whenever it happens that a man can claim nothing according to the rules of commerce, and the principles of justice, he passes out of that department and comes within the jurisdiction of mercy. In that province the magistrate has nothing at all to do: his interference is a violation of the property which it is his office to protect.[13]

Above all, the state must not intervene

> to supply to the poor those necessaries which it has pleased the Divine Providence for a while to withhold from them. We, the people [Burke's use of the phrase made famous eight years earlier in constituting the United States of America is curious here], ought to be made sensible, that it is not in breaking the laws of commerce, which are the laws of nature, and consequently the laws of God, that we are to place our hope of softening the Divine displeasure to remove any calamity under which we suffer, or which hangs over us.[14]

The extent of Burke's acceptance not only of the market economy but also of the market society is now apparent. Burke was under no misapprehension about the market. He knew that if it was to be self-regulating as an economic system, it would have to penetrate and transform all other social relationships. He knew that if the market economy was to work, a man's labour had to be wholly subjected to the market, and that when this happened human beings were brought into a different relation to each other. When labour becomes a commodity, the market economy becomes a market society. All this Burke knew and accepted.

We can now see the full extent of the apparent paradox in Burke's social philosophy. Let the cash nexus prevail in social relations, he tells us, root out the idea that society has any obligation to the individual, break up the institutions of poor relief and wage and price regulation in which the English state had acknowledged such obligation for hundreds of years—do all this, and so maintain the traditional organic English society. Could there be a more striking paradox? By leaving the fundamental relation of men as producers to the absolute

11 *Ibid.*, p. 6.
12 *Ibid.*, p. 10.
13 *Ibid.*, p. 13.
14 *Ibid.*, p. 22.

determination of the impersonal market, the organic unity of society is to be maintained.

The contradiction to which I am drawing attention here is not, it must be noticed, the one that is sometimes, wrongly, read into the principles of the Utilitarians and the classical economists. I find no contradiction, in their thinking or in Burke's, between belief in a self-regulating market economy and belief in the necessity of a strong and rather pervasive state. Far from it. For to the extent that the productive work of a society, and the apportioning of the product among the members of the society, is removed from traditional arrangements and handed over to the market, in which men meet each other simply as bargaining proprietors of labour-power, capital, land, and other commodities, to that extent a stronger state is needed, a state more meticulous about contract and property rights and much else besides. Thomas Hobbes had seen this very clearly in the middle of the seventeenth century: having reduced all justice to the performance of contract, and all moral relations to the relations of the market, he demonstrated the need for a strong state with positive functions in morals, education and religion, as well as in property and contract. By the end of the eighteenth century the need was more obvious, for the transformation of social relations into market relations had gone somewhat farther than in Hobbes's day. It is not surprising, then, that the eighteenth century advocates of laissez-faire were advocates also of a strong state, nor that the classical economists gave the state rather more positive functions, in, for instance, health and education, than did Herbert Spencer's caricature version of laissez-faire.

So we may set aside any supposed contradiction between the self-regulating market and the powerful and sedulous state, either in the classical economists or in Burke. But what remains, and is thrown into sharper relief in Burke's thinking, is an apparent contradiction between the market society on the one hand, in which man is reduced to a commodity and justice is determined by the market, and on the other hand the traditional society with its older notions of commutative and distributive justice, and of a moral order in which one's rights and duties were related to rank and status rather than to the market or contract.

Burke apparently spoke for both. Were there then two Burkes, wildly inconsistent? Not at all. It was Burke's genius to grasp intuitively something that his less politically involved friends, the classical economists, overlooked or at least did not see as of central importance. Burke saw that the self-regulating market could not work, indeed could not hope to establish itself fully, unless there was a widespread belief in a divine and natural order of subordination of ranks in society. Unless labourers, farmers, capitalists and rentiers all knew their place, unless all were convinced that the rewards the market gave them were just and hallowed, the market system could not operate, for its attempted operation would engender an overwhelming resentment.

We can see Burke's mind working this way again and again. He does not blush, for instance, to take over from the ancients the classification of animate and inanimate instruments of a master, and apply it to the modern farmer: the human labour which the farmer employs is the *instrumentum vocale*, the working stock of cattle the *semivocale*, and the carts, ploughs, and spades the *instrumentum mutum*. Between all these there is a natural chain of subordination: "the beast is as an informing principle to the plough and cart; the labourer is as reason to the beast; and the farmer is as a thinking and presiding principle to the labourer. An attempt to break this chain of subordination in any part is equally absurd." [15] This, it should be noticed, is offered as a proof that the interests of the farmer and the labourer "are always the same."

For a clearer assertion that the market economy cannot work unless a traditional class subordination is carried over into it, we may turn to the *Reflections*. Burke is arguing that the accumulation of capital is of fundamental importance to any society. To make accumulation possible, the people

> must be tractable and obedient. . . . The body of the people must not find the principles of natural subordination by art rooted out of their minds. They must respect that property of which they cannot partake. They must labour to obtain what by labour can be obtained; and when they find, as they commonly do, the success disproportioned to the endeavour, they must be taught their consolation in the final proportions of eternal justice. Of this consolation whoever deprives them, deadens their industry, and strikes at the root of all acquisition as of all conservation. He that does this is the cruel oppressor. . . .[16]

A substantial part of the labour force had to be engaged in "the innumerable servile, degrading, unseemly, unmanly, and often most unwholesome and pestiferous occupations, to which by the social economy so many wretches are inevitably doomed." But it would be "pernicious to disturb the natural course of things, and to impede, in any degree, the great wheel of circulation which is turned by the strangely-directed labour of these unhappy people." [17] Burke's regret for the miseries of the labourer was matched by his appreciation of the function of the capitalist (Burke's own word):

> Monied men ought to be allowed to set a value on their money; if they did not, there could be no monied men. This desire of accumulation

15 *Ibid.*, p. 9.
16 *Reflections*, p. 271.
17 *Ibid.*, pp. 177–8.

is a principle without which the means of their service to the state could not exist. The love of lucre, though sometimes carried to a ridiculous, sometimes to a vicious excess, is the grand cause of prosperity to all states. . . . this natural, this reasonable, this powerful, this prolific principle. . . .[18]

It is clear that Burke fully accepted the morality of *bourgeois* society. Nothing was to be allowed to interfere with the operation of the market. With all its misery it was naturally just. But it had to be supported by the consolation that could be found "in the final proportions of eternal justice." The great body of the people could be taught this consolation provided that "the principles of natural subordination" were not "by art rooted out of their minds." The functioning of the capitalist market system, in short, depended on the continuance, into the capitalist era, of the traditional notion of natural subordination of ranks. The traditional notion might, in a logical view, seem inconsistent with the notion of a purely contractual market society, but Burke knew that historically they were fully consistent.

There were not, after all, two Burkes, one the defender of the cash nexus, the other the defender of the earlier traditional social values. There was one Burke, with the perspicacity to see that the cash nexus could hold only if there was a "natural" order of subordination to support it. Burke was the first to see this, or at least the first to make it the central point of a political and social theory. He was so fully persuaded of it that he usually presented market society as if it were traditional society. The notion that market society *was* traditional society would have seemed extravagant nonsense to most social thinkers of the sixteenth and seventeenth centuries, when the market society was breaking through in England. The conflict between the two societies had been real; the controversy between the proponents of Christian Natural Law and the proponents of *bourgeois* morality and justice had been bitter. Some writers, indeed, notably Locke, had smudged over the difference, and by the eighteenth century the controversy had pretty well died down. Why then did Burke so powerfully state both the Natural Law view and the new view, and present them as complementary?

We need not credit Burke with a degree of insight altogether surpassing that of his predecessors in the English tradition of *bourgeois* political thought; the point is that the circumstances had changed. By Burke's time the old conflict between the market morality and the earlier morality was being replaced by a new conflict—that between any unequal social morality, market or traditional, on the one hand, and on the other a new equalitarian moral theory which, in the hands of the Jacobins or of Tom Paine, had menacing democratic implica-

---

[18] "Third Letter on Regicide Peace," *Works*, VI, p. 270.

tions. Burke's achievement was to see that in the new circumstances it was necessary and possible to fuse the two hitherto competing moral theories. If traditional ideas of subordination had to be accepted by the bulk of the people in order to make the self-regulating market work, then the traditional Christian Natural Law must be rescued from the depredations of the materialists Hobbes and Locke, and revived for use in shoring up the utilitarian market morality.

That was Burke's real insight. Several generations of his admirers, both those who have placed him in the Utilitarian tradition and those who (more recently) have insisted that he was not a Utilitarian at all but a strong Christian Natural Law man, have come short of seeing the true measure of his achievement. He covered with a mantle of traditional Natural Law a set of pure *bourgeois* moral relations. He could do it because he saw deeper than the theoretical contradiction between the old Natural Law and the new morality of the market. He saw that market society, while treating all men equally as contractors and equally as free, required also that they should be vastly unequal and that they should feel themselves to be so. There could be no better instrument for reconciling them to inequality than the Natural Law that Burke espoused, a Natural Law brought again under the sway of Divine Law and freed of the temporal equalitarian implications that had been read into it in its seventeenth-century transformation. The old Natural Law, before Hobbes and Locke had got at it, had upheld hierarchy and subordination as natural and necessary principles of social organization. Burke saw that the old Natural Law was needed again, and that it could be married to Utility.

Thus the interpretation of Burke that is now coming into fashion, which focuses attention on Burke's revival of Christian Natural Law, has something to be said for it. But its exponents,[19] dazzled by the prospect of making Burke over into an adherent of an unchanging and profound moral theory, have failed to see the skill with which he altered the content of that moral theory; they have missed Burke's *tour de force*, which consisted not in emptying out the old contents to make room for the morality of the market, but in inserting the new contents beside or beneath the old.

Are we to say, then, that the Utilitarian interpreters of Burke, who have seen him as the great empiricist, rooted in history, are more nearly right than the Natural Law apologists? We can hardly say so, for to fit Burke into the Utilitarian pattern (even by creating for him a special historical division of Utilitarianism) is also to miss the point. It was not that Burke's feeling for concrete problems and historical

[19] E.g., Charles Parkin, *The Moral Basis of Burke's Political Thought* (Cambridge, 1956); Peter J. Stanlis, *Edmund Burke and the Natural Law* (Ann Arbor, 1958); Francis P. Canavan, S.J., "Burke's Conception of the Role of Reason in Politics," *Journal of Politics* (Feb., 1959).

solutions made him impatient of metaphysics, and so made him amenable to factory-spun Utilitarian principles. It is rather that Burke was impatient of the logic of any moral theory because he grasped, however obscurely, that history sometimes transcends logic; that these were times when English society, to enter fully into its heritage, needed capitalism, and that capitalist society could not operate unless traditional morality was maintained and reinforced. If logical confrontation would show that capitalist morality and traditional morality were incompatible, so much the worse for logic.

Burke was no dialectician. He could not or would not formulate clearly either the logical contradiction or its historical resolution. Had he done so, his work might not now be getting such extravagant praise from proponents of a Natural Law revival, for it would have been evident that his historical resolution of the conflict of moralities was pretty narrowly time-bound. The most we can say of Burke is that, for his own age, he had the root of the matter in him as the Utilitarians had not.

14

Alexander Bickel: Reconsideration: Edmund Burke

Alexander Bickel is Professor of Law at Yale and contributing editor to the liberal weekly The New Republic. *In this piece, which appeared on St. Patrick's Day, 1973, Bickel makes the case for the relevance of Burke to America in the 1970s. Our age, Bickel suggests, is not unlike the 1790s—long on ideological excess and short on real principles of belief. There is, he concludes, much we can learn from Burke.[1]*

"Who now reads Bolingbroke? Who ever read him through?" asked Burke in 1790 in the *Reflections*. And who now reads Burke? Perhaps whoever—meaning no offense—compiles *Bartlett's Familiar Quotations,* although even he, more probably, just reads the previous editions of *Bartlett's.* English schoolboys no doubt hear of Burke, and maybe they are exposed to an occasional excerpt. American schoolboys scarcely know him. If they are exposed to anything, it is likely to be no more than the passage about the function and duty of a representative in the Speech to the Electors of Bristol at the Conclusion of the Polls, and that is presented as a curiosity. No, though always brilliantly quotable, the prose is unfashionable and there is too much of it. It takes a lot of digging to get to the quotations. As for the substance, Burke speaks for the side that lost, resoundingly, quite a while ago. "When our grandchildren have made up their minds, once for all," wrote John Morley in 1888, "as to the merits of the social transformation which dawned on Europe in 1789, then Burke's *Reflections* will become a mere literary antiquity, and not before." Morley's grandchildren, if not his children, did make up their minds, and his great-great-grandchildren do not remember what the problem was that called for the making up of minds.

[1] "Reconsideration: Edmund Burke" (editor's title). From Alexander Bickel, "Edmund Burke: A Retrospective," *The New Republic,* March 17, 1973. Reprinted by permission of *The New Republic,* © 1973, Harrison-Blaine of New Jersey, Inc.

But there was a problem. Enormous, in our eyes incredible, social injustices have been gradually remedied in the nearly two centuries since the French Revolution, although others remain or have newly appeared. Perhaps the good that has been achieved is a legacy of the revolution, and perhaps it is not. But this is certain. The French Revolution was the first of the totalitarian movements that have drenched the Western world in blood, particularly in our own century. This is what Burke prophetically saw and this is what he hated.

"Is it an infirmity to wish," asked Morley, that some "phrase of generous hope," such as "lighted up in the spirits" of Wordsworth, of Coleridge and of Charles James Fox, "had escaped from Burke" on the fall of the Bastille? The large-hearted Fox exclaimed: "How much the greatest event it is that ever happened in the world, and how much the best." It was a fatuous remark, like Lincoln Steffens' when he came back from the Soviet Union thinking he had been into the future and seen it work, or like many a now charitably forgotten celebration of one or another wave of the future in the 1930s. And it is an infirmity to wish that Burke had said something of the sort. For it would have been the expression at best of a "fine illusion," as Morley himself implies, and not necessarily fine at that.

Burke saw further and deeper instantly and without illusion. He saw a "chaos of levity and ferocity." He was no more given to automatic adulation of "the people" than of kings, knowing that "liberty, when men act in bodies, is *power*," and that power is to be judged by the use that is made of it, by its distribution, and by the limits put on it. Simply the seizure of power by a great many enthusiastic people is in itself no cause for rejoicing. Burke knew that to begin by despising everything is to set up "trade without a capital," and he saw that the French revolutionaries, despising all about them, all their predecessors and all their contemporaries, must also "despise themselves until the moment in which they become truly despicable." Their liberty was not liberal, he wrote, their humanity was "savage and brutal." He was clear that moderation and reason—the very reason in whose name the revolution was made—would count for nothing in an escalation of fervor from one assembly to the next, until a soldier who could secure the obedience of the armies to himself "on his personal account" would become "the master of your Assembly, the master of your whole republic." Thus in 1790 did Burke unhesitatingly foretell the rise of Napoleon.

Then and for some years more, Burke beheld in England the spectacle of well-born, high-living swells—Fox's companions, despite all Fox's virtues and talents—and of high-minded dissenting divines, seeing only what they wanted to see and extolling the Parisian mobs ("excuse the term, it is still in use here," Burke remarked) from Brooks' or from their pulpits. The French, these safely distanced people were pleased to believe, had merely and at long last acted on the principles of the English Revolution of 1688 and emulated the recent American one. Revolutionary principles were all one, all equal, all good. They had, in fact, too long been neglected in England itself. For the flaws of English government were also gross. The rhetoric of these people was ever apocalyptic. All that was wrong was wrong at the root and all remedies had to be applied at the root. "Something they must destroy," said Burke, "or they seem to themselves to exist for no purpose." Mere reform would not do.

Burke understood his radical compatriots. He did not delude himself about their steadiness of purpose. "Almost all the high-bred republicans of my time have, after a short space," he observed, "become the most decided, thorough-paced courtiers; they soon left the business of a tedious, moderate, but practical resistance to those of us whom, in the pride and intoxication of their theories, they have slighted as not much better than Tories. . . . These professors, finding their extreme principles not applicable to cases which call only for a qualified or, as I may say, civil and legal resistance, in such cases employ no resistance at all. It is with them a war or a revolution, or it is nothing."

Though not often amused, Burke could sometimes dwell on the radical chic hilarity of it all. "Is it not a singular phenomenon," he wrote in a public letter to the Duke of Bedford, after the *Reflections,* "that whilst the *sans-culotte* carcase-butchers, and the philosophers of the shambles are pricking their dotted lines upon his hide, and like the print of the poor ox that we see at the shop-windows at Charing-cross, alive as he is, and thinking no harm in the world, he is divided into rumps, and sirloins, and briskets, and into all sort of pieces for roasting, boiling, and stewing, that all the while they are measuring *him,* his grace is . . . fawning on those who have the knife half out of the sheath—poor innocent!"

Such were the flirtations of the upper class and of assorted visionaries. One reason, not the chief reason but an interesting if marginal one, why Burke was never taken in is that he was invincibly middle class and something of an Irish upstart at that; certainly not, as Sir Philip Magnus writes, "the best of good fellows," like Fox. Burke did not gamble, he did not hunt, he cared nothing for horseflesh. He was Church of England all right—and so, later, less seriously, was Disraeli —but he not only began at a considerable remove from the upper-class establishment, he never, like Disraeli, with whatever degree of detachment, became an establishment-follower. "I was not," Burke wrote, "like his grace of Bedford, swaddled, and rocked, and dandled into a legislator. . . . I possessed not one of the qualities, nor cultivated one of the arts, that recommend men to the favor and protection of the great. . . . At every step of my progress in life (for in every step was I traversed and opposed), and at every turnpike I met, I was obliged to show my passport, and again and again to prove my sole title to the honor of being useful to my country. . . . Otherwise no rank, no toleration even, for me." Burke was, of course, very far from being a philistine. He was a man of letters before, after and while he was a politician, and his circle was that of the finest spirits and intellects of the day. But this was not a time or a place in which the artistic and intellectual elite, which was Burke's class, aspired to mingle with the social aristocracy.

The greatly more significant, the decisive reason why Burke did not for a moment go along with the gilded Whig radicals was that Burke confronted events in France with a coherent set of attitudes. He had what he once noted that Shelburne, with whom he served briefly and unhappily in 1782 in the second Rockingham government, and who now as the Marquis of Lansdowne was befriending various radical divines, signally lacked. "He wants what *I* call principles," Burke said of Shelburne, "not in the vulgar sense of a deficiency of honor, or conscience—but he totally wants a uniform rule and scheme of life." Burke had principles, he had a coherent rule and scheme, which he applied to the revolution in France. These principles are of enduring interest, as is Burke's steady sense of their limits. For one of his principles was the principle that on most occasions in politics principle must not be allowed to be controlling. His mind, Christopher Hobhouse wrote, was equal to the application to every question of both tests: principle, and expediency or prudence. "It was this double approach to political thought that made Burke the colossus that he is. He strides the gulf between the reactionary and the progressive, between the empiricist and the doctrinaire."

In our own time of dogma to the left and dogma to the right, and also curious though it be, of unvarnished populism to the left and to the right, when on numerous issues, in a phrase of Burke, "rival follies" mutually wage an unrelenting war, a time when change is widely counted a self-evident virtue, an age of futurism and millenarianism —there is much to learn from Burke. Our problem is the totalitarian tendency of the democratic faith, to which we have become increasingly committed, and the apparent inconsistency and arbitrary tendency of most remedies against the totalitarian tendency of populist democracy. Our problem has been, and is most acutely now, the tyrannical tendency of ideas and the suicidal emptiness of a politics without ideas, "the opposite evils," in another phrase of Burke, "of intolerance and of indifference." These are problems Burke addresses. There is in our past a usable Burke.

His thought yields no systematic philosophy, but it proceeds from a whole view. And a number of fully developed and firmly held propositions can be readily extracted from it. The first of these is that no-where should there be any lodgment of uncontrolled, arbitrary power, not in any person, not in any electorate, not in any institution of government. Burke fought the King's prerogative, of course. That was what the Whig Party was about, that is what the *Thoughts on the Cause of the Present Discontents*, published in 1770, was about. And that was why Burke supported the American side in the War of the Revolution. He said much later, when accused of inconsistency in op-posing the French Revolution although he had held with the Ameri-can, that he considered "the Americans as standing at that time, in that controversy, in the same relation to England, as England did to King James II, in 1688." He fought the exercise of arbitrary power in his native Ireland. He fought arbitrary power as exercised in the ad-ministration of Warren Hastings in India, securing Hastings' indict-ment by the House of Commons and pursuing Hastings through seven long years of trial.

Arbitrary power in the people was no more tolerable than in kings or colonial proconsuls. "These old fanatics of single arbitrary power," he wrote in the *Reflections*, "dogmatized as if hereditary royalty was the only lawful government in the world, just as our new fanatics of popular arbitrary power maintain that a popular election is the sole lawful source of authority." Men thirst after power, he wrote a few years later, and whether they want it "vested in the many or the few" depends chiefly on their estimate of their own chance to exercise it. What mattered was less the source of the power than whether it was arbitrary or limited. And the way to prevent power being arbitrary was to ensure that it was nowhere total. A good constitution, therefore, distributed power so that no man or institution held it all, and all who held it balanced and checked one another.

So it was in the British constitution, the Crown, the Lords and the Commons sharing power, and limiting the power of each. What had gone wrong early in the reign of George III was that Parliament had become an instrument of the Crown, joining it in exercising control over the people, rather than controlling it in behalf of the people. An additional safeguard against arbitrary power was an independent ju-diciary, not as a sharer of power, but as a counterweight. "Whatever is supreme in a state," Burke wrote in the *Reflections*, "ought to have, as much as possible, its judicial authority so constituted as not only not to depend upon it, but in some sort to balance it. It ought to give a security to its justice against its power. It ought to make its judica-ture, as it were, something exterior to the state."

But it was not enough that power be distributed, in no place ar-bitrary, and in no single place total. The entire edifice of power, with its many interior chambers and partitions, must rest on consent. Nei-ther the distribution of power nor its basis in consent ensure good and wise government. Power is to be limited so that the chances of its wielders doing the bad and the unwise thing may be minimized; and so that when they do it anyway, the harm they cause will be less than total. And power should seek to rest on consent so that its distribution and its exercise may be stable—stability being a prime value, both as an end and as a means; as an end, because though truth may be preferable to peace, "as we have scarcely ever the same certainty in the one that we have in the other, I would, unless the truth were evident indeed, hold fast to peace"; and as a means, because stability is a source as well as a fruit of consent, making the beneficent exercise of power possible though by no means certain.

A representative, electorally responsible institution was critical, therefore, not merely as a sharer of power, but as a generator of consent. Yet it was not the sole generator of consent, nor did it need to be elected by universal suffrage, or to mirror its constituents' desires with perfect fidelity in order to be effective.

Actually a parliament that is a creature strictly of a majority of the people "told by the head" was in Burke's view a menace, because it was all too likely to regard itself as sovereign, and to seize total power, riding roughshod over other institutions.

But it is necessary here to emphasize Burke's pragmatism, and his sense of place and circumstance. "Circumstances," he says in the *Reflections*, "give in reality to every political principle its distinguishing color and discriminating effect. The circumstances are what render every civil and political scheme beneficial or noxious to mankind." Even though he saw clearly and in great detail what had gone wrong in France, he would not be drawn, in the course of controversies that raged following publication of the *Reflections*, into making affirmative recommendations for the structure and composition of French institutions. "I must see with my own eyes," he said, "touch with my own hands, not only the fixed, but the momentary circumstances, before I would venture to suggest any political project whatsoever. I must know the power and disposition to accept, to execute, to persevere. . . . I must see the means of correcting the plan, where correctives would be wanted. I must see the things; I must see the men. . . . The eastern politicians never do anything without the opinion of the astrologers on the *fortunate moment*. . . . Statesmen of a more judicious prescience look for the fortunate moment too; but they seek it, not in the conjunctions and oppositions of the planets, but in the conjunctions and oppositions of men and things. These form their almanac."

In a system like the present one in the United States, therefore, where the executive and a bicameral legislature have both evolved toward election by universal suffrage, but from different constituencies and with staggered terms, Burke would not likely have perceived the dangers that were so evident in the sovereign French Assembly, and that might have arisen in 18th-century England from a sovereign House of Commons elected by universal suffrage; although he would likely have diagnosed the same danger in a Gaullist type of presidency, little countervailed by parliamentary institutions and acting on the basis of the presumed consent to its actions of the people, "told by the head" at the last election or referendum. Even so, Burke wrote two years after the *Reflections* that the English constitution was "not made for great, general, and proscriptive exclusions [from the franchise, as of Irish Catholics]; sooner or later it will destroy them, or they will destroy the constitution."

The fundamental point was, and remains, that consent and stability are not produced simply by the existence and function of popularly elected institutions, although absolute power may be. Elections, even if they are referenda, do not establish consent, or do not establish it for long. They cannot mean that much. Masses of people do not make clear-cut, long-range decisions. They do not know enough about the issues, about themselves, their needs and wishes, or about what those needs and wishes will appear to them to be two months hence. "The will of the many and their interest must very often differ"—an echo here, in some part, of Rousseau, but Burke did not suggest that anything positive followed from this observation, such as the right of a minority, seized somehow of the Rousseauian "general will," to rule. He argued only that there was nothing natural or necessary about allowing a majority to prevail. Rule by a majority obtained where it did, he pointed out, by convention and habit, and did not obtain universally on all occasions and for all purposes even where established. And where a majority does rule unrestrained, it is capable of great and cruel oppression of minorities.

The people are something else than a majority registered on election day, although by convention and for lack of any other suitable method, we let various majorities, including electoral ones, settle various things in various contexts on various occasions. The people begin with "the little platoon we belong to in society," what today we call groups, and they are found in places to which they are attached, in divisions of the country, what we call constituencies, which "have been formed by habit, and not by a sudden jerk of authority"—not by the assembly in Paris dividing France into equal squares, or by a reapportioning federal district judge, one might add, using a computer to so divide a state. No man will ever "glory in belonging to the Chequer No. 71," and yet "public affections," meaning consent to the institutions of government, must begin "in our families . . . pass on to our neighborhoods and our habitual provincial connexions," and so on to the nation. No jet age can change that.

The people then form into parties, under leadership they trust and find natural. Their temper, the temper of both the greater number and weight of them or of significant groups of them, is readily determinable, and no one can long govern against it, except by suppression, which is not government, as Burke remarked when urging conciliation with America. A nation, he said, "is not governed, which is perpetually to be conquered." Widespread dissatisfaction with government does not need the ballot box to express itself—Burke was far from deprecating direct political action, including civil disobedience in cases of necessity—and it must be met and conciliated, even if not shared by a numerical majority of the population, for law cannot deal with it. "I do not know the method," goes one of his most famous sentences, "of drawing up an indictment against an whole people."

Such was the people, as Burke used the term, in place, gathered, led, manifesting its temper in many ways and over a span of time as a people, or as one or another sizable community within the body of the people, not speaking merely on occasion in momentary numerical majorities. The influence of the people, so conceived, must be a dominant one because their consent is essential. That consent may be withdrawn regardless of elections, it must be preponderant, not merely majority consent, and is yielded not only and not even chiefly to the electoral verdict, but to institutions validated by time and familiarity and composed from time to time of men who are trusted because they are seen to have "a connexion with the interest . . . the sentiments and opinions of the people."

George III's slogan, "not men, but measures," was pernicious precisely because consent is in large part the consequence of confidence in, and identification with, men. "The laws reach but a little way. Constitute government how you please, infinitely the greater part of it must depend upon the exercise of the powers which are left at large to the prudence and uprightness of ministers of state." Consent will not long be yielded to faceless officials, or to mere servants of one man, who themselves have no "connexion with the interest of the people." In opposing the cant of "not men, but measures," Burke therefore resisted rule by non-party ministers who lacked the confidence of the Commons. By the same token we may today oppose excessive White House staff-government by private men whom Congress never sees. There are substantial differences of degree in the case of an elected executive seeking to control a large, permanent civil service, but it was not for nothing that the American Constitution provided for "executive Departments" and for Senate confirmation of the appointments of great officers of state.

Safeguards against arbitrary power, resistance to total power, assurance of stable government which is responsive and capable of generating long-term consent—these are agnostic objectives. Any true believer will want total power to achieve the true ends of government, and will be a democrat or an authoritarian depending, as Burke said, on which scheme or system he thinks will bring him nearer to total power. But any thorough-going agnostic might well also be a radical democrat, believing that nothing matters and that the merest whim of the majority is as good a guide to social action as anything else; and perhaps this is simply another form of true belief, like reliance on astrology or oracles. In any case Burke was neither a true believer nor a thorough-going agnostic. He was a Christian, and if anything something of a mystic, but no ideologue.

True believers—though not Christians—theorists and ideologues made the French Revolution, and for Burke a politics of theory and ideology, of abstract, absolute ideas was an abomination, whether the idea was the right of the British Parliament to tax the American colonies or the rights of man. Such a politics cannot work as politics. It begins and ends by sacrificing peace, and it must proceed from one bloodbath to another, and from one tyranny to another. Ideas are the inventions of men and are as arbitrary as their will. The business of politics is not with theory and ideology but with accommodation.

"All government, indeed every human benefit and enjoyment," Burke said in 1775 in urging conciliation with America, "every virtue, and every prudent act, is founded on compromise and barter. We balance inconveniences; we give and take; we remit some rights, that we may enjoy others; and we choose rather to be happy citizens, than subtle disputants." He would not enter into "distinctions of rights . . . these metaphysical distinctions; I hate the very sound of them." They were, he found later, what the French Revolution was about. These revolutionaries build their politics, he wrote in the *Appeal from the New to the Old Whigs,* a year after the *Reflections,* "not on convenience but on truth; and they profess to conduct men to a certain happiness by the assertion of their undoubted rights. With them there is no compromise. . . . Their principles always go to the extreme."

The presumption, the arrogance of these Frenchmen's assurance in their new discovery appalled Burke. Those "rights of man" were an invitation to another round of religious wars and persecutions, not likely to be any the less fanatical or bloody for the irreligiousness of the new dogma. "The foundation of government is . . . not in imaginary rights of men," Burke argued, "but in political convenience, and in human nature. . . ." Government thus stops short "of some hazardous or ambiguous excellence," but it is the better for it.

Men do have rights, Burke wrote in the *Reflections,* but as civil society is made for the advantage of man, "all the advantages for which it is made become his right." The rights of man, this is to say, have no independent, theoretical existence. They do not preexist and condition civil society. They are in their totality the right to decent, wise, just, responsive, stable government in the circumstances of a given time and place. Under such a government, a partnership Burke calls it, "the restraints on men, as well as their liberties, are to be reckoned among their rights," and "all men have equal rights, but not to equal things," since a leveling egalitarianism which does not reward merit and ability is harmful to all and is unjust as well.

Civil society is a creature of its past, of "a great mysterious incorporation," and of an evolution which in improving never produces anything "wholly new," and in conserving never retains anything "wholly obsolete." It may malfunction—the English constitution did in 1688—and then drastic measures may be called for to restore it to its true self, but that true self ought never be altered, and certainly society ought never be uprooted, never be razed to the ground and replaced with some wholly new construct. This passionately held faith and his deprecation of the rights of man form the basis of Burke's reputation as the purveyor of a conservative doctrine unfit for modern consumption, as the last apologist for an oppressive social order now long dead and unlamented, as an obscurantist reactionary, an opponent not only of humanitarian reform, but of reason itself.

The conservative reputation does not fit the Whig of the 1770s and '80s, to be sure, the advocate of consent and limited power, the friend of the American Revolution, or even the critic of the totalitarian tendencies of the French Revolution. But Burke's contemporary adversaries and his later detractors resolve the contradiction by accusing him of having abandoned his earlier convictions. He got frightened, he got old, his sympathy dried up, he went Tory, perhaps he was not even altogether of sound mind. John Morley's opinion, however—and Morley was critical of much in the *Reflections*—was that Burke "changed his front, but he never changed his ground," and this opinion can be shown to be correct. The same principles, the same "uniform scheme and rule of life" that informed the earlier Whig animated the author of the *Reflections*. The latter work is, therefore, not to be so simply rejected. "Fly from the French Revolution," Burke cried in Parliament in 1791. The liberal tradition did not fly from the revolution. It fled from Burke instead, and that was a mistake.

Of course there are moments in the *Reflections* that are nothing but sterile reaction. There is the passage that Tom Paine tellingly picked up in which Burke makes love to Marie Antoinette, that "Roman matron," and laments that "the age of chivalry is gone . . . gone— that . . . charity of honor which felt a stain like a wound . . . which ennobled whatever it touched, and under which vice itself lost half its evil by losing all its grossness." With this passage, says Sir Philip Magnus, "the Romantic Movement in English literature had begun," which is certainly too bad. But even here Burke exaggerates a valid point, namely that manners, civility, certain forms and standards of behavior, what he calls the "public affections," are founded in custom and are all easily exploded by a shallow reason. They are nothing but "pleasing illusions which make power gentle and obedience liberal"; they are "the decent drapery of life." But without them society and government are brutal, conflict is naked. It is all too easy and it is fatal to keep tearing them off until not only is a king merely a man and a queen just a woman, but also "a woman is but an animal, and an animal not of the highest order."

Again there is the passage where we are told that the poor must be trained to obedience and labor, "and when they find, as they commonly do, the success disproportioned to the endeavor, they must be taught their consolation in the final proportions of eternal justice." Not an edifying sentence. But Burke had a social conscience, if a perplexed one. He puzzled, with feeling, over how to rescue people doomed to "servile, degrading, unseemly, unmanly . . . unwholesome . . . pestiferous occupations," but asked, "What is the use of discussing a man's abstract right to food or medicine? The question is upon the method of procuring and administering them." And yet again Burke surely treated much too lightly the abuses of the French monarchy, aristocracy and clergy, and the misery they bred. France needed a revolution, if anything more than England in 1688 or America in 1776, though not the one it got, and Burke should have seen this. Nor, finally, was Burke without his share of anti-Semitism, though it was of a variety that barely rises to the notice of anyone who has lived through the first half of the 20th century.

But all this cannot on any fair reading be taken as central to the *Reflections*, and much will be missed by those who do so take it. First there is in the worst, as it might be viewed, of Burke's so-called conservatism a powerful realism that any political thought denies or ignores at its peril. You cannot start from scratch, he maintained, and expect to produce anything but a continual round of chaos and tyranny, until you return to the remnants of what you sought to destroy. Perfection is unlikely in human contrivances, and so the professed purpose of any scheme that attempts to start fresh will be defeated. The old vices tend to reappear in new institutions, if their causes have not been attacked, but only their outward manifestations, which were the old institutions. Meanwhile the price has been paid of teaching men to yield as little respect to new institutions as was shown for the old, and in a continual round of change, men unmoored from their past "become little better than the flies of summer." Even in pursuit of the most radical reforming ends, it is, moreover, simple practical common sense "to make the most of the existing materials." A politician, Burke lectured, contemplating in sheer unbelieving wonder the destruction of the church in France and the confiscation and dismantling of productive church property, a politician, "to do great things, looks for a *power*, what our workmen call a *purchase*." Here, in the church, were revenues, here was a bureaucracy. To destroy all this and scatter it rather than to use it seemed to Burke the height of stupidity —and subsequent French history proved him right. In the same spirit, reading Condorcet's dictum that the American Constitution "had not grown, but was planned," that it had taken no weight from the centuries but was put together mechanically in a few years, John Adams commented in the margin: "Fool! Fool!"

Continuity—a practical necessity, if nothing else—was for Burke the principle of reform, not of opposition to it. Even revolutionary reform, as in England in 1688 and in America a century later, might be called for by a "grave and overruling necessity," in order to conserve by correcting. But the science of government is practical and intended for practical purposes. Cause and effect are most often obscure, and it is, therefore, "with infinite caution that any man ought to venture upon pulling down an edifice which has answered in any tolerable degree for ages the common purposes of society." This is conservatism, no doubt, but what is behind it is not wish, or tired old age, or romantic delusion, or moral obtuseness, or class interest, but good practical wisdom.

Burke's conservatism, however, served another purpose as well. In order to survive, be coherent and stable and answer to men's wants, a civil society had to rest on a foundation of moral values. Else it degenerated—if an oligarchy, into interest government, a government of jobbers enriching themselves and their friends, and ended in revolution; or if a full democracy, into a mindless, shameless thing, freely oppressing various minorities and ruining itself. Burke's pragmatism, strong as it is, did not go the length of taking mind out of politics. Metaphysics, yes; mind and values, no. But where are a society's values to be found? In theory? Metaphysics, abstract rights would always clash with men's needs and their natures, and with various unforeseeable contingencies.

Theories were not fit to live with, and any attempt to impose them would breed conflict, not responsive government enjoying the consent of the governed. The rights of man cannot be established by any theoretical definition; they are "in balances between differences of good, in compromises sometimes between good and evil, and sometimes between evil and evil. Political reason is a computing principle: adding, subtracting, multiplying, and dividing, morally and not metaphysically, or mathematically, true moral denominations." The visions of good and evil, the denominations to be computed—these a society draws from its past and without them it dies. Burke was strong for the union of church and state, since he viewed religion as a major source of the values that held a society together. He even praised, on the same score, the ancient prejudices of the people, using the word in a somewhat different sense than we do, and warned against exchanging the people's old superstitions—"the religion of feeble minds"—for new.

For many millions of us, organized religion no longer plays the role Burke assigned to it, and we want nothing of superstition and prejudice. Burke may have regretted the Enlightenment, but it did occur. The Age of Reason continues, if not quite as pretentiously and self-confidently as it began. Precisely for that reason, however, the problem to which Burke spoke is even more acute for us. A valueless politics and valueless institutions are shameful and shameless, and what is more, man's nature is such that he finds them, and life with and under them, insupportable. Doctrinaire theories of the rights of man, on the other hand, serve us no better than Burke thought they would. The computing principle is still all we can resort to, and we always return to it following some luxuriant outburst of theory in the Supreme Court, whether the theory is of an absolute right to contract, or to speak, or to stand mute, or to be private. We find our visions of good and evil and the denominations we compute where Burke told us to look, in the experience of the past, in our tradition, in the secular religion of the American republic. The only abiding thing, as Brandeis used to repeat, and as Burke might not have denied, is change, but the past should control it, or at least its pace. We hold to the values of the past provisionally only, in the knowledge that they will change, but we hold to them as guides.

This is not, as Holmes once remarked, a duty, it is a necessity. How else are we to know anything? What is the use of empty "rationalists," such as were discovered at many a university some years ago, who being confronted with various demands for instant change, found that they believed nothing and could not judge any change as better or worse than another? They drove the very seekers after change up the wall in frustration. Nobody wants everybody not to believe in anything. And who wants politicians who, as Burke said, "see no merit or demerit in any man, or any action, or any political principle" except in terms of a desired political end, and who "therefore take up, one day, the most violent and stretched prerogative, and another time the wildest democratic ideas of freedom, and pass from one to the other. . . ."

Our problem, as much as Burke's, is that we cannot govern, and should not, in submission to the dictates of abstract theories, and that we cannot live, much less govern, without some "uniform rule and scheme of life," without principles, however provisionally and skeptically held. Burke's conservatism, if that is what it was, which at any rate belongs to the liberal tradition, properly understood and translated to our time, is the way.

Bibliographical Note

The most easily available complete edition of Burke's writings and speeches in American libraries is the twelve-volume "Boston" edition, 1865–67. This is closely patterned on the complete Bohn British Classics edition published in 1853. Several collections of selected Burke material are also available: Edward J. Payne, ed. (Oxford, 1874–78), in three volumes; World Classics (1906–7), in six volumes; and three excellent recent American collections—Ross J. S. Hoffman and Paul Levack, eds., *Burke's Politics: Selected Writings and Speeches* (New York, 1949); Louis I. Bredvold and Ralph G. Ross, eds., *The Philosophy of Edmund Burke* (Ann Arbor, 1960); and Walter J. Bate, ed., *Edmund Burke: Selected Works* (New York, 1960). There are many separate editions of *Reflections on the Revolution in France* available, several in paperback. Burke's first publication, *Philosophical Enquiry into the Origin of Our Ideas of the Sublime and Beautiful*, has also recently been published in a separate edition, edited by James T. Boulton (London and New York, 1958). Not only is it useful in reconstructing the impact he made on the literary world in the 1750s, but also it is in its own right an important landmark in eighteenth-century aesthetic theory.

As an active man of affairs whose interests were deeply involved in parliamentary maneuverings and, beyond Parliament, Ireland, America, France, and India, Burke was, not surprisingly, a voluminous letter writer. The standard edition of his correspondence was, until very recently, the four volumes edited by Earl Fitzwilliam and Richard Bourke in 1844. In 1972, however, the definitive edition of Burke's letters was completed in ten volumes separately edited, jointly published by the University of Chicago Press and Cambridge University Press. Whereas the 1844 edition contained under 400 letters, the definitive edition has over 2000 pieces of correspondence.

There are several important biographies of Burke that are rewarding reading. James Prior's *Life of the Right Honorable Edmund Burke* was a popular nineteenth-century study, replaced by what has become the classic life —John Morley's *Burke* in the English Men of Letters series (1874). Twentieth-century biographies include: R. H. Murray, *Edmund Burke: A Biography* (London, 1931); Philip Magnus, *Edmund Burke, A Life* (London, 1939); Carl B. Cone, *Burke and the Nature of Politics*, 2 vols. (Lexington, Ky., 1957). Several important books have helped clarify particular aspects of Burke's life; for example: Ernst Barker's *Burke and Bristol* (Bristol, 1930); Dixon Wector's *Edmund Burke and His Kinsmen* (Boulder, 1939); and Thomas H. D. Mahoney's *Edmund Burke and Ireland* (Cambridge, Mass., 1960).

For interpretations of Burke and his writings, one could look at this cross section of scholarship: Alfred Cobban's *Edmund Burke and the Revolt against the Eighteenth Century* (London, 1929); Thomas W. Copeland, *Our Eminent Friend Edmund Burke* (New Haven, 1949); Steven Graubard, *Burke, Disraeli and Churchill: The Politics of Perseverence* (Cambridge,

Mass., 1961); John McCunn, *The Political Philosophy of Burke* (London, 1913); Russell Kirk, *The Conservative Mind* (Chicago, 1953); Charles Parkin, *The Moral Basis of Burke's Political Thought* (Cambridge, 1956); Peter J. Stanlis, *Edmund Burke: The Practical Imagination* (Cambridge, Mass., 1967); Harvey Mansfield, Jr., *Statesmanship and Party Government* (Chicago, 1965); Francis Canavan, *The Political Reason of Edmund Burke* (Durham, N.C., 1960); and Peter Stanlis, ed., *Edmund Burke. The Enlightenment and the Modern World* (Detroit, Mich.: 1972).

A selection from the interpretive-article literature on Burke would include: Mario Einandi, "The British Background of Burke's Political Philosophy," *Political Science Quarterly*, XLIX (1934): 576–98; Victor M. Hamm, "Burke and Metaphysics," *New Scholasticism*, XVIII (January, 1944): 3–18; Robert M. Hutchins, "The Theory of the State: Edmund Burke," *Review of Politics*, V (1943): 139–55; M. F. K. Millar, "Burke and the Moral Basis of Political Liberty," *Thought*, XVI (1916): 79–101; L. B. Namier, "The Character of Burke," *Spectator* (December 19, 1958): p. 895; C. B. Mapherson, "Edmund Burke and the New Conservatism," *Science and Society*, XXII (1958): 231–39; Isaac Kramnick, "The Skeptical Tradition in English Political Thought," *Studies in Burke and His Times*, XII (1970): 1627–1660; John C. Weston, "Edmund Burke's View of History," *Review of Politics*, XXIII (1961): 203–29; J. G. A. Pocock, "Burke and the Ancient Constitution," *Historical Journal*, III (1960): 125–43; and Arnold A. Rogaw, "Edmund Burke and the American Liberal Tradition," *Antioch Review*, XVII (1957): 255–65.

Index